Restaurant & Bar Design

Selected by the
**Restaurant & Bar
Design Awards**

TASCHEN

Contents

Preface

Marco Rebora
Founder of the Restaurant & Bar Design Awards

Marco Rebora founded the
Restaurant & Bar Design Awards
in 2008. An Italian, he was born
in Belgium and lives in the UK.
He studied Fashion Design and
Marketing, and previous to founding
the Awards he created and ran the
Neon restaurant in Brixton, London.

Marco Rebora gründete 2008 die
Restaurant & Bar Design Awards.
Als Italiener wurde er in Belgien
geboren und lebt in Großbritannien.
Er studierte Modedesign und
Marketing. Bevor er den Preis schuf,
etablierte und führte er das Restau-
rant Neon in Brixton, London.

Marco Rebora a fondé les
Restaurant & Bar Design Awards
en 2008. D'origine italienne, il est né
en Belgique et réside actuellement
au Royaume-Uni. Il a suivi des études
de design de mode et de marketing.
Avant les Awards, il a fondé et
dirigé le restaurant Neon dans le
quartier de Brixton, à Londres.

Editor's Note
The dollar signs in the fact-sheets for
the different projects indicate the
relative building costs in US Dollars:

$ up to 50 K
$$ up to 100 K
$$$ up to 250 K
$$$$ up to 1 million
$$$$+ more than 1 million

The Restaurant & Bar Design Awards are the only awards in the world dedicated to the design of food and beverage spaces. This covers every imaginable type of space, from ships to airports, museums to burger vans, and from revered Michelin-starred establishments to the fleeting dynamism of pop-ups.

Food and beverage spaces have long been understood as places that enrich people's lives, where people come together and creatives meet. The most influential designers and artists have designed restaurants or bars, and the majority of innovators – in fashion, music, art or design – would have eaten, drunk and been seen in one. They are the spaces where revolutionaries, world-changers and game-players interact and as such, they are very important places in the fabric of our towns and cities.

The design of restaurants and bars is also one of many indicators in the evolution of urban living. As a country modernises it undergoes intense periods of change. The design of these spaces is a reflection of the progression of the social and economic climate, showing us how people develop their thoughts and ideas and giving us an important insight into our society.

Over the last five years the Awards have been a survey of this statement of creativity and modernisation, making it a focal point of the most impressive things happening across the industry worldwide. This book is an opportunity to bring a selection of the best of these projects together for the first time.

I had been approached by many publishers before wanting to turn the Awards into a book. It is only with TASCHEN, who have always understood the ethos of art and design, and whom I respect greatly, that I decided to make a statement by publishing what we consider to be the most creative designs in the first Restaurant & Bar Design Awards book.

The Restaurant & Bar Design Awards is completely dependent on what is happening in the industries of design, architecture and gastronomy. The most important and creative people, who are part of an inspiring international community we work with – from the big names to the small names – are reflected in the projects and through our outstanding judges.

Our aim for the Awards ceremony is to inspire our guests by creating amazing interactive experiences. Every year the selection of restaurants and bars we see keeps getting better and each Award is different from the last, which is why it is such an exciting place to be.

The Awards would not be possible without the sponsors and partners, for which we are very grateful. I'd like to extend special thanks to Leslie Brissett, Rupert Davies and Ceri Richmond, for their hard work over the years in ensuring that the Awards is a success each time.

Die Restaurant & Bar Design Awards sind die weltweit einzige Auszeichnung, die sich der Gestaltung von Orten zum Speisen und Trinken widmet. Dies betrifft alle nur vorstellbaren Arten von Einrichtungen: von Schiffen zu Flughäfen, Museen zu Burger-Vans und von angesehenen Sterne-Etablissements zu flüchtigen dynamischen Pop-up-Lokalen.

Stätten zum Speisen und Trinken wurden von alters her als Orte zur Bereicherung des menschlichen Lebens betrachtet, wo Leute zusammenkommen und Kreative sich treffen. Die einflussreichsten Designer und Künstler haben Restaurants oder Bars ausgestattet, und viele Innovatoren der Mode, Musik, Kunst oder Design haben dort gegessen, getrunken und Zeit verbracht. Es sind die Orte, an denen Revolutionäre, Weltverbesserer und Insider agieren, und darum sind sie von Bedeutung für unsere Stadtstruktur.

Die Gestaltung von Restaurants und Bars ist auch einer von zahlreichen Indikatoren für die Entwicklung städtischen Lebens. Im Zuge der Modernisierung durchläuft ein Land intensive Perioden des Wandels. Das Design dieser Räume spiegelt den Fortschritt der sozialen und wirtschaftlichen Verhältnisse und zeigt uns, wie Menschen ihre Gedanken und Ideen entwickeln. Das bietet uns einen wichtigen Einblick in unsere Gesellschaft.

In den vergangenen fünf Jahren haben die Awards uns einen Überblick über den Stand von Kreativität und Modernisierung gegeben und über die eindrucksvollsten Entwicklungen der Branche weltweit informiert. Dieses Buch bietet erstmalig die Gelegenheit, eine Auswahl der besten Entwürfe zu präsentieren.

Viele Verleger hatten mich aufgefordert, die preisgekrönten Projekte in einem Buch zu veröffentlichen. Aber erst, als TASCHEN, ein Verlag mit stetigem Verständnis für den Wert von Kunst und Design und den ich sehr schätze, mich ansprach, habe ich mich dafür entschieden, die unserer Ansicht nach kreativsten Entwürfe im ersten Buch über diesen Preis zu publizieren.

Die Restaurant & Bar Design Awards sind gänzlich davon abhängig, was sich in den Bereichen Design, Architektur und Gastronomie abspielt. Die wichtigsten und kreativsten Persönlichkeiten, die der inspirierenden internationalen Gemeinschaft angehören – von den großen bis zu den kleinen Namen –, werden in ihren Projekten und durch unsere hervorragenden Juroren vorgestellt.

Ziel der Preisverleihung ist es, unsere Gäste durch verblüffende interaktive Erlebnisse zu begeistern. Jedes Jahr wird die Auswahl der vorgestellten Restaurants und Bars besser, und jedes Ergebnis unterscheidet sich vom vorhergehenden. Und genau das macht die Beteiligung daran zu einem so faszinierenden Ereignis.

Die Awards wären nicht realisierbar ohne die Sponsoren und Partner, denen ich sehr zu Dank verpflichtet bin. Besonderer Dank gebührt Leslie Brissett, Rupert Davies und Ceri Richmond für ihre jahrelange aktive Arbeit, die den Erfolg der Preisverleihung immer wieder garantiert.

Les Restaurant and Bar Design Awards sont les seuls prix au monde récompensant le design de lieux de restauration. Cette catégorie englobe une quantité infinie de types d'espaces : bateaux, aéroports, musées, camions à burgers, établissements étoilés au Michelin, ou encore installations éphémères.

Voilà longtemps que les lieux de restauration sont considérés comme des endroits enrichissant la vie de leurs clients, où des personnes s'y retrouvent et où des créatifs s'y rencontrent. Les designers et artistes les plus influents ont conçu des restaurants ou des bars dans lesquels nombre d'innovateurs (du monde de la mode, de la musique, de l'art ou du design) ont mangé, bu ou été vus. Pour être des lieux où se côtoient révolutionnaires, décideurs et protagonistes, ces espaces jouent un rôle clé dans le développement des villes.

Le design de restaurants et de bars sert aussi de baromètre de l'évolution de la vie urbaine. Quand il se modernise, un pays passe par des périodes intenses de changements. Le design de ces espaces reflète la progression du climat socio-économique : en montrant comment les individus élaborent leurs pensées et leurs idées, il offre un instantané pertinent de notre société.

Depuis cinq ans, ces prix illustrent cette déclaration de créativité et de modernisation, au point d'en faire la référence de ce qu'il se fait de mieux dans le domaine à travers le monde. Le présent ouvrage présente une sélection des meilleurs projets pour la première fois réunis.

De nombreux éditeurs ont voulu me convaincre de faire un livre de ces prix. C'est avec Taschen, qui a toujours compris la philosophie de l'art et du design et que je respecte grandement, que j'ai accepté ce projet. Ensemble, nous publions le premier livre Restaurant & Bar Design Awards qui rassemble les designs les plus créatifs à notre sens.

Les prix Restaurant & Bar Design Awards dépendent entièrement des nouveautés dans les domaines du design, de l'architecture et de la gastronomie. Les personnes les plus importantes et créatives, membres plus ou moins renommés d'une communauté internationale stimulante, sont reflétées dans les projets et par nos éminents juges.

Pour la cérémonie des prix, nous cherchons à inspirer nos invités par le biais d'expériences interactives surprenantes. Chaque année, la sélection de restaurants et de bars va plus loin et chaque prix est différent du précédent, d'où le rayonnement de l'événement.

Ces prix ne seraient pas possibles sans nos sponsors et partenaires, auxquels nous exprimons toute notre reconnaissance. J'aimerais également remercier Leslie Brissett, Rupert Davies et Ceri Richmond pour faire au fil des ans que ces prix soient un succès sans cesse renouvelé.

Changing Tastes

Tony Chambers
Editor-in-Chief
at *Wallpaper*

Tony Chambers has twice been named Art Director of the Year in the Periodical Publishers Association Awards, as well as New Editor of the Year by the British Society of Magazine Editors. He is a graduate of Central Saint Martins School of Art and started his career as art editor at *The Sunday Times Magazine* before becoming art director of *British GQ* magazine. In 2003 he joined *Wallpaper** magazine as creative director and was appointed editor-in-chief in 2007.

Once upon a time, in a gastronomic land far away, a restaurant or bar that merely sated our appetite was deemed good enough. This land no longer exists. Our attitudes and expectations about where we want to meet, play, drink and eat have drastically changed. It's now as much about pleasing the eye as pleasing the tastebuds – and regular restaurant-goers will agree that sometimes it takes more than a delectable menu to ensure a fulfilling dining experience.

As a keen observer and consumer, I'm particularly sensitive to trends and to overbearing clichés. 'Artisanal' locally sourced ingredients, 'heritage' vegetables, 'mixologist-designed' beverages and 'curated' menus are all attractive and intriguing, but have become far too ubiquitous.

As product differentiation becomes increasingly difficult and competition between restaurateurs and bar-owners fiercer, the visual appeal of new establishments is more important than ever. A distinctive and intelligent design is essential to separate the ordinary from the extraordinary and to imprint a brand on the consumer's mind. And while aesthetics are of huge psychological importance, functionality also plays a critical role in an environment's navigation and flow.

Along with the expectation of alluring interiors, an all-round experience is just as covetable. Venues that successfully combine great service with good lighting, excellent acoustics and a comfy chair prove to be long-term winners. My all-time favourite has to be the Philip Johnson/Mies van der Rohe-designed Four Seasons in New York. Opened in 1959, every element from chairs to curtains, glassware to cutlery, menu typography to artwork was created to celebrate the ultimate in the Modernist, International Style. It remains one of the most talked-about restaurants in the world and should act as the benchmark for any designer, restaurateur or foodie.

This book is a timely celebration of a brave new wave of restaurant and bar design. It features work by long-time *Wallpaper** friends such as Jaime Hayon (Le Sergent Recruteur, Paris), Thomas Heatherwick (East Beach Cafe, Littlehampton, UK) and Isay Weinfeld (Las Piedras Fasano Swimming Pool Bar, Uruguay). Experienced designers creating modern spaces for a new generation.

We are all part of this new generation of well-read, well-connected, food-loving consumers. We are sophisticated, globally savvy and demanding. We have higher expectations, and we search for more creativity and individuality in our daily lives. This poses great challenges to the hospitality industry, but makes it the most exciting time to be a designer in this field.

Geschmack im Wandel

Tony Chambers wurde von den Periodical Publishers Association Awards zweimal zum Art Director des Jahres ernannt und von der British Society of Magazine Editors zum New Editor of the Year. Er ist Absolvent der Central Saint Martin's School of Art und begann seine Karriere als Kunstredakteur des *Sunday Times Magazine*; danach war er Art Director bei der Zeitschrift *British GQ*. Im Jahre 2003 ging er als Creative Director zum Magazin *Wallpaper** und wurde 2007 dessen Chefredakteur.

Vor langer, langer Zeit, in einem fernen gastronomischen Land, hielt man ein Restaurant oder eine Bar, die nur unseren Appetit stillten, für ausreichend. Dieses Land gibt es nicht mehr. Unsere Vorstellungen und Erwartungen gegenüber den Orten, an denen wir uns begegnen, spielen, trinken oder essen wollen, haben sich drastisch verändert. Heute geht es eher darum, das Auge ebenso wie die Geschmacksnerven anzusprechen – und regelmäßige Restaurantbesucher werden zustimmen, dass zu einem wirklich zufriedenstellenden kulinarischen Genuss manchmal mehr gehört als ein köstliches Menü.

Als scharfer Beobachter und hinterfragender Konsument reagiere ich besonders sensibel auf Trends und herrschende Klischees. Vor Ort „handwerklich" hergestellte Zutaten, „überlieferte" Gemüsesorten, „Mixologist"-Getränke und „ausgewählte" Menüs sind alle attraktiv und spannend, aber viel zu allgegenwärtig geworden.

Da die Unterscheidung von Produkten zunehmend schwieriger und der Wettbewerb zwischen Restaurant- und Barbesitzern härter wird, hat das optische Erscheinungsbild neu eingerichteter Lokale immer mehr an Bedeutung gewonnen. Ein unverwechselbares und intelligentes Design ist wichtig, um das Gewöhnliche vom Ungewöhnlichen zu unterscheiden und im Gedächtnis des Konsumenten einen Eindruck zu hinterlassen. Und wenngleich die Ästhetik von großer psychologischer Bedeutung ist, spielen auch die Funktionalität eines Betriebs und dessen geordneter Ablauf eine entscheidende Rolle.

Natürlich erwartet man ansprechende Räumlichkeiten, aber viel bedeutsamer ist der zufriedenstellende Gesamteindruck. Lokale, die perfekten Service erfolgreich mit guter Beleuchtung, ausgezeichneter Akustik und einem bequemen Sessel vereinen, gehören langfristig zu den Gewinnern. Mein absoluter Favorit ist nach wie vor das von Philip Johnson und Mies van der Rohe gestaltete Four Seasons in New York. In diesem 1959 eröffneten Lokal wurde jedes Element – von Stühlen bis zu Vorhängen, von Gläsern bis zu Bestecken, von der Typografie der Speisekarte bis zur künstlerischen Ausstattung – in hochqualifiziertem modernistischen International Style gestaltet. Es gehört immer noch zu den bekanntesten Restaurants der Welt und sollte jedem Designer, Restaurantbesitzer oder Feinschmecker als Maßstab dienen.

Dieses Buch ist eine Hommage an einen interessanten, neuartigen Trend in der Gestaltung von Restaurants und Bars. Es zeigt Arbeiten von langjährigen *Wallpaper**-Freunden wie Jaime Hayon (Le Sergent Recruteur, Paris), Thomas Heatherwick (East Beach Cafe, Littlehampton, UK) und Isay Weinfeld (Las Piedras Fasano Swimming Pool Bar, Uruguay). Erfahrene Designer schaffen moderne Räume für eine neue Generation.

Wir alle gehören zu dieser neuen Gesellschaftsschicht gut informierter, vernetzter, das Essen liebender Konsumenten. Wir sind gebildet, global versiert und anspruchsvoll. Wir haben hohe Erwartungen und streben verstärkt nach Kreativität und Individualität in unserem täglichen Leben – eine große Herausforderung an die Gastronomie. Zugleich macht es die Arbeit eines Designers auf diesem Gebiet und in unserer Zeit besonders spannend.

Les goûts changent

Tony Chambers a été nommé deux fois Art Director of the Year dans le cadre des Periodical Publishers Association Awards, ainsi que New Editor of the Year par la British Society of Magazine Editors. Il est diplômé de la Central Saint Martins School of Art et a débuté sa carrière en tant que rédacteur pour *The Sunday Times Magazine*, avant de devenir directeur artistique du magazine *British GQ*. En 2003, il a rejoint le magazine *Wallpaper** comme directeur de la création, puis est passé rédacteur en chef en 2007.

Il était une fois, dans des contrées gastronomiques éloignées, un restaurant ou un bar auquel nous demandions simplement d'être rassasiés. Cette réalité a disparu. Notre approche et nos attentes quant aux lieux que nous choisissons pour nous restaurer et nous amuser ont changé de façon radicale. Le plaisir des yeux est désormais tout aussi important que celui du palais, et les amateurs de restaurants s'accordent pour dire qu'une expérience gastronomique réussie tient plus qu'à un menu élaboré.

À la fois fin observateur et consommateur, je suis particulièrement sensible aux tendances et aux clichés qui s'imposent trop. Ingrédients locaux, légumes du terroir, boissons signées de mixologues et menus d'auteur sont aussi attirants qu'intrigants, mais par ailleurs trop courus.

La différentiation de produits est chaque fois plus difficile et la concurrence entre les propriétaires de restaurants et de bars toujours plus féroce. L'attrait visuel des nouveaux établissements est donc déterminant : un design original et intelligent est la clé pour distinguer l'ordinaire de l'extraordinaire et pour que les clients retiennent un nom. L'esthétique a un poids psychologique très important, mais la fonctionnalité est aussi essentielle pour la dynamique d'un environnement.

Outre des intérieurs séduisants, une expérience complète est recherchée. Les locaux sachant marier un service de qualité, un bon éclairage, une excellente acoustique et des assises confortables s'avèrent être des gagnants à long terme. Mon grand classique reste le Four Seasons de New York, conçu par le tandem Philip Johnson/Mies van der Rohe. Ouvert en 1959, chaque élément, des chaises aux rideaux en passant par les coupes, les couverts, la typographie du menu et le graphisme, a été pensé pour rendre hommage au summum du style moderniste international. Il s'inscrit comme l'un des restaurants les plus emblématiques au monde et mérite d'être pris comme référence par tous les designers, restaurateurs et gastronomes.

Cet ouvrage salue la nouvelle vague audacieuse en matière de design de restaurants et de bars. Il présente des créations d'amis de longue date de *Wallpaper** comme Jaime Hayon (Le Sergent Recruteur, Paris), Thomas Heatherwick (East Beach Cafe, Littlehampton, Royaume-Uni) et Isay Weinfeld (Las Piedras Fasano Swimming Pool Bar, Uruguay). Des designers expérimentés qui conçoivent des espaces modernes pour une nouvelle génération.

Nous appartenons tous à cette nouvelle génération de consommateurs informés, connectés et gourmets. Nous avons des goûts sophistiqués, une vision globale et sommes exigeants. Nous avons des attentes plus poussées et voulons plus de créativité et d'individualité dans notre quotidien. Autant de défis de taille pour le secteur de la restauration, et une bonne dose de motivation pour les designers dans ce domaine.

Americas

Americas

William Russell
Pentagram Partner

William Russell studied architecture at the University of Newcastle-upon-Tyne and the Royal College of Art. His recent clients have included Alexander McQueen, Cass Art, Margaret Howell and the Tate Gallery. His work has been published in the architectural press, design journals and numerous books and his projects have received prestigious awards. He has taught and lectured at South Bank University, the RCA and has been an invited lecturer at the Royal Institute of the Architects of Ireland (RIAI).

William Russell studierte Architektur an der Universität Newcastle-upon-Tyne und am Royal College of Art. Zu seinen aktuellen Auftraggebern zählen Alexander McQueen, Cass Art, Margaret Howell und die Tate Gallery. Seine Arbeiten wurden ausführlich in Architektur- und Design-zeitschriften sowie in zahlreichen Büchern veröffentlicht, seine Projekte mit renommierten Preisen ausge-zeichnet. Gelehrt und Vorlesungen gehalten hat er an der South Bank University, am Royal College of Art (RCA) und am Royal Institute of the Architects of Ireland (RIAI).

William Russell a suivi des études d'architecture à l'Université de Newcastle-upon-Tyne et au Royal College of Art. Parmi ses récents clients, il compte Alexander McQueen, Cass Art, Margaret Howell et la Tate Gallery. Son travail est apparu dans nombre de publications et ouvrages, et ses projets ont été primés. Il a été enseignant et conférencier à la South Bank University et au RCA, ainsi que professeur invité du Royal Institute of the Architects of Ireland (RIAI).

There is a unique freedom in designing spaces for social engagement such as these. Once all the basic functional requirements are covered, even the wildest concepts can work if they are carried through with enough conviction and attention to detail.

However frequently we go out, we are always looking for a memorable unrepeatable experience. When we take that first step over the threshold into one of these spaces, we do so with the expectation that all our senses will be stimulated and provoked, and therefore are more open and willing to accept the dramatic and extreme than we are in our day-to-day life.

The architectural space is one of the core components of this hoped-for sensory indulgence, but it is vital that the vision of the client, chef or club-owner, is clearly defined and understood so that all the individual elements work together. The details are so important, down to the wine glass we drink from or the jacket of the waiter serving our food – all combine to create a heightened sense of occasion.

For example, when I was designing Matter, a large night-club in London, the clients Keith and Cameron had a clear concept from the outset. It was to be a 'concrete playground', a series of volumes each fully serviced with cutting-edge sound systems, projectors and lighting rigs completely integrated into the architecture. These spaces should be a blank canvas which could then be taken and transformed into a different experience for every night by whoever was the promoter or DJ for that evening.

The designers of all the spaces documented in the following pages demonstrate a keen understanding of the theatrical possibilities that open up when working on this type of project. Unfortunately I have not had the opportunity to visit every one, but purely from the beautiful images it is clear the visitors to each establishment will be taken on a unique and distinct journey.

Every interior in this chapter has a different blend of elegance, opulence and restraint and shows a remarkable attention to detail. They all are carefully orchestrated designs which evoke a strong symbiotic relationship between the original distinctive concepts of the client and the designers.

The projects I am most drawn to and inspired by are those where there is a fine balance achieved between the theatricality required and an elegant economy in the number and type of materials utilised to fulfil the vision. The Pump Room in Chicago and the Tsujita LA Artisan Noodle in Los Angeles are great examples of this approach. Both places are immersive and beautiful while employing a small palette of materials.

They are all, however, on my ever-expanding list of places I must visit.

Dem Designer werden bei Räumen für gesellschaftliche Begegnungen dieser Art ungeahnte Freiheiten gewährt. Wenn die grundlegenden funktionalen Erfordernisse erfüllt sind, können sogar die unglaublichsten Konzepte funktionieren, sofern sie mit entsprechender Überzeugung und sorgfältiger Behandlung der Details ausgeführt werden.

Wann immer wir ausgehen, wünschen wir uns ein einprägsames, einmaliges Erlebnis. Sobald wir die Schwelle eines solchen Raumes überschreiten, erwarten wir, dass alle unsere Sinne angeregt und gefordert werden. Wir sind daher offener und eher als im alltäglichen Leben bereit, das Dramatische und Extreme zu akzeptieren.

Der architektonische Raum ist die Grundvoraussetzung für diesen erhofften sensorischen Genuss, aber es ist auch absolut notwendig, dass die Vorstellung des Auftraggebers, des Chefs oder des Besitzers, klar definiert und verstanden wird, damit alle Einzelelemente zusammenwirken. Die Details – bis zu den Weingläsern, aus denen wir trinken, oder dem Jackett des Kellners, der uns das Essen serviert – sind wichtig, weil sie alle zum Gefühl eines besonderen Erlebnisses beitragen.

Als ich zum Beispiel den großen Londoner Nightclub Matter plante, hatten die Auftraggeber Keith und Cameron von Anfang an eine klare Vorstellung. Es sollte ein „Spielplatz aus Beton" werden, eine Folge von Räumen mit voller Dienstleistung, mit modernsten, in die Architektur integrierten Tonanlagen, Projektoren und Lichtinstallationen. Diese Räume sollten eine freie Fläche darstellen, die dann jeden Abend von jedem beliebigen Promoter oder DJ für unterschiedliche Zwecke genutzt und verändert werden könnte.

Die Designer all der auf den folgenden Seiten vorgestellten Räume zeigen ein großes Verständnis für das in derartigen Projekten enthaltene dramatische Potenzial. Leider hatte ich nicht die Möglichkeit, sie alle zu besuchen, aber schon aus den wunderbaren Abbildungen wird deutlich, dass sich die Besucher jedes dieser Lokale auf eine einzigartige und jeweils unterschiedliche Reise begeben.

Jeder Raum zeigt eine andere Verbindung von Eleganz, Opulenz und auch Einschränkungen sowie eine besondere Beachtung der Details. Alle sind sie Ergebnisse sorgfältig inszenierter Entwürfe, die eine starke Symbiose zwischen den ursprünglich unterschiedlichen Konzepten von Auftraggeber und Designer herstellen.

Die mich am meisten ansprechenden und inspirierenden Projekte sind diejenigen, bei denen ein gelungenes Gleichgewicht von gewünschter Dramatik und ökonomischer Eleganz durch Anzahl und Art der verwendeten Materialien erreicht wurde. Der Pump Room in Chicago und das Tsujita LA Artisan Noodle sind hier großartige Beispiele. Beide Orte sind beeindruckend und ansprechend bei Anwendung einer nur kleinen Materialpalette.

Aber alle stehen sie auf meiner immer länger werdenden Liste von Lokalen, die ich besuchen muss.

La conception d'espaces visant l'engagement social offre une totale liberté. Une fois tous les aspects fonctionnels résolus, les idées même les plus audacieuses sont viables si elles sont exécutées avec une dose suffisante de conviction et de sens du détail.

Que nous allions souvent ou non restaurant, nous sommes toujours en quête d'une expérience unique et mémorable. En franchissant le seuil de l'un de ces locaux, nous espérons que tous nos sens seront stimulés et provoqués ; nous sommes donc plus disposés à accepter quelque chose de surprenant et d'inattendu que dans notre quotidien.

L'espace architectural est l'un des composants clés de cet apport sensoriel attendu. Toutefois, la vision du client, du chef ou du propriétaire doit être clairement exposée et comprise afin que tous les éléments se combinent en harmonie. Chaque détail compte, du verre dans lequel nous buvons à la veste du serveur, pour qu'ensemble ils confèrent un sentiment d'exception.

Pour le design de la discothèque Matter à Londres par exemple, mes clients Keith et Cameron avaient dès le départ une idée claire en tête. Elle devait être un « espace ludique en béton », avec une série de volumes équipés de systèmes audio sophistiqués, de projecteurs et de supports d'éclairage entièrement intégrés à l'architecture. Les espaces devaient être transformables à souhait et offrir une nouvelle expérience chaque nuit, en fonction du promoteur ou du DJ en charge.

Les designers de tous les locaux présentés dans ces pages font preuve d'une grande maîtrise des possibilités créatives liées à ce type de projet. Je n'ai malheureusement pas eu la chance de tous les visiter, mais les superbes photos suffisent pour savoir que les clients de chaque établissement seront invités à un voyage unique.

Chaque intérieur dans ce chapitre mêle à sa façon élégance, opulence et retenue, avec un soin remarquable du détail. Tous ces designs subtilement agencés dénotent la relation symbiotique entre les concepts d'origine du client et ceux des designers.

Les projets qui me parlent et m'inspirent le plus sont ceux affichant un parfait équilibre entre la théâtralité recherchée et l'élégante économie des matériaux employés pour donner corps à une vision. The Pump Room à Chicago et Tsujita LA Artisan Noodle à Los Angeles illustrent parfaitement cette approche, avec des intérieurs immersifs et élégants reposant sur une palette réduite de matériaux.

Tous s'inscrivent en tous cas dans ma liste toujours croissante de lieux à visiter absolument.

Aura Light & Sound Suite

Website auranightclubli.com
Date Opened September 2011
Designer Bluarch Architecture + Interiors + Lighting
Cost of Build $$$$
Size of Build 557 m² / 6,000 ft²
Award Longlist 2012
Address 1900 Hempstead Turnpike
East Meadow, NY 11554
USA

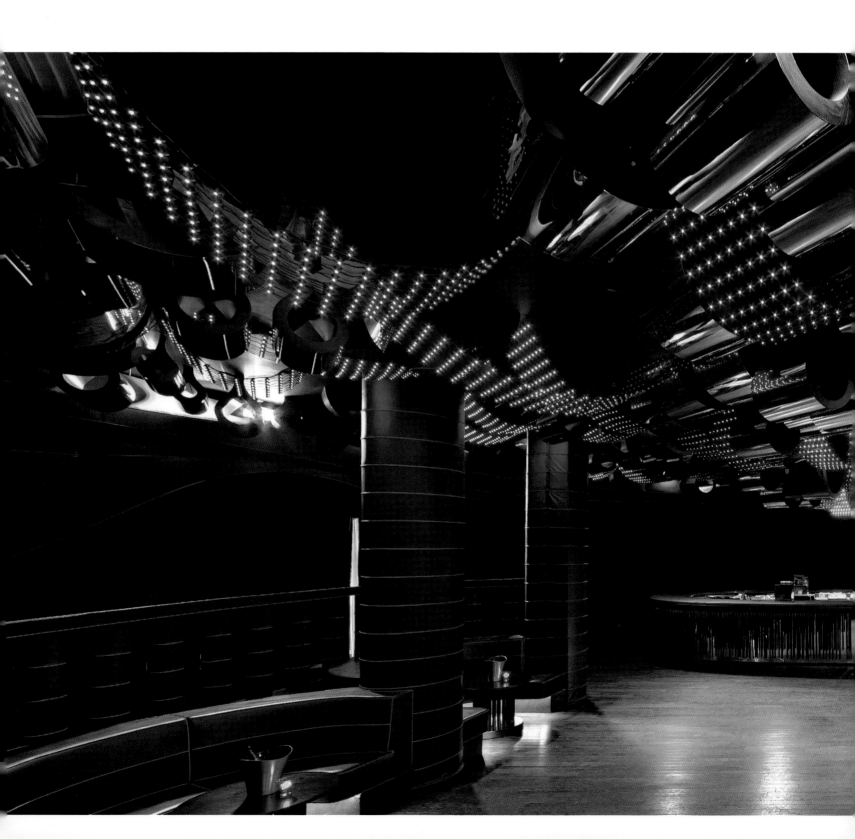

The dazzling interior of this night-club in upstate New York captures the spirit of euphoria to be found in dance music and the light shows that go with it, integrating the visual and auditory into one continuous space.

The design extends over two main levels, with spiralling vertical planes leading to a sunken dance-floor. This area is bathed in neon with the focal point being very much the vibrant, sculptural light installation overhead.

Keeping things lit up, flexible LED tape has been used to line the three bars, offset by walnut rods lining their vertical faces while a similar structure supports the tables embraced by the banquettes. The d&b audiotechnik electroacoustics were designed by KM Productions.

01

Der strahlende Innenraum dieses Clubs außerhalb von New York fängt die euphorische Stimmung ein, welche die Musik und die dazugehörigen Lichteffekte vermitteln. Gesehenes und Gehörtes treffen in einem durchgehenden Raum aufeinander.

Das Lokal erstreckt sich über zwei große Ebenen; spiralförmige Flächen führen hinunter zu einer vertieften Tanzfläche. Dieser Bereich ist in Neonlicht getaucht, zentrales Element ist vor allem die darüber angebrachte pulsierende, skulpturale Lichtinstallation.

Um die Helligkeit zu verstärken, wurden flexible LED-Bänder zur Einfassung der drei Theken verwendet. Die vertikalen Flächen sind mit Latten aus Walnussholz verkleidet. Eine ähnliche Struktur haben die von Sitzbänken umgebenen Tische. Die elektroakustische d&b audiotechnik wurde von KM Productions geplant.

01 Waves of large neon pleats ribbon along the ceiling illuminating the dance-floor below

02 A combination of reflective chrome panelling and flexible LED lighting were used to create the sinuous shapes

03 The mesh screens are video-operated using software and an LED light controller

Grâce à son intérieur éblouissant, cette discothèque dans le nord de l'État de New York restitue l'esprit d'euphorie propre à la *dance music* et au jeu de lumières qui va de pair. Les aspects visuels et acoustiques sont intégrés dans un espace continu.

Sur deux niveaux, le design est fait de surfaces verticales en spirale conduisant à une piste de danse en contrebas. Cette zone est baignée de néons, l'élément central étant de loin l'installation lumineuse sculpturale au plafond.

Pour l'éclairage, une bande de LED souple dessine les trois bars. La composition verticale de baguettes en noyer vient neutraliser l'effet des LED, et les tables entourées de banquettes reposent sur une structure similaire. L'électroacoustique d&b audiotechnik a été conçue par KM Productions.

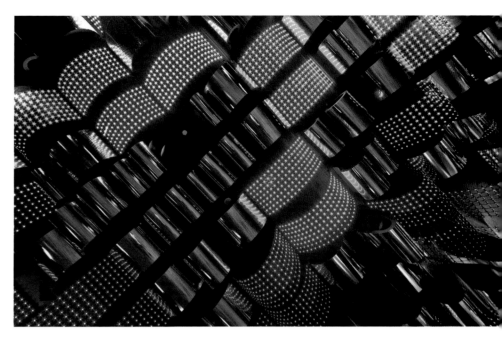

03

02

Cienna Ultralounge

Website	ciennany.com
Date Opened	December 2010
Designer	Bluarch Architecture + Interiors + Lighting
Cost of Build	$$$$
Size of Build	325 m² / 3,500 ft²
Award	Shortlist 2011
Address	2818 31st Street
	Astoria, NY 11102
	USA

Stepping into Cienna Ultralounge is like being transported to a subterranean wonderland, and one in which the overall design is modelled on the form of a silk cocoon.

Upholstered leather flows across the ceiling and down into the semi-circular booths lining the walls, providing a sumptuous backdrop for the stalactite curtains dangling overhead. 3D software was used to map the 88,888 soft acrylic threads on to the space, which were then applied by tufting each strand to a button.

Down-lit with LED lights, the strands pick up the continuously changing fluorescent colours as they rotate. They have also been synchronised to react to the music, thereby drawing sound and design together into one fluid experience.

Der Eintritt in dieses Lokal gleicht dem in ein unterirdisches Wunderland, und zwar in eins, das durchgehend nach der Form eines Seidenraupenkokons gestaltet wurde.

Die Decke und die Wände der halbrunden Nischen sind mit gepolstertem Leder verkleidet; es bildet einen prächtigen Hintergrund für die darüber aufgehängten Stalaktitenvorhänge. 3D-Software diente zur Verteilung der 88.888 weichen Acrylfäden über den Raum, die dann jeweils an einem Knopf festgemacht wurden.

Im Licht von LED-Strahlern nehmen diese rotierenden Stränge die ständig wechselnden fluoreszierenden Farben auf. Sie können auch synchronisiert werden, um auf die Musik zu reagieren, wobei Klang und Gestaltung sich zu einem eindruckvollen Erlebnis vereinen.

En pénétrant dans Cienna Ultralounge, les clients sont transportés dans un monde sous-terrain merveilleux, dont le design prend la forme d'un cocon de soie.

Un revêtement en cuir capitonné recouvre le plafond et les parois des banquettes semi-circulaires, une toile de fond somptueuse pour les rideaux de stalactites tombant du haut. Les 88.888 fils acrylique ont été répartis dans l'espace à l'aide d'un logiciel 3D et fixés en touffes à des boutons.

Éclairés du haut par des LED, les bandes captent les couleurs fluorescentes pendant leur rotation. Elles ont également été synchronisées pour réagir à la musique, mêlant naturellement audio et design.

01 An incandescent honey onyx bar joins the Cienna restaurant to the lounge space, adding a dramatic lustre to the shadowy setting

02 Lacquered poplar tables accompany curved white-leather seating, echoing the shapes created by the fringe detailing overhead

03 The LED lighting which illuminates the strands is tucked into recesses in the ceiling

03

02

Conga Room

Website	congaroom.com
Date Opened	December 2008
Designer	Belzberg Architects
Cost of Build	$$$$+
Size of Build	1,300 m² / 14,000 ft²
Award	Category winner 2010
Address	LA Chicago
	800 W Olympic Boulevard
	Los Angeles, CA 90015
	USA

This Latin night-club has been a Los Angeles cultural landmark for years, so when it relocated to the LA Live complex this was an opportunity to design a new version, housing a big dance-floor and a stage, multiple VIP areas, three bars and a full-service restaurant – completely transforming a space previously used as office premises.

With Latin American influences being naturally the guiding principle in the general design, the central attraction is an organic bloom in the form of a six-metre light installation.

The light erupts through a circular opening in the floor to form a stunning array that stretches upwards and saturates both the interior spaces in colour. Each 'step' creates an impressive pattern that works its way across the club's ceiling.

01

Dieser lateinamerikanische Club war über Jahre hinweg ein kultureller Mittelpunkt in Los Angeles. Als er in den LA Live Complex umzog, bot sich die Gelegenheit für eine Umgestaltung, die jetzt eine große Tanzfläche und eine Bühne, verschiedene VIP-Bereiche, drei Bars und ein Full-Service-Restaurant umfasst – wobei früher als Büroräume genutzte Flächen vollkommen umgestaltet wurden.

Während lateinamerikanische Einflüsse naturgemäß die Leitlinie für den Gesamtentwurf darstellten, bildet ein organischer Strahl in Form einer sechs Meter großen Lichtinstallation die zentrale Attraktion.

Das große Lichtobjekt stößt in eine runde Öffnung im Boden und bildet eine fantastische Plastik, das sich über beide Innenbereiche austreckt und sie in Farbe taucht. Jeder „Schritt" erzeugt ein eindrucksvolles Muster, das die Decke des Raumes überzieht.

01 Amongst the kaleidoscope of back-lit shapes covering the walls, the Papaya Bar and 'Surface Tattoos' were designed by Cuban artist Jorge Pardo and Mexican muralist Sergio Arau

02 The intricately arranged shapes of the panelling are dance 'footprints' taken from the Cuban rumba and play an important functional role as an integral part of the building's infrastructure, housing a state-of-the-art acoustic control system

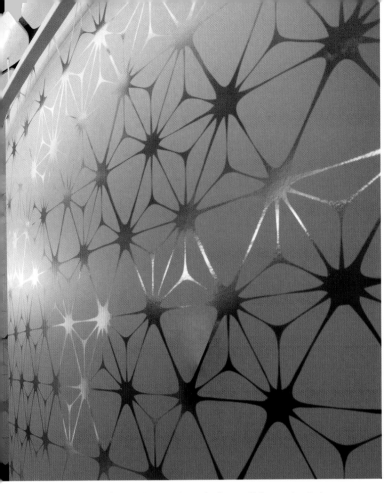

"The ceiling panels converged into a 20-foot-tall glowing tornado that penetrated the dance floor, inviting and guiding patrons up to the activities in the club."

Belzberg Architects

Cette discothèque de musique latine a été pendant des années une référence culturelle à Los Angeles. Son installation dans le complexe LA Live a été l'excuse pour en revoir le design et la doter d'une piste de danse généreuse, de plusieurs espaces VIP, de trois bars et d'un restaurant, supposant la complète métamorphose d'un local auparavant destiné à des bureaux.

Les influences d'Amérique latine ont naturellement dicté le design dans son ensemble. L'attraction centrale est une installation lumineuse de six mètres de haut qui rappelle la forme d'un bourgeon.

Un éclairage suspendu sort d'une ouverture circulaire au sol pour éclore et s'étendre au plafond, saturant de couleur les espaces intérieurs. Chaque « étape » crée un motif surprenant qui se propage sur tout le plafond du club.

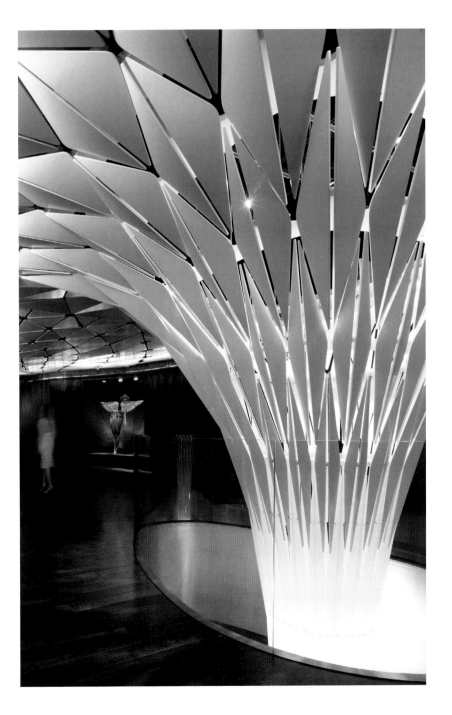

Innuendo

Date Opened	May 2011
Designer	Bluarch Architecture + Interiors + Lighting
Cost of Build	$$$
Size of Build	158 m² / 1,700 ft²
Award	Shortlist 2011
Address	75 Main Street
	Port Washington, NY 11050
	USA

Although it is now no longer open, the Innuendo restaurant was an engaging fusion of awe-inspiring ceiling installation combined with creative lighting techniques.

The concept behind the massed ceiling design was derived from geometry and the self-replicating patterns produced by fractals, which was then developed into the impressive maze of clustered cubes suspended overhead.

The repeating unit-shapes of the poplar-wood structure hung together in such a way that they evoked the sensation of being caught inside some futuristic hive. Large in mass, but not in density, the structure was given life by use of rotational lighting, in turn emphasising its ephemerality.

In dem heute geschlossenen Restaurant Innuendo sind Lichttechnik und Deckeninstallation auf beeindruckende Art und Weise miteinander verschmolzen.

Das der kumulativen Deckengestaltung zugrunde liegende Konzept war von der Geometrie und sich wiederholenden, von Fraktalen produzierten Mustern bestimmt. Daraus entwickelte sich ein eindrucksvoller Irrgarten aus gruppenweise aufgehängten Kuben.

Die standardisierten Formelemente der Konstruktion aus Pappelholz hingen so zusammen, dass man meinen konnte, man wäre in einem futuristischen Bienenstock gefangen. Die in der Masse, aber nicht der Dichte ausgedehnte Struktur wurde durch rotierende Beleuchtung zum Leben erweckt, die sie wiederum flüchtig hervorhob.

01

01 A kinetic lighting system created a fluid and ever-changing environment

02 A mirrored surface in the centre of the ceiling gave the impression of additional space

03 The self-similar cubes created an illusionary space beneath which diners sat at their tables

Désormais fermé, le restaurant Innuendo combinait parfaitement une installation grandiose au plafond et des techniques d'illumination créatives.

Le design volumineux au plafond s'inspirait de la géométrie et des motifs reproduits par fractales. Le résultat était un gigantesque labyrinthe de cubes assemblés et suspendus.

La répétition et l'assemblage des éléments cubiques de cette structure en bois de peuplier donnaient la sensation d'être pris au piège dans une sorte de ruche futuriste. Volumineuse en termes de masse mais de faible densité, la composition prenait vie grâce à un éclairage rotatif, lequel en soulignait aussi l'aspect éphémère.

03

Las Piedras Fasano
Swimming Pool Bar

Website	fasano.com.br
Date Opened	January 2011
Designer	Isay Weinfeld
Cost of Build	$$$
Size of Build	110 m² / 1,180 ft²
Award	Category winner 2012
Address	Cno. Cerro Egusquiza y Paso del Barranco La Barra 20400 Punta del Este Uruguay

Sitting in harmony with its beautiful surroundings, this structure within the Las Piedras Fasano hospitality complex is a stunning design for a space balanced in affinity with the region's vast and rocky landscape.

Positioned on a mound overlooking the whole complex, the bar's main draw is its panoramic views. A large rectangular corten steel container balances gracefully on the edge of the plateau, hovering over the low vegetation of lavender and cactus below.

So as not to disturb the continuity of the countryside, each element in the complex has been designed to mimic the surrounding *piedras*, or rock formations. As a result, the bar and swimming pool constitute just one of several architectural ecosystems here, self-contained yet connected by the terrain.

Dieses harmonisch in seine schöne Umgebung eingefügte Gebäude in der Ferienanlage Las Piedras Fasano ist das Ergebnis eines großartigen Entwurfs für einen Ort im Einklang mit der weiträumigen Felslandschaft der Region.

Die besondere Attraktion des auf einen Hügel oberhalb der ganzen Anlage errichteten Gebäudes ist vor allem der Panoramaausblick. Wie ein großer, rechteckiger Container aus Corten-Stahl balanciert es anmutig am Rande des Plateaus und schwebt über der niedrigen Vegetation aus Lavendel und Kaktus.

Um den Fortbestand der Landschaft nicht zu beeinträchtigen, wurde jedes Element des Komplexes in Anlehnung an die *piedras*, die umgebenden Felsformationen, geplant. Folglich bilden die Bar und der Pool hier nur eins von mehreren architektonischen Ökosystemen, sie sind eigenständig und doch mit dem Terrain verbunden.

02

Totalement en harmonie avec la beauté de son environnement, cette structure logée dans le complexe hôtelier de Las Piedras Fasano présente un design original pour un espace équilibré, en affinité avec le vaste paysage rocheux.

Planté sur une butte surplombant le complexe, le point fort du bar est la vue panoramique. Un grand conteneur en acier Corten semble en équilibre au bord du plateau et chapeaute les lavandes et les cactus en dessous.

Pour ne pas rompre la continuité du paysage, chaque aspect du complexe a été conçu pour imiter les *piedras* (formations rocheuses) alentours. Le bar et la piscine forment donc l'un des écosystèmes architecturaux de l'endroit, à la fois autonomes et connectés par le terrain.

01 The blockish and brutalist modern structure creates a space for an open-air lounge, bar and changing-room area

02 The russet colour of corten steel, an alloy of copper, nickel and chromium, blends into the arid setting whilst acting as a counterpoint to the turquoise pool nearby

03 The swimming pool is an elegant response to a natural depression within the surrounding rock formation, creating the seductive illusion of a waterhole

03

33

Mistral Wine & Champagne Bar

Date Opened	November 2012
Designer	Studio Arthur Casas
Size of Build	100 m² / 1,100 ft²
Award	Shortlist 2013
Address	Shopping JK São Paulo
	São Paulo-SP, 04543-011
	Brazil

With the majority of sales for Mistral Wines being made over the Internet, the design for this concept store aimed to provide a physical interaction with the product being sold. The impressive contemporary space also complements the status of the wines and champagnes on display.

The resulting design creates an intimate journey that shows off the many vintages on offer. Each of the interconnected areas encourages individual responses, much like the relationship we share with fine wines.

Making use of the narrative potential of long, curved spaces, the store itself becomes a story through which customers move as they learn. A long hallway opens into a bar area, with a large, free-standing pentagonal table used for tastings. The space also includes a cellar, interactive gallery, reading-room and sales area.

Weil die Mistral-Weine überwiegend durch das Internet vertrieben werden, sollte das Design dieses Concept Stores eine konkrete Begegnung mit dem angebotenen Produkt ermöglichen. Der eindrucksvolle, moderne Raum entspricht darüber hinaus dem Status der ausgestellten Weine und Champagner.

Der ausgeführte Entwurf bietet eine ausgedehnte Tour durch das Gebäude, bei der die vielen angebotenen Jahrgänge vorgeführt werden. Jeder der miteinander verbundenen Räume löst individuelle Reaktionen aus, genauso wie unser Verhältnis zu guten Weinen.

Der Store macht vom narrativen Potenzial der langen, gekrümmten Räume Gebrauch und wird selbst zu einer Geschichte, durch die sich die Kunden lernend bewegen. Ein langer Korridor führt zur Bar mit einem großen, frei stehenden Tisch für Verkostungen. Der Bau enthält auch einen Keller, eine interaktive Galerie, einen Lesesaal und einen Verkaufsraum.

01 Vertical wooden ribbing is complemented by the black mirror and glossy white plastic in the long hallway, in which bottles are displayed using holes cut into the walls

02 Mirrored glass conceals a digital screen which provides information about the different wines

03 The reading-room features a floor-to-ceiling wine rack

Le gros des ventes de Mistral Wines se faisant sur Internet, le design pour cette boutique concept recherche l'interaction physique avec le produit. Cet espace contemporain et impactant permet également de consulter le statut des vins et des champagnes en vente.

Le design choisi conduit à un voyage intime parmi les nombreux millésimes. Chacune des zones interconnectées encourage des expériences individuelles, à l'instar de la relation avec les grands crus.

Le recours au potentiel narratif de longs espaces courbes fait de cette boutique une histoire à elle seule que les clients parcourent tout en apprenant. Un long couloir débouche sur un bar, où une grande table pentagonale autoporteuse est destinée aux dégustations. L'espace compte également un cellier, une galerie interactive, une salle de lecture et une salle de vente.

03

02

Pio Pio

Website	piopio.com
Date Opened	November 2009
Designer	Sebastian Mariscal Studio
Cost of Build	$$$$+
Size of Build	325 m² / 3,500 ft²
Award	Category winner 2010
Address	604 Tenth Avenue
	New York, NY 10036
	USA

01

Drawing visitors in from the busy streets, this restaurant is a highly choreographed space disguising a series of well-crafted wooden rooms. The wholesale transformation from the world outside is designed to evoke a sense of Latin America, but without directly referring to it.

Entry via the ground floor leads to rooms clad entirely in sustainable wood, with a floating hosting table, a 12-metre marble bar and a brass-lined vestibule. Downstairs opens out into the main dining area where the walls are covered with 4,000 ocotillo branches.

This sustainable Mexican desert plant adds to the palette of textures and materials and frames a series of deconstructed poured-concrete cubes which divide the lower-ground floor into different areas. The use of concrete adds to the strange sense that the space is full of discovery, whilst artfully concealing functional elements.

Dieses Restaurant lockt die Besucher von der belebten Straße in einen attraktiv inszenierten Bereich, der aus einer Folge kunstvoll mit Holz verkleideter Räume besteht. Dieser drastische Unterschied zur Außenwelt soll die Atmosphäre Lateinamerikas herbeirufen, aber keinen direkten Bezug herstellen.

Der Eingang vom Erdgeschoss führt in ganz mit nachhaltig gewonnenem Holz ausgestattete Räume mit einem schwebenden Bewirtungstisch, einer 12 Meter langen Marmorbar und einem mit Messing ausgeschlagenen Vestibül. Im Untergeschoss liegt der große Speisesaal, dessen Wände mit 4.000 Ocotillozweigen überzogen sind.

Diese nachhaltige mexikanische Wüstenpflanze gehört zur Palette der Texturen und Materialien und umgibt eine Anzahl von zerlegten Gussbetonkuben, die das Untergeschoss in verschiedene Bereiche aufteilen. Die Verwendung von Beton trägt zum seltsamen Eindruck bei, dass es an diesem Ort viel zu entdecken gibt, während die funktionalen Elemente kunstvoll verborgen bleiben.

02

"The spaces of Pio Pio are interwoven with mystery, discovery, and contradiction."

Sebastian Mariscal Studio

Ce restaurant attire les clients par son espace très sophistiqué qui renferme une série de salles en bois soignées. La transformation globale vise à évoquer l'Amérique latine, sans pour autant faire de référence directe.

L'entrée se fait au rez-de-chaussée et conduit à des salles entièrement revêtues de bois durable, avec une table flottante à la réception, un bar en marbre de 12 mètres de long et un vestibule aux parois en laiton. Des escaliers mènent au sous-sol à la salle principale, dont les murs sont recouverts de 4 000 branches d'ocotillo.

Cette plante durable du Mexique enrichit la palette de textures et de matériaux ; elle encadre aussi une série de cubes déstructurés en béton coulé qui compartimentent l'espace du bas. L'emploi de béton confère de l'originalité à l'ensemble, tout en dissimulant habilement les éléments fonctionnels.

01 The seating was designed and built by a Californian carpenter, local to the Sebastian Mariscal Studio office

02 All the wood comes from a sustainable forest in Mexico

03 The marble floating table was built by New York stone-mason T. D. Smith

Pump Room

Website	pumproom.com
Date Opened	2011
Designer	Yabu Pushelberg
Size of Build	409 m² / 4,400 ft²
Award	Category winner 2012
Address	Public Chicago
	1301 North State Parkway
	Chicago, IL 60610
	USA

Originally the famous Ambassador East, this lounge and late-night supper club has now reopened in a re-imagined format as part of the Public hotel. The first Pump Room restaurant was a renowned celebrity haunt and the new design wanted to capture this glamour but in a fully 21st-century context.

The dining space is split across two levels, with four eating areas. Special touches mark the former glory, such as keeping Frank Sinatra's personal 'booth' intact or the 3,000-plus photos of the rich and famous who visited the restaurant, from David Bowie to Queen Elizabeth.

In contrast, the five-metre-high ceiling boasts a fantastical lighting structure built like a constellation. 500 different-sized marbled orbs – each individually cast – connected with iron rods form an elaborate mobile running down one length of the space.

Diese Lounge mit nächtlichem Speiselokal war ursprünglich das berühmte Ambassador East. In umgestalteter Form wurde es nun als Teil des Hotels Public wiedereröffnet. Das frühere Pump Room Restaurant war ein beliebter Treffpunkt von Prominenten, und der Umbau sollte diesen Glamour bewahren, jedoch ganz im Kontext des 21. Jahrhunderts.

Der Speisebereich ist über zwei Ebenen in vier Abteilungen aufgeteilt. Einzelne Elemente verweisen auf die glorreiche Vergangenheit, zum Beispiel der Erhalt von Frank Sinatras persönlicher „Nische" oder die mehr als 3.000 Fotos der Reichen und Berühmten, die das Restaurant besucht haben, von David Bowie bis zu Queen Elizabeth.

Als Kontrast dazu prangt an der fünf Meter hohen Decke ein fantastischer Beleuchtungskörper in Form eines Sternbilds. 500 unterschiedlich große, marmorierte Himmelskörper – jeder von ihnen separat gegossen – bilden, verbunden durch Eisenstäbe, ein ausgeklügeltes Mobile über die gesamte Länge des Raumes.

01 A recess lined with 12-carat white-gold leaf bathes the liquor bottles in a precious glow

02 Chic half-round banquettes with oak tables provide seating, as does the 7.5-metre bar in dark cerused oak

03 The lighting installation was a special commission designed by Milan's Dimore Studio

02

Anciennement Ambassador East, ce *lounge* et restaurant nocturne a rouvert ses portes dans un nouveau format au sein de l'hôtel Public. Le prédécesseur de Pump Room était un repère de célébrités ; le nouveau design voulait traduire ce glamour, mais dans le contexte du XXIᵉ siècle.

L'espace se répartit sur deux niveaux et compte quatre salles. Des touches spéciales évoquent la gloire d'antan, comme la banquette personnelle de Frank Sinatra laissée intacte, ou les plus de 3 000 photographies de personnalités qui sont passées par le restaurant, de David Bowie à la reine Elizabeth.

A cinq mètres de hauteur, le plafond arbore une incroyable structure de lampes, telles une constellation de 500 globes marbrés de différentes tailles. Éclairés individuellement, ces globes sont reliés par des tiges de fer et forment un mobile élaboré sur toute la longueur de l'espace.

Salon Urbain

Website laplacedesarts.com/rooms/area/
salon-urbain.en.html
Date Opened May 2012
Designer Sid Lee Architecture
Size of Build 553 m² / 5,950 ft²
Award Shortlist 2013
Address Place des Arts
175 Sainte-Catherine Street West
Montreal, QC H2X 1Z8
Canada

Located next door to Montreal's cultural centre, the Place des Arts, this spectacular communal space was partly inspired in its design by live art and musical performances. Another consideration meant using straight lines to offset the room's natural curve, making the ceiling look taller in this former underground car-park.

A free-standing fibreglass bar works as one continuous element. With an alluring glossy black finish the apparently seamless curvature of the shape becomes a visual manifestation of a sound-wave.

Continuing with this theme, the ceiling installation echoes the behaviour of sound, endlessly refracting and diffracting across the space. White geometric panels laced with dazzling LED lights open and close, folding out across the textured and moulded ceiling. Made from lacquered metal, they form a beguiling pattern that sets a futuristic tone.

Das Design für diese neben Montreals Kulturzentrum Place des Arts gelegene, spektakuläre kommunale Einrichtung sollte ein Forum für künstlerische und musikalische Aufführungen bieten. Außerdem wollte man mit geraden Linien einen Kontrast zu den natürlichen Krümmungen des Raumes setzen und die Decke dieser früheren Tiefgarage höher wirken lassen.

Die frei stehende Bar aus Glasfaser bildet ein durchgehendes Element. Mit ihrer ansprechenden, schwarz glänzenden Beschichtung wird die scheinbar nahtlose Krümmung zur sichtbaren Manifestation einer Klangwelle.

Als Fortsetzung dieses Themas nimmt die Deckeninstallation das Klangverhalten auf in unaufhörlicher Brechung und Ablenkung im Raum. Weiße, geometrisch geformte Tafeln mit blendenden LED-Leuchten öffnen und schließen sich und entfalten sich über die strukturierte und profilierte Decke. Sie sind aus lackiertem Metall und bilden ein attraktives Muster mit futuristischen Akzenten.

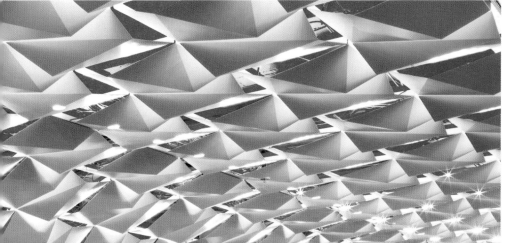

01 Different-coloured lighting changes the mood in this multi-functional event space

02 The shimmering curved pillars are strong sci-fi elements, whilst the translucent red plastic curtain allows for versatility when the venue is in use

03 A flowing metal sink in the toilets continues the sound-wave theme

03

À côté du centre culturel de Montréal, la Place des Arts forme un espace public spectaculaire dont le design a été en partie inspiré par les concerts et performances artistiques qui s'y produisent. L'emploi de lignes droites était aussi recherché pour compenser la courbe naturelle de la pièce : le plafond de cet ancien parking sous-terrain semble ainsi plus haut.

Un bar autoporteur en fibre de verre marque une continuité. Sa finition brillante et séduisante fait de cette forme courbe apparemment d'un bloc la représentation visuelle d'une onde sonore.

Sur la même thématique, l'installation au plafond fait écho au déplacement du son et à ses réfractions et diffractions constantes à travers l'espace. Des panneaux géométriques blancs éclairés de LED éblouissantes s'ouvrent et se ferment. En métal laqué, ils se déploient sur le plafond texturé et à moulures et composent un assemblage attrayant aux allures futuristes.

STK Midtown

Website	togrp.com/togrp-stk-midtown/about
Date Opened	December 2011
Designer	ICRAVE
Cost of Build	$$$$+
Size of Build	557 m² / 6,000 ft²
Award	Shortlist 2013
Address	1114 6th Avenue
	New York, NY 10036
	USA

01

Rising up from Manhattan's Avenue of the Americas, the sloped black-and-white façade of the 50-storey Grace Building is a monumental feat of architectural engineering. At its base, where street level meets the columned façade, is the fifth outlet for steakhouse chain STK.

The sleek and contemporary design of the two-floored dining-space lends elegance to the traditional American steakhouse. In this, the chain's key stylistic elements are adapted to fit into distinguished premises.

Banquette seating in the dining area promotes an intimate and relaxed atmosphere while eating. The soft leather furnishing is by Ultrafrabrics and the seats have been cut into a lightbox that runs down the centre of the main space, creating inviting half-circle inlets.

02

01 White travertine used on the building's exterior continues into the lobby and main bar, with streetlight-inspired lighting

02 Alongside moulded columns, the bar is made from calacatta marble veneer, laminated with honeycomb backer and edged with solid marble

03 The undulating Formglas ceiling is modelled on the shape of a cattle horn, and is echoed in the building's ribbed façade

04 Tables by ISA International have a luxurious polished rosewood finish

03

Die von der Avenue of the Americas in Manhattan schräg aufsteigende, schwarz-weiße Fassade des 50-geschossigen Grace Buildings ist ein monumentales Meisterstück der Architektur- und Ingenieurkunst. An seiner Basis, bei den Stützen auf Straßenebene, befindet sich die fünfte Filiale der Steakhouse-Kette STK.

Die schicke und moderne Gestaltung des zweigeschossigen Speiselokals verleiht dem traditionellen amerikanischen Steakhouse Eleganz. Hier wurden die wichtigen Stilelemente des Unternehmens einem hochklassigen Restaurant angepasst.

Gepolsterte Sitzbänke im Essbereich vermitteln eine intime und entspannte Atmosphäre. Die weichen Ledermöbel stammen von Ultrafabrics; die Sitzgruppen sind in eine Lichtbox im Zentrum des großen Saales integriert und bilden einladende, halbkreisförmige Einbuchtungen.

Du haut de ses 50 étages se dressant sur l'Avenue of the Americas, en plein Manhattan, la façade noire et blanche inclinée de l'immeuble Grace est un exploit monumental de génie architectural. Au pied de la façade à colonnes se trouve le cinquième local ouvert par la chaîne de restaurants à viande STK.

Le design épuré et contemporain de la salle distribuée sur deux étages confère une touche d'élégance au traditionnel restaurant à viande américain. La chaîne s'attache d'ailleurs à adapter les éléments stylistiques à chacun de ses locaux.

Assis sur des banquettes, les convives peuvent profiter de l'atmosphère intime et détendue. Le mobilier revêtu de cuir doux est signé Ultrafrabrics, et les côtés d'un caisson lumineux traversant la salle principale ont été découpés en demi-cercles pour former des espaces accueillants.

04

The Gourmet Tea

Website	thegourmettea.com.br
Date Opened	February 2011
Designer	Alan Chu
Cost of Build	$$$
Size of Build	90 m² / 970 ft²
Award	Shortlist 2012
Address	Rua Mateus Grou 89
	Pinheiros
	São Paulo-SP, 05415-050
	Brazil

Located amongst the lively bars and graffiti-lined alleyways of São Paulo's Vila Madalena district, this bright but minimal tea-room was the first home for the brand, The Gourmet Tea.

To encourage an uptake in tea-drinking amongst the Brazilian people, tea is infused at the table so that customers can see the process in action. The glass teapots each come with their own timer, ensuring that the tea is brewed to just the right strength.

Originally a small house, in its new incarnation the site functions as a café and concept store. 35 blends have been given their own identifying colour and this in turn informed the rest of the design, which relies on patterns and colour to punctuate the otherwise bleached interior.

Diese heitere, und kleine, inmitten der mit Bars und Graffiti angefüllten Gassen in São Paulos Bezirk Vila Madalena gelegene Teestube war das erste Lokal der Marke The Gourmet Tea.

Um den Brasilianern das Teetrinken näherzu bringen, wird der Tee am Tisch aufgegossen, sodass die Kunden den Prozess in Aktion sehen können. Jede gläserne Teekanne hat einen eigenen Timer, um sicherzustellen, dass der Tee genau die richtige Stärke hat.

Ursprünglich nur ein kleines Haus, funktioniert das Gebäude jetzt in seiner neuen Gestalt auch als Café und Concept Store. 35 Mischungen haben ihre eigene Farbe, und das wiederum bestimmte auch die Gestaltung mit Mustern und Farben, die im ansonsten einfarbig hellen Innenraum Akzente setzen.

01 An open display unit storing canisters of tea runs the entire length of the space

02 The counter was made simply from plywood, with a vinyl adhesive giving it a colourful makeover

03 Brightly coloured pendant lamps vary in shape and size and stand out against the exposed brickwork, painted white

"It's for those willing to live the real tea experience."

The Gourmet Tea

03

02

Trouvant sa place parmi les bars animés et les ruelles pleines de graffiti du quartier Vila Madalena de São Paulo, ce salon de thé clair et minimal est le premier ouvert par la marque The Gourmet Tea.

Pour inciter la population brésilienne à boire plus de thé, celui-ci est infusé à la table des clients, ainsi témoins du processus. Les théières en verre sont équipées d'un minuteur pour garantir la bonne intensité du thé.

Cette ancienne petite maison s'est réincarnée en un café et une boutique concept. Chacun des 35 mélanges est identifié par une couleur, et cette palette conditionne le reste du design, dont les motifs et les tons agrémentent l'intérieur blanchi.

Toy

Website toyrestaurant.com
Date Opened July 2012
Designer Jeffrey Beers International
Size of Build 186 m² / 2,000 ft²
Award Longlist 2013
Address 18 9th Avenue
New York, NY 10014
USA

A fusion of dining and nightlife in the Gansevoort Hotel, this contemporary-Asian restaurant takes classic Oriental imagery and recasts it with startling futuristic effect. After hours the atmospheric surroundings host special DJ nights, complete with laser lighting and dancers suspended in mid-air.

For speed of completion, 3D design was linked to a CNC cutting machine, enabling the design to be transferred on to the space immediately. A range of ready-made materials, customised to fit, also helped give the difficult original layout a more free-flowing arrangement.

A mirrored structure (weighing 680 kg) descends from the ceiling to cover the DJ booth, its angled surfaces reflecting light through the venue and each triangular panel being animated individually by projected images. The blown-up image of a Ming vase was applied with sheeting directly to the graphic wall.

Dieses zeitgenössisch asiatische Restaurant im Gansevoort Hotel, ein Speiselokal mit Nachtleben, übernimmt klassische orientalische Darstellungen und überträgt sie in aufregende futuristische Effekte. In dieser besonderen Atmosphäre werden auch DJ-Nächte veranstaltet, mit Laserlicht und einer in der Luft schwebenden Tanzfläche.

Um die Fertigstellung zu beschleunigen, wurde die 3D-Planung mit einem CNC-Schneider verbunden, sodass der Entwurf direkt auf den Raum übertragen werden konnte. Verschiedene Fertigmaterialien, die passend gemacht wurden, trugen dazu bei, dem ursprünglichen Bereich eine offenere Raumwirkung zu verleihen.

Eine verspiegelte, 680 Kilogramm wiegende Konstruktion an der Decke über dem DJ-Pult reflektiert mit ihren schrägen Flächen das Licht durch den ganzen Raum; auf jede der dreieckigen Tafeln werden unterschiedliche Bilder projiziert. Das vergrößerte Abbild einer Ming-Vase wurde direkt an der grafischen Wand befestigt.

01 Gauze scrim with projected images separates the main dining-room from the upstairs area

02 Triangular projection mapping hides the DJ booth, transforming it into this eye-catching feature

03 An outdoor oyster bar and dining area features sculpted wooden chairs

04 Communal tables are raised to bar-stool level, providing an alternative dining option

Au sein de l'hôtel Gansevoort, ce restaurant asiatique contemporain et club à ses heures remanie l'imagerie orientale avec des effets futuristes surprenants. Pour les *after hours*, le cadre dynamique accueille des DJ pour des nuits spéciales, avec une illumination laser et des danseurs suspendus dans les airs.

Pour accélérer les travaux, une machine-outil à commande numérique a permis de transposer le design 3D immédiatement dans l'espace. Grâce à une série de matériaux prêts à l'emploi et personnalisés, l'agencement complexe a pu se faire plus aisément.

Une structure en miroir de 680 kg descend du plafond et enveloppe la cabine du DJ. Ses surfaces obliques reflètent la lumière dans la pièce et chaque panneau triangulaire est animé par des images projetées. L'agrandissement sur bâche de la photo d'un vase Ming a été directement appliqué sur un mur.

03

04

Tsujita LA Artisan Noodle

Website	tsujita-la.com
Date Opened	July 2011
Designer	SWeeT co., ltd.
Cost of Build	$$$$
Size of Build	79 m² / 850 ft²
Award	Shortlist 2012
Address	2057 Sawtelle Blvd
	Los Angeles, CA 90025
	USA

Recalling Japanese ink-wash painting, subtle cloud-forms cover the ceiling of this Japanese restaurant. Light plays a key role in giving the space its special charm as the warm, gentle glow suggests golden rain falling from the clouds above.

The textured, artistic installation captivates viewers from any perspective, whether passers-by looking in from the street through the large windows or seen directly from beneath when dining. The meticulously crafted structure is made from 2,500 wooden rods and appears to change with each new viewing.

The overall concept came from the ancient Shinto shrine of Izumo and the calm of such a place does, quite literally, shine through. Many of the elements in the handcrafted interior were produced in Japan, reinforcing the aim to create an authentic Japanese setting in downtown LA.

Zarte, an japanische Tuschmalereien erinnernde Wolkenformationen zieren die Decke dieses japanischen Restaurants. Das warme und milde Licht spielt hier eine wichtige Rolle; es verleiht dem Raum einen besonderen Charme und lässt an goldenen Regen denken, der aus den Wolken herabfällt.

Die strukturierte, künstlerische Installation fängt die Betrachter aus jeder Perspektive ein: Vorübergehende, die von der Straße durch die großen Fenster hereinschauen, oder Speisegäste, die von unten hinaufsehen. Die handwerklich exakt verarbeitete Konstruktion besteht aus 2.500 Holzstäben und scheint sich von jedem Blickwinkel aus zu verändern.

Das Gesamtkonzept stammt vom alten Shinto-Schrein von Izumo, und die Ruhe eines solchen Ortes scheint hier im wörtlichen Sinne durch. Viele Elemente des handwerklich gestalteten Innenraumes wurden in Japan produziert und haben dazu beigetragen, dass in Downtown Los Angeles ein authentisch japanischer Ort entstanden ist.

02

Les subtiles formes de nuages ornant le plafond de ce restaurant japonais rappellent la technique du lavis d'encre. La lumière joue un rôle essentiel et donne tout son charme au local, avec une lueur blonde telle une pluie dorée tombant des nuages.

L'installation artistique et pleine de texture est fascinante depuis tous les angles de vue, tant pour les passants l'observant de la rue à travers les grandes fenêtres que pour les convives mangeant juste en dessous. Cette structure assemblée avec soin compte 2 500 tiges de bois et semble changer constamment.

Le concept global s'inspire de l'ancien sanctuaire shinto d'Izumo et de la paix qu'un lieu de culte transmet. Nombre d'éléments de l'intérieur ont été élaborés à la main au Japon, plantant au cœur de Los Angeles un décor japonais authentique.

01 Hanging tubular lights create a glow right across the ceiling, casting shadows over the dining area and paved black floor tiles

02 Two walls either side of the bar are constructed out of neatly woven bamboo

03 Lanterns with the brand's simple flower identity sit in blonde-wood cube-shelving units, a neat partition that divides the dining space from the entrance area and glass door

W Seattle

Website   wseattle.com
Date Opened May 2012
Designer   Skylab Architecture
Cost of Build $$$$+
Size of Build 498 m² / 5,360 ft²
Award   Shortlist 2013
Address   1112 4th Avenue
                 Seattle, WA 98101
                 USA

Mixing elements of historic North American woodland culture with futuristic style, this restaurant and bar-space is described as a "Sonic Lodge", housed in a 26-storey building in the creative quarter of Seattle.

The stout columns of the original architecture have been augmented by the further installation of six-metre pilings and treating the interior generally with the same 'lodge-pole' aesthetic. Like exaggerated rings on a totem-pole each column is masked with stacked modular wooden elements, a direct reference to the natural surroundings and indigenous inhabitants.

A rich palette of golds, browns, pinks and silvers washes over the walls and furnishings, creating a magical atmosphere. In the centre of the Living-room, interconnected panels of textured silver scaling veil a hybrid form, part science-fiction monolith with a cosy woodcabin fireplace below.

In diesem Restaurant mit Bar verbinden sich Elemente der nordamerikanischen Waldkultur mit futuristischem Stil. Es wird als „Akustik-Hütte" bezeichnet und befindet sich in einem 26-geschossigen Hochhaus im Künstler-viertel von Seattle.

Zu den gedrungenen Stützen der ursprünglichen Architektur wurden weitere, sechs Meter hohe Pfähle aufgestellt, damit der gesamte Innenraum die gleiche „Hütten-Pfosten"-Asthetik annimmt. Wie mit vergrößerten Ringen an einem Totempfahl ist jede Stütze mit modularen Holzelementen bedeckt – ein unmittelbarer Bezug zur natürlichen Umgebung und ihrer Urbevölkerung.

Eine reiche Palette aus Gold, Braun, Rosa und Silber überzieht Wände und Mobiliar und erzeugt eine verzauberte Atmosphäre. Im Mittelpunkt des Aufen-thaltsraums verbergen verbundene Tafeln mit silbernen Schuppen eine hybride Form, eine Art Science-Fiction-Monolithen, mit einem gemütlichen offenen Kamin darunter.

01

Ce restaurant-bar se loge dans un immeuble de 26 étages dans le quartier créatif de Seattle. Pour mélanger des éléments des régions boisées d'Amérique du Nord et un style futuriste, il a été qualifié de « *lodge* sonore ».

Les robustes colonnes de l'architecture d'origine ont été amplifiées par des palplanches de six mètres, avec un intérieur qui renforce cette esthétique de refuge. Telle un totem entouré d'anneaux démesurés, chaque colonne est recouverte d'éléments en bois modulaires et empilés, un clin d'œil au paysage environnant et aux habitants indigènes.

Une riche palette de dorés, de bruns, de roses et d'argents inonde les murs et le mobilier, créant une atmosphère magique. Au centre de la salle, un assemblage de panneaux argentés et texturés crée une forme hybride, sorte de monolithe de science-fiction sous lequel se trouve une cheminée digne d'une confortable cabane en bois.

02

01 A six-metre stacked record collection hovers beside a fusion of pink and grey, the spines of the records echoing the vertical lines created by the fringe wall

02 Fringe curtains have been used as a subtle way of dividing up the space

03 Orange *Ribbon* stools by Cappellini stand out against the silver centrepiece

03

What Happens When

Date Opened	January 2011
Date Closed	July 2011
Designer	The Metrics
Cost of Build	$
Size of Build	74 m² / 800 ft²
Award	Shortlist 2012
Address	25 Cleveland Place
	New York, NY 10002
	USA

An all-changing temporary restaurant in an abandoned ground-floor space is What Happens When chef John Fraser, designer Emilie Baltz, three sound engineers and Elle Kunnos de Voss joined forces.

Operating on a 30-day rhythm lasting nine months, each month saw a completely new menu, interior space and soundscape. Despite a tight budget and only a 15-hour turnaround, this creative collaboration wowed customers with settings ranging from Nordic-inspired minimalism to jazz improvisation to an intimate hideaway after Renoir's *Luncheon of the Boating Party*.

This 'work in progress' aesthetic nevertheless kept certain features in place throughout, such as the black walls and floor inspired by the theatre, the white tables, chairs and lighting. A grid of hooks attached to the ceiling offered different possibilities as a flexible canvas overhead.

Es war ein temporäres, sich ständig veränderndes Restaurant im Erdgeschoss eines aufgegebenen Hauses, das die vereinten Kräfte des Chefs von What Happens When, John Fraser, der Architektin Emilie Baltz, drei Toningenieuren und Elle Kunnos de Voss herausforderte.

Das Lokal wurde über neun Monate in einem 30-Tage-Rhythmus betrieben, jeden Monat mit einer neuen Speisekarte, neu gestaltetem Innenraum und veränderter Klanglandschaft. Trotz geringem Etat und nur 15-stündiger Betriebszeit begeisterte dieses kreative Team die Besucher mit Ausstattungen, die von nordisch inspiriertem Minimalismus über Jazz-Improvisationen bis zu intimen Rückzugsbereichen nach Renoirs Gemälde *Das Frühstück der Ruderer* reichten.

Diese Work-in-Progress-Ästhetik hielt dennoch durchweg an gewissen Elementen fest: den vom Theater inspirierten schwarzen Wänden und Fußböden, den weißen Tischen und Stühlen und der Beleuchtung. Ein System an der Decke befestigter Haken bot verschiedene Möglichkeiten für eine textile Gestaltung über den Köpfen der Gäste.

Installé au rez-de-chaussée d'un local abandonné, ce restaurant temporaire et évolutif est le résultat de la collaboration entre le chef John Fraser, la designer Emilie Baltz, trois ingénieurs du son et Elle Kunnos de Voss.

Ouvert tous les jours pendant neuf mois, le menu, la décoration intérieure et le paysage sonore ont été entièrement modifiés chaque mois. Malgré les limites du budget et un service sur 15 heures seulement, cette collaboration créative a conquis les clients avec des agencements allant du minimalisme scandinave à l'improvisation de jazz, en passant par un refuge secret inspiré du tableau *Le déjeuner des canotiers*, de Renoir.

L'esthétique d'inachevé a toutefois maintenu certains aspects, comme le sol et les murs noirs (tels une scène de théâtre), les tables et les chaises blanches, ainsi que l'éclairage. Au plafond, la grille assortie de crochets servait de canevas pour des créations diverses et variées.

01 Intricate square mosaics symbolised the various countries along the Silk Road

02 7.5-metre awning in the colours of spring formed the third incarnation of the design, inspired by Renoir's *Luncheon of the Boating Party*

03 Architectural drawings on the walls added to the design's transitional feel

03

Workshop Kitchen + Bar

Website	workshoppalmsprings.com
Date Opened	September 2012
Designer	SOMA
Lighting	.PSLAB
Cost of Build	$$$$
Size of Build	279 m² / 3,000 ft²
Award	Category winner 2013
Address	800 N Palm Canyon Dr. Suite G
	Palm Springs, CA 92262
	USA

A delight for concrete enthusiasts, this sophisticated redesign in the colonial El Paseo building is the latest incarnation of a space used in many ways in its history. Now an 'Americana' restaurant serving seasonal produce, it was also designed as a new go-to destination.

Instead of hiding the original structural features, they were built around, using a palette of concrete, black metal and leather drawn from the owners' love of industrial materials. The polished walls are softened by pendant lights, with naked bulbs adding warmth and ambience.

More private seating in the form of tall booths in a 'blockish' design, fitted with leather banquettes, extend upwards to wooden trusses overhead. The majestic concrete enclosures and banquet-style communal table were made using ten-metre moulds that allowed the forms to be created on site.

Dieser intelligente Umbau im kolonialen El Paseo Building begeistert Betonliebhaber und ist die neueste Inkarnation eines Raumes, der im Verlauf seiner Geschichte vielfach umgenutzt wurde. Jetzt ist er ein „Americana" Restaurant, das Speisen aus saisonalen Produkten anbietet, und ein beliebter Treffpunkt.

Anstatt das originale Tragwerk zu verbergen, wurde mit Beton, schwarzem Metall und Leder, gemäß der Vorliebe der Eigentümer für industrielle Materialien, darum herumgebaut. Die polierten Wände werden durch Hängeleuchten weicher; nackte Glühbirnen bewirken Wärme und Ambiente.

Der allgemeine Aufenthaltsbereich in Form hoher, „blockweise" angeordneter Nischen ist mit ledergepolsterten Sitzbänken ausgestattet und erstreckt sich bis aufwärts zu den oberen Holzbindern. Die schweren Betoneinfassungen und Bankett-Tische wurden vor Ort in zehn Meter langen Formen gegossen.

01 In the main dining-room
a row of 'ancient bronze ceiling
pendants' drops down close
to the tables, suspended from
a ridge beam in the roof

Véritable régal pour les amateurs de béton, ce nouveau design sophistiqué dans l'immeuble colonial El Paseo est la dernière incarnation d'un espace utilisé de diverses façons au fil du temps. Ce restaurant « americana » qui offre des produits de saison a été pensé pour devenir une destination prisée.

Au lieu de dissimuler les éléments structurels d'origine, la construction s'est faite autour d'eux, l'emploi de béton, de métal noir et de cuir révélant le goût des propriétaires pour les matériaux industriels. Les murs polis sont adoucis par des lampes suspendues, et les ampoules nues apportent de la chaleur et créent l'ambiance.

Les tables sont encaissées dans de hautes cabines, telles des blocs individuels, et assorties de banquettes en cuir ; des fermes en bois surplombent l'ensemble. Les imposantes séparations en béton et la table de banquet ont été réalisées avec des moules de dix mètres de long permettant la taille de formes sur place.

Yojisan Sushi

Website yojisan.com
Date Opened April 2012
Designer Dan Brunn Architecture
Cost of Build $$$$
Size of Build 186 m² / 2,000 ft²
Award Shortlist 2013
Address 260 N Beverly Drive
Beverly Hills, CA 90210
USA

A subtle and seductive setting combines a modernist aesthetic with a minimalist colour palette, using natural forms and imagery to evoke Japanese culture.

Cedar planks form the upper half of the façade and subdivide the glass entrance, framing the interior and drawing the eye into the space. As a meditation on Japanese tradition, the design is an interplay between the strong and the ephemeral.

A hanging garden and inverted forms representing oversized bento boxes in bold red are the first features seen upon entering, their organic shadows brushing the floor and interior. A long curtain gives movement and texture to the otherwise smooth surfaces and runs parallel to a bamboo wall of light opposite; an illusion between shadow and light, they enhance the design's transcendental qualities.

01

Ein raffiniertes und verführerisches Ambiente verbindet moderne Ästhetik mit einer minimalistischen Farbpalette und der Verwendung natürlicher Formen und Bilder mit Bezug zur japanischen Kultur.

Bretter aus Zedernholz bedecken die obere Hälfte der Fassade und unterteilen den verglasten Eingangsbereich, rahmen den Innenraum ein und ziehen den Blick hinein. Der Entwurf, vom Respekt vor der japanischen Tradition getragen, ist ein Zusammenspiel aus Kräftigem und Ephemerem.

Herabhängende Bepflanzung und umgekehrte Formen, die übergroße Bentoboxen in leuchtendem Rot darstellen, sind das erste, was man beim Betreten des Lokals sieht. Ihre organischen Schatten streichen über Boden und Innenwände. Ein langer Vorhang verleiht den ansonsten glatten Oberflächen Bewegung und Textur und führt parallel zu einer gegenüberliegenden Lichtwand aus Bambus. Wie eine Illusion aus Schatten und Licht verstärken sie den transzendentalen Charakter der Gestaltung.

02

01 Illuminated negative space on one wall was achieved using custom-formed cloth and plastic composite

02 Custom-made tables are a fusion between Modernism and Japanese simplicity, as realised through a special process of bluing to replicate the fashioning of Japanese tools and cutlery

03 The reception desk is made from board-formed concrete

03

Cette composition délicate et attrayante marie une esthétique moderniste et une palette de couleurs minimaliste. Les formes naturelles et l'imagerie adoptées rappellent la culture japonaise.

Des planches en cèdre forment la moitié supérieure de la façade et divisent l'entrée vitrée en encadrant l'intérieur pour attirer l'attention. Telle une réflexion sur la tradition japonaise, le design combine le solide et l'éphémère.

En entrant, les clients voient d'abord un jardin suspendu et des formes inversées symbolisant des bentos géants rouge vif ; leurs ombres organiques se projettent sur le sol et les murs. Un long rideau confère mouvement et texture aux surfaces lisses et fait face à un mur illuminé en bambou. L'illusion entre ombres et lumières met en valeur les qualités transcendantales du design.

"We stepped 'through the looking-glass' – sushi signifiers are upended."

Dan Brunn Architecture

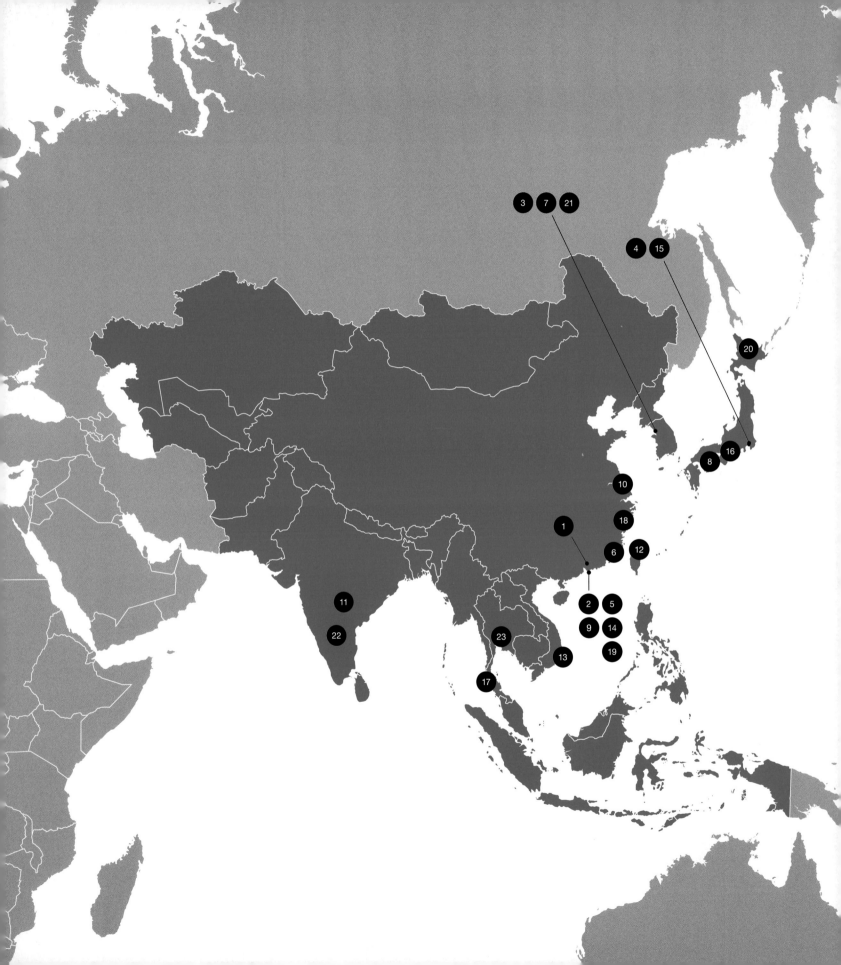

Asia

Asia

Stephen Alden
Chief Executive Officer
Maybourne Hotel Group

Stephen Alden is responsible for the development of three world-renowned hotels, Claridge's, the Connaught and the Berkeley, while respecting the individual personality of each hotel and its staff and guests. Prior to joining Maybourne, he headed Starwood's St. Regis hotels based in New York and from 1996–2003 operated Ciga Hotels, based in Rome. Stephen graduated from the Centre International de Glion, Switzerland.

Stephen Alden ist verantwortlich für den Betrieb von drei weltberühmten Hotels: Claridge's, Connaught und Berkeley, unter Wahrung des individuellen Charakters jedes einzelnen mit Hinblick auf Personal und Gäste. Bevor er zu Maybourne ging, leitete Alden die Starwood's St. Regis Hotels in New York und von 1996 bis 2003 die Ciga Hotels in Rom. Er studierte am Centre International de Glion in der Schweiz.

Stephen Alden est en charge du développement de trois hôtels de renommée mondiale : Claridge's, The Connaught et The Berkeley. Sa mission vise aussi à respecter la personnalité de chacun d'eux, de leur personnel et de leur clientèle. Avant de rejoindre le groupe Maybourne, il a dirigé pour Starwood l'hôtel St. Regis à New York et de 1996-2003, l'hôtel Ciga à Rome. Stephen est diplômé du Centre International de Glion, en Suisse.

I have been fascinated by hotels in Asia from the days I lived in Singapore in my early career. My love affair for the industry then whisked me around three continents, and finally to London, where I now live. But despite – or perhaps because of – the fact that I have been charged with the transformation and continuing stewardship of three iconic London hotels, I am still intrigued by hotels in Asia.

One of the most fascinating ways to observe the rich and diverse cultures of this continent, rapidly changing in some ways, is through local hotels, restaurants and bars. In Asia the relationship between discerning city-dwellers and their hotels appears to be almost full-time. Dining out seems to have become an integral part of city life. I love great restaurants for their vitality and pace, normally with a crowd that transcends generations and is quite international, and nowhere is this more apparent to me than in Asia today.

Indeed at the time of writing I have recently returned from an Asian tour and have had the opportunity to reflect on this with two designers whose work I admire: Guy Oliver, who resides in London, and Andre Fu, who is based in Hong Kong. We spoke at length about the transformation of restaurant and bar venues across the region in the past 20 years and the sheer magnificence of some of these projects. Asia has a restaurantscape that ranges from underwater-world inspiration in Shenzhen to artificial forests in South Korea and simulations of clouds around the summit of Mount Fuji in Japan. There certainly does not appear to be any limit to creativity (nor should there be for that matter!) and a tendency towards theatre and drama is a pattern.

Andre reflected that, as most new restaurants are not at street level, the lack of street presence can be compensated for by using the dramatic physical ambience of a destination outlet as a differentiator. Guy pointed out that restaurant designers in Asia are creating a new genre of design in much the same way that designers like Gaudí challenged architectural norms in Europe at the turn of the 20th century. Interiors are innovative and whimsical and sometimes humorous, but all are visually stimulating.

For me, to create a great interior you need clear design intent, and a notion of how the place should make you feel. Purposeful design and inventive techniques in the kitchen are a magical formula. I believe that good restaurants and bars can make or break a hotel. They generate the vibrancy that permeates throughout the hotel and public areas, and the hotel becomes the address for guests and local residents.

Today, excellent design plays a more important role than ever with that first visual stimulation that sets the tone for the multi-sensory experience that will follow. How a place makes you feel is ultimately what counts and excellent design is a key component of that success.

Asiatische Hotels begeistern mich, seitdem ich zu Beginn meiner beruflichen Laufbahn in Singapur gelebt habe. Meine Liebe zu dieser Branche hat mich dann in drei Kontinente entführt und schließlich nach London, wo ich jetzt wohne. Aber trotz – oder vielleicht wegen – der Tatsache, dass ich mit der Umgestaltung und danach mit der Leitung von drei Londoner Kult-Hotels beauftragt wurde, faszinieren mich die Hotels in Asien noch immer.

Ein hervorragender Weg zum Studium der reichen und vielfältigen Kulturen dieses sich rapide im Umbruch befindenden Kontinents ist der Besuch von Hotels und Restaurants. In Asien besteht fast über den ganzen Tag eine Bindung zwischen den Stadtbewohnern und ihren Hotels. Auswärts zu essen ist anscheinend ein wichtiger Bestandteil des städtischen Lebens geworden. Mir gefallen große Restaurants wegen ihrer Vitalität und ihres Tempos; normalerweise besteht das Publikum aus Menschen aller Generationen und Nationen, und nirgendwo ist dies sichtbarer als heutzutage in Asien.

Als ich diesen Text schrieb, war ich gerade von einer Asienreise zurückgekehrt und hatte Gelegenheit, mit zwei Designern über das Thema zu sprechen, deren Arbeit ich bewundere: Guy Oliver, der in London lebt, und Andre Fu, sesshaft in Hongkong. Wir sprachen ausführlich über die Veränderung von Lokalen in dieser Region während der letzten 20 Jahre und die schiere Pracht einiger dieser Projekte. Asien hat eine Restaurantlandschaft, die von Inspirationen aus der Unterwasserwelt in Shenzhen bis zu künstlichen Wäldern in Südkorea und Wolkensimulationen um den Gipfel des Fuji in Japan reicht. Der Kreativität scheinen tatsächlich keine Grenzen gesetzt zu sein (und sollten es auch nicht!), und eine Tendenz zu Theatralik und Dramatik ist unverkennbar.

Weil die meisten Restaurants nicht auf Straßenebene liegen, meinte Andre, müsse dieser Mangel im Gegenzug durch ein dramatisches Ambiente kompensiert werden. Guy wies darauf hin, dass Restaurantdesigner in Asien ein neues Genre der Gestaltung kreieren, vergleichbar mit Architekten wie Gaudí, der Anfang des 20. Jahrhunderts den Architekturkanon in Europa in Frage stellte. Die neue Innengestaltung ist innovativ, ungewöhnlich und manchmal humorvoll, aber immer visuell ansprechend.

Ich selbst benötige für die Gestaltung eines großartigen Innenraums ein klares Planungsziel und eine Vorstellung, welche Empfindungen dieser Ort auslösen soll. Zielgerichtete Planung und einfallsreiche Technik in der Küche sind wundertätige Voraussetzungen. Ich glaube, dass gute Restaurants für den Erfolg eines Hotels entscheidend sind. Hier entsteht die Lebendigkeit, die durch das Haus fließt, und so wird das Hotel zu einer guten Adresse für Gäste und Anwohner.

Heutzutage spielt herausragendes Design eine wichtigere Rolle als je zuvor, denn der erste optische Eindruck bestimmt den Grad des darauffolgenden multisensorischen Erlebnisses. Letztlich zählt, welche Gefühle ein Ort in uns auslöst, und der Schlüssel für diesen Erfolg ist eine exzellente Gestaltung.

Ma fascination pour les hôtels en Asie remonte à l'époque où j'habitais à Singapour, au début de ma carrière. Cette histoire d'amour m'a amené à voyager à travers trois continents et à m'installer finalement à Londres. Mais même si (ou peut-être parce que) j'ai été chargé de la transformation et de la gestion de trois hôtels londoniens emblématiques, je reste attiré par les hôtels en Asie.

Les hôtels, les restaurants et les bars permettent d'apprécier la richesse et la diversité culturelles de ce continent en constante mutation. En Asie, les citadins sont très liés aux hôtels de leur ville, et sortir au restaurant fait partie intégrante de la vie urbaine. J'aime les grands restaurants pour leur vitalité et leur dynamique, pour leur clientèle normalement intergénérationnelle et plutôt internationale ; une réalité qui, à mon sens, se vérifie plus que nulle part en Asie.

J'ai écrit ces lignes au retour d'un voyage sur ce continent, après avoir eu la chance de réfléchir au sujet avec deux designers dont j'admire le travail : Guy Oliver, qui vit aussi à Londres, et Andre Fu, installé à Hong Kong. Nous avons conversé longtemps sur la transformation des restaurants et des bars dans cette partie du monde au cours des 20 dernières années, ainsi que sur la splendeur de certains de ces projets. La palette de restaurants en Asie est des plus riches : inspiration du monde sous-marin à Shenzhen, forêts artificielles en Corée du Sud, simulations de nuages au sommet du Mont Fuji au Japon, il semble n'y avoir (heureusement d'ailleurs !) aucune limite à la créativité. La tendance est clairement à la théâtralisation.

Pour Andre, les nouveaux restaurants, dont la plupart n'occupent pas un rez-de-chaussée, doivent compenser ce manque de visibilité par un intérieur spectaculaire afin de faire la différence. Pour Guy, les designers de restaurants en Asie sont en train de créer un nouveau genre de design, tout comme Gaudí a révolutionné au début du XXe siècle les règles architecturales en Europe. Les intérieurs sont innovants, fantaisistes, parfois amusants et toujours visuellement stimulants.

Je crois pour ma part que la conception d'un intérieur demande de savoir l'intention recherchée et quel sentiment l'espace doit transmettre. La formule magique allie un design réfléchi et des techniques inventives en cuisine. Les restaurants et bars de qualité sont décisifs dans le succès d'un hôtel. La vitalité qu'ils transmettent à l'établissement et aux zones publiques fait de l'endroit une référence pour les touristes et les résidents.

Un excellent design joue plus que jamais un rôle important car la première stimulation visuelle conditionne l'expérience multisensorielle qui suivra. L'essentiel est la façon dont un espace vous fait sentir, un design réussi étant à la clé de ce succès.

Aix Arôme Café

Date Opened	May 2012
Designer	One Plus Partnership
Cost of Build	$$
Size of Build	150 m² / 1,600 ft²
Award	Longlist 2013
Address	OCT Harbour Theme Park
	Shenzhen Bay
	Shenzhen
	China

A sleek and modern underwater world was the concept for this ground-floor café, a calm space away from the bustling city, with a timber floor and dazzling surfaces made from plastic laminate and stainless steel.

Coffee is served from a central silver ovoid whose form adds a science-fiction veneer to the basic shape at the heart of the café, the coffee bean. Vibrant blues stand out against the otherwise flawlessly white interior whilst a five-metre grey Corian communal table mimics an octopus's tentacle down one side of the space. Brightly coloured bubble-like seating resembles sea anemones or schools of fish.

Electric-blue rods were used for the lighting – fitted with neon striplights and suspended from the ceiling, each one appears to be falling randomly, a physical manifestation of sunlight rippling across water.

Eine schicke und moderne Unterwasserwelt war das Konzept für dieses Erdgeschoss-Café, ein ruhiger Ort fern von der turbulenten Stadt, mit hölzernem Fußboden und schillernden Flächen aus Kunststoff-Laminat und Edelstahl.

Kaffee wird aus einer zentralen, eiförmigen Bar serviert, deren Gestalt dem Grundelement des Cafés, der Kaffeebohne, einen Hauch Science-Fiction verleiht. Leuchtende Blautöne heben sich vom ansonsten makellos weißen Innenraum ab; und ein fünf Meter langer, grauer Gemeinschaftstisch aus Corian auf einer Seite des Raumes gleicht den Tentakeln eines Oktopus. Ballonförmige Sitze in leuchtenden Farben gleichen Seeanemonen oder Fischschwärmen.

Blaue Elektrostäbe dienen als Leuchtkörper – sie sind mit Neonröhren bestückt und an der Decke aufgehängt. Sie scheinen willkürlich herunterzufallen, ein Symbol für Sonnenstrahlen, die über das Wasser gleiten.

01 Zipped together, the black elements of Ueli Berger's sofa snake through the back of the room and create a free-flowing arrangement

02 Keen to combine functionality and beauty, One Plus Partnership are celebrated for their themed out-of-the-box designs, the huge openings of the 'big bean' here serving as a good source of ventilation and natural light

01

Tel un monde sous-marin moderne et élégant, ce café au rez-de-chaussée offre un espace paisible, loin de l'agitation de la ville. Il arbore un plancher en bois et des surfaces brillantes en plastique stratifié et en acier inoxydable.

Au centre se trouve le bar couleur argent et au contour ovoïde, qui ajoute une touche de science-fiction à la forme caractéristique du grain de café. Des notes bleu vif se détachent sur l'intérieur parfaitement blanc ; longue de 5 mètres, une grande table grise en Corian rappelle un tentacule de pieuvre. Très colorés, les sièges boules font penser à des anémones de mer ou à des bancs de poissons.

Pour l'éclairage, des baguettes bleu électrique pendues au plafond entourent des rampes de néon. Elles semblent tomber de façon aléatoire, comme les rayons du soleil ridant l'eau.

02

AMMO

Website	ammo.com.hk
Date Opened	May 2012
Designer	Joyce Wang
Cost of Build	$$$
Size of Build	112 m² / 1,200 ft²
Award	Shortlist 2013
Address	HK Asia Society Center
	9 Justice Drive
	Admiralty
	Hong Kong

The stunning interior design of this restaurant and bar derives from its location, the building having originally served the British Army in the mid-19th century as an explosives depot. It is now home to the Asia Society, a not-for-profit arts and education centre.

Adding sharp modern touches to this historical underlay, the result is spacious as well as luxurious, replete with velvets, silks and leather, offset against curved metals, concrete and glass. Copper is used continuously throughout, which gradually transforms through shades of pink, orange, green and brown as it oxidises over time.

Large windows and a seven-metre ceiling made it important to manage the acoustics. A fabric-clad mirror feature was fitted to the ceiling, while the granite columns were masked with special sound-minimising panels.

Die fantastische Innenausstattung dieses Restaurants mit Bar geht auf seinen Standort zurück: Das Gebäude diente ursprünglich Mitte des 19. Jahrhunderts der Britischen Armee als Sprengstoffdepot. Jetzt gehört es der Asia Society, einem gemeinnützigen Kunst- und Bildungszentrum.

Dem historischen Bestand wurden klare, moderne Elemente hinzugefügt. Dadurch entstand ein geräumiges und zugleich luxuriöses Lokal, ausgestattet mit Samt, Seide und Leder im Kontrast zu gebogenem Metall, Beton und Glas. Kupfer ist überall präsent und verändert sich im Lauf der Zeit durch Oxidation in Rosa-, Orange-, Grün- und Brauntöne.

Große Fenster und eine sieben Meter lange Deckenfläche erforderten akustische Maßnahmen. Ein mit Stoff ausgekleideter Spiegel wurde an der Decke angebracht; die Stützen aus Granit wurden mit speziellen schalldämpfenden Tafeln verhüllt.

Le fabuleux design d'intérieur de ce bar-restaurant tient à son emplacement : au milieu du XIXe siècle, ce bâtiment servait d'entrepôt d'explosifs à la British Army. Aujourd'hui, il est occupé par l'Asia Society, un centre artistique et d'enseignement à but non lucratif.

En ajoutant des touches détonantes au décor historique, l'espace obtenu est généreux et luxueux, et il regorge d'éléments en velours, en soie et en cuir venant trancher avec le métal, le béton et le verre. Le cuivre est omniprésent et prend des teintes roses, orange, vertes et brunes en s'oxydant avec le temps.

L'acoustique a dû être étudiée en raison des baies vitrées et des 7 mètres de hauteur de plafond. Un revêtement en tissu a été fixé au plafond et les colonnes de granite ont été logées derrière des panneaux absorbant le bruit de fond.

"Cinematic references and interdisciplinary inspirations elicit a sense of drama."

Joyce Wang

01 Various seating arrangements were developed to offer privacy in the otherwise open space: bar-stools, counter-stools, dining chairs, or the olive and brown velvet and leather cocktail banquettes

02 References to Jean-Luc Godard's film *Alphaville* (1965) can be seen in the chandeliers, which take the shape of spiral staircases

03 Floor-to-ceiling glass windows overlook a lush green forest and high-rise towers in the distance

Coffee'n LoaF

Date Opened	October 2010
Designer	design BONO
Cost of Build	$$$
Size of Build	197 m² / 2,150 ft²
Award	Shortlist 2013
Address	Square 1, 926
	Dongchun-dong
	Incheon
	South Korea

Set in a busy area of the South Korean capital, this café was specifically designed as a peaceful setting away from the commotion of the city.

To this end, the design aim was to create an indoor landscape in the form of an artificial forest. Having entered via a flight of stairs, you pass through tree-like columns and between long wooden rods which symbolise fallen branches.

Inside the main café area the woodland theme continues, with tree-columns supporting a minimalistic canopy and spreading branches beneath which diners can sit in the different areas created. Spotlights shining through the forest openings imitate a starry sky over a lake, whilst the misty glaze on the surrounding glass façade conjures up the atmosphere of a dense fog in the early dawn.

Dieses Café in einer belebten Straße der südkoreanischen Hauptstadt wurde bewusst als friedlicher Ort fern von der turbulenten Stadt geplant.

Ziel der Planung war es deshalb, eine Innenlandschaft in Form eines künstlichen Waldes zu gestalten. Nach Eintritt über eine Treppe führt der Weg vorbei an Baumstützen und zwischen langen Holzstäben, die abgebrochene Zweige symbolisieren.

Im großen Caféraum wird das Waldthema fortgesetzt: Baumstützen tragen einen minimalistischen Baldachin und breiten Zweige aus, unter denen die Gäste in den dadurch gebildeten unterschiedlichen Bereichen sitzen können. Strahler scheinen durch die Waldlichtungen und imitieren einen Sternenhimmel über einem See, während eine dunstige Beschichtung der umgebenden Glasfassade die Atmosphäre dichten Nebels in früher Dämmerung heraufbeschwört.

01

Ce café se trouve dans un quartier animé de la capitale de la Corée du Sud. Il a été spécialement conçu pour offrir un environnement calme, étranger aux bruits de la ville.

Dans ce but, le design a cherché à créer un paysage intérieur sous la forme d'une forêt artificielle. Après l'entrée et sa volée d'escaliers, les clients passent entre des colonnes, telles des arbres, et de longues tiges en bois, à l'image de branches tombées.

Dans la zone principale, la thématique se poursuit. Des colonnes-troncs soutiennent une canopée minimaliste, dont les branches surplombent les différentes zones où les convives prennent place. Les spots qui brillent à travers les ouvertures de la forêt font penser à un ciel étoilé au-dessus d'un lac. La pellicule brumeuse sur la façade vitrée finit de créer l'atmosphère d'un brouillard dense à la prime aurore.

01 Simple lightwood seating reflects the curves of the white tree-like columns, made from ironwood and painted with white vinyl

02 The words "time to rest" and "time to taste" have been written on the epoxy finish of the exposed concrete floor

03 Vertical sheets of glass have been suspended in a row to form the entrance to the toilet facilities

02

03

Cronus Private Bar & Lounge

Date Opened   June 2012
Date Closed   December 2013
Designer   Doyle Collection
Cost of Build $$$$
Size of Build   150 m² / 1,650 ft²
Award   Shortlist 2013
Address   2-25-23, Nishi-azabu
Minato-ku
Tokyo 106-0031
Japan

Entering the luxurious interior of this private members' bar and lounge is like being transported inside a secret cave, hidden deep underground, a triumph of this glorious piece of design in presenting a space so detached from the outside world.

The calculated opulence disorients the senses: large mirrors mounted on the ceiling, plush velvet and leather seating and Swarovski crystal chandeliers combine to open up the shadows into a sparkling champagne glow that reveals a series of discreetly tucked-away spaces.

This sensual atmosphere was obtained chiefly by means of materials and textures; heavy-set seating upholstered in crushed velvet balances the jagged rock of the exposed wall to the rear, whilst the custom-built wine cellar serves to divide the space at the same time as displaying its luxury goods.

Der Eintritt in diese luxuriöse Bar und Lounge eines privaten Klubs gleicht dem Gang in eine verborgene Höhle. Tief im Untergrund verborgen präsentiert diese prächtige Architektur einen total von der Außenwelt abgesonderten Raum.

Die gewollte Üppigkeit verwirrt die Sinne: Große Spiegel sind an der Decke montiert, mit Plüsch und Leder bezogene Sessel und Kronleuchter aus Swarovski-Kristall vertreiben die Schatten und versetzen den Bereich in ein strahlendes Champagnerlicht, das eine Reihe von diskret verborgenen Räumen offenlegt.

Diese die Sinne ansprechende Atmosphäre wurde durch entsprechende Materialien und Strukturen erreicht. Schwere, samtgepolsterte Sessel bilden einen Kontrast zum zackigen Fels der frei liegenden Mauer an der Rückseite, während der neu eingerichtete Weinkeller als Raumteiler dient und zugleich seine luxuriöse Ware ausstellt.

01

Se plonger dans l'intérieur luxueux de ce bar-lounge privé revient à pénétrer dans une cave secrètement dissimulée sous terre. C'est là tout le succès de ce design spectaculaire, qui met en scène un espace coupé du monde extérieur.

L'opulence bien dosée trouble les sens. Grands miroirs installés au plafond, sièges en velours peluche et cuir, chandeliers en cristal de Swarovski : le jeu entre les ombres et la lumière couleur champagne révèle une série de recoins discrètement nichés.

Cette atmosphère sensuelle tient principalement aux matériaux et aux textures. Des sièges généreux en velours écrasé s'alignent devant la roche dentelée au mur du fond, alors que la cave à vins sur mesure divise l'espace et sert de présentoir des grands crus.

01 A library wall lined with *faux* monochrome book spines surrounds the rock-face feature

02 Mirrored ceilings have been used to reflect light and make the intimate dens appear more spacious

02

French Window

Website   thefrenchwindow.hk
Date Opened   December 2009
Designer   AB Concept
Cost of Build $$$$+
Size of Build 500 m² / 5,400 ft²
Award   Shortlist 2010
Address   3101, Podium Level 3
               IFC Mall
               Central
               Hong Kong

This classic brasserie interior captures all the romance and style of French culture. Boasting stunning views of Hong Kong's harbour, the restaurant is situated on the third floor of the dining-hall of the IFC Mall.

The unusual architecture set the template for the design, with entry via a 50-metre tunnel walkway which opens out into the open-plan restaurant area. The passage is clad with blonde-wood panels, whilst floor lanterns and elaborate copper-framed vertical gardens line one wall, making the already grand entrance more stylish still.

Inside, wrought iron and classic furnishings create a timeless, yet modern impression. French windows, in the form of textured glass panelling, feature throughout alongside a subtle palette of mink, cream, green and brown, making the space feel elegant, but not uptight.

Dieses klassische Brasserie-Ambiente vertritt die ganze Romantik und den Stil französischer Kultur. Das Restaurant ist stolz auf seine fantastische Aussicht auf den Hafen von Hongkong; es befindet sich im dritten Geschoss der Speisehalle an der IFC Mall.

Die ungewöhnliche Architektur setzte Maßstäbe für die Planung. Der Eingang erfolgt durch einen 50 Meter langen, tunnelartigen Korridor, der sich zum offenen Restaurantbereich weitet. Der Durchgang ist mit hellen Holztafeln verkleidet. Bodenleuchten und gepflegte, in Kupfer eingefasste vertikale Bepflanzung schmücken eine Wand und gestalten den an sich schon prächtigen Zugang noch stilvoller.

Im Innern erzeugen schmiedeeisernes und klassisches Mobiliar einen zeitlosen und dennoch modernen Eindruck. Französische Fenster mit Strukturverglasung an allen Seiten und eine Farb-palette aus Braun, Creme, Grün und Braun lassen den Raum elegant, aber nicht steif wirken.

Cet intérieur typique d'une brasserie transmet toute la romance et le style propres à la culture française. Bénéficiant d'une vue imprenable sur le port de Hong Kong, le restaurant occupe le troisième étage de l'espace de restauration de l'IFC Mall.

L'architecture singulière a déterminé le design. L'entrée se fait par un tunnel de 50 mètres de long débouchant sur la salle de restaurant ouverte. Éclairé par des lanternes au sol, le passage est revêtu de panneaux en bois clair d'un côté, alors que des jardins verticaux dessinent de l'autre côté des tableaux dans des cadres en cuivre.

Le mobilier classique et en fer forgé habille un intérieur moderne et intemporel. L'espace est ponctué par des portes-fenêtres formant des panneaux en verre texturé. Il combine une subtile palette de tons vison, crème, verts et bruns pour créer un sentiment d'élégance sans être guindé.

01 The old-fashioned lanterns in iron and glass recall the type that hangs outside rural French manor-houses

02 Glass panels act as elegant dividers that help to create a sense of natural flow across the open-plan design

03 Small vintage-style framed pictures are hung in a Parisian Salon, exaggerating the brasserie's high ceiling

01

02

"The key words in the brief for designing the French Window were: upscale, not uptight."

AB Concept

03

Haneda Japanese Restaurant

Date Opened	October 2009
Designer	Kris Lin Interior Design
Size of Build	600 m² / 6,450 ft²
Award	Longlist 2012
Address	Jiang Bing Zhong Da Dao
	350001 Fuzhou
	China

This striking and almost austere Japanese restaurant has been conceived as an exercise in Zen. In accordance with the motto "the vitality of activity in silence", stone is the material employed here to create a feeling of stillness and serenity.

With a layout and formality reminiscent of a temple, the interior couples calmness with a robust and handsome aesthetic. A dramatically placed rock – originating in Jerusalem – occupies the centre space on the marble floor, with a backdrop of cement walls marked with horizontal bands in low relief.

Metal cross-hatching acts as a partition wall while iron strut-work cubes have been inset into the ceiling recess, giving the restaurant a decidedly graphic tone.

Dieses bemerkenswerte und fast strenge japanische Restaurant wurde als Übung in Zen-Buddhismus geplant. Nach dem Motto „Vitalität durch Aktivität in der Stille" wurde hierfür Naturstein verwendet, um ein Gefühl von Ruhe und Heiterkeit anzuregen.

In Aufteilung und Formalität erinnert der Innenraum an einen Tempel. Er verbindet Ruhe mit einer robusten und ansprechenden Ästhethik. Ein eindrucksvoll auf dem Marmorboden platzierter – aus Jerusalem stammender – Felsbrocken nimmt den Mittelpunkt des Raumes ein. Die Betonwände im Hintergrund zeigen ein flaches Relief aus horizontalen Bändern.

Metallgitter in Schrägschraffur dienen als Trennwand, während die Kuben aus eisernen Streben dem Restaurant deutliche grafische Akzente verleihen.

01

Ce restaurant japonais au décor original et presque austère a été conçu comme un exercice zen. Fidèle à la devise « la vitalité de l'activité en silence », la pierre est la matériau employé pour transmettre calme et sérénité.

À l'intérieur, la distribution et les formes ne sont pas sans rappeler celles d'un temple, où une esthétique élégante et robuste accompagne le calme ambiant. Une pierre provenant de Jérusalem a été placée au centre de l'espace, sur le sol en marbre blanc. En toile de fond, les bandes horizontales sur les murs en ciment créent un léger relief.

Les séparations sont faites par des barres métalliques en oblique, alors qu'une structure de barreaux en acier a été fixée dans le renfoncement du plafond pour doter le local d'un ton clairement graphique.

02

01 The temple-style furniture was also designed by the architects

02 Large white candles sit in iron holders

03 Fringe curtains and walnut partitions with inset mirrors offer privacy between neighbouring tables

03

HoHum

Website	hohum.co.kr
Date Opened	December 2012
Designer	m4
Cost of Build	$
Size of Build	59 m² / 635 ft²
Award	Longlist 2013
Address	Seogyo-dong
	Mapo-gu
	395-20 Seoul
	South Korea

Shining like an oversized screen against the night sky, this fusion restaurant is a scene of bright lights and billowing drapery. The simple canteen combines Korean cuisine with Moroccan tagine, a traditional North-African dish not readily available in South Korea.

With its name translating as an onomatopoeic exhalation of breath, HoHum is fitted with a series of puffy animated clouds suspended from the whole ceiling of the interior. Hidden fans breathe life into the fabric, whilst spotlights help to create a soft ambience in the otherwise flat surfaces of the box-like space.

Given the restrictions of a low ceiling, narrow space and modest budget, blonde-wood furniture is coupled with white walls and a leather banquette to form the backdrop of this monochromatic, playful and minimalist design.

Dieses Fusion-Restaurant leuchtet wie ein übergroßer Bildschirm in den Nachthimmel und bildet einen Schauplatz aus strahlendem Licht und bauschenden Vorhängen. Die einfache Kantine serviert koreanische Küche und marokkanische Tagine, ein traditionelles nordafrikanisches Gericht, das in Südkorea sonst nur schwer zu bekommen ist.

Zu seinem Namen HoHum, der onomatopoetischen Übersetzung für Ausatmen, passen die an der ganzen Decke des Raumes aufgehängten aufgeblähten und sich bewegenden Wolken. Verborgene Ventilatoren blasen die Stoffe auf. Lichtstrahler tragen zu einem sanften Ambiente in den ansonsten ebenen Flächen des kastenförmigen Raumes bei.

Trotz aller Einschränkungen durch eine niedrige Decke, den schmalen Raum und einen bescheidenen Etat bilden das helle Holzmobiliar vor den weißen Wänden und die lederne Sitzbank die Kulisse zu einem monochromen, verspielten und minimalistischen Design.

Aussi lumineux qu'un écran géant sur fond de ciel nocturne, ce restaurant de cuisine fusion dégage une lumière éclatante et arbore une jolie draperie. Le menu propose des plats coréens et des tajines marocains, une recette traditionnelle d'Afrique du Nord autrement introuvable en Corée du Sud.

Le nom « Ho-Hum » traduit par onomatopée une expiration. Semblable à une boîte avec des surfaces plates, le plafond du local est décoré de nuages gonflés et animés. Des ventilateurs cachés donnent vie au tissu, alors que des spots créent une atmosphère douce.

En raison des limitations imposées par le plafond bas, un espace étroit et un budget réduit, le choix s'est porté sur un mobilier en bois clair et la couleur blanche pour le murs et la banquette en cuir ; le design monochromatique est ainsi agréable et minimaliste.

01 To create the soft and undulating cloudscape, white fabric was attached to the ceiling with mesh plates

02 Black-lettered murals in bold typography stand out on the white walls, supplying background information about the exotic cuisine

03 Graphics, in the form of a tree, continue outside on the glass façade of the restaurant

02

03

Hoto Fudo

Website	hosakatakeshi.com
Date Opened	December 2009
Designer	Takeshi Hosaka Architects
Cost of Build	$$$
Size of Build	726 m² / 7,810 ft²
Award	Longlist 2011
Address	Funatsu 2458
	Fujikawaguchiko-machi
	Minamisturu-gun
	Yamanashi-ken 4010301
	Japan

The four white hemispheres of this stunning environmental design, built in conjunction with structural engineers Arup, are intended to simulate clouds on the summit of nearby Mt. Fuji.

Modelled using polygon mesh points, giving the building its organic, shell-like appearance, the soft architectural form envelops guests as they look out on the majestic landscape. Aside from the seating area, just under half of the expansive interior is taken up by the stainless-steel kitchen.

Heat and light circulate naturally through semi-circular entrances, which are left open to frame sections of the landscape and allow fog and air to enter the restaurant and add to the dining experience. Rain and snow can also fall just inside but the curved acrylic sliding-doors are only shut in the most extreme weather, so that the views may be enjoyed almost all year round.

Die vier weißen Halbkugeln des eindrucksvollen ökologischen Designs, das in Zusammenarbeit mit dem Ingenieurbüro Arup entstand, sollen Wolken auf dem Gipfel des Mount Fuji simulieren.

Die mit Hilfe von polygonem Geflecht modellierten weichen architektonischen Elemente geben dem Gebäude seine organische, schalenähnliche Form und umhüllen die Gäste bei ihrem Blick in die majestätische Landschaft. Neben dem großen Restaurantbereich nimmt die Edelstahlküche fast die Hälfte des weitläufigen Innenraums ein.

Wärme und Licht zirkulieren natürlich durch die halbkreisförmigen Eingänge, die offen gelassen werden, um Teile der Landschaft einzurahmen sowie Dunst und Luft in das Restaurant einzulassen, was zu dem Speiseerlebnis beiträgt. Auch Regen und Schnee dürfen herein. Die gebogenen Schiebetüren aus Acryl werden nur bei extremem Wetter geschlossen, sodass man die Ausblicke fast das ganze Jahr über genießen kann.

Les quatre hémisphères blancs de ce surprenant design environnemental, pour lequel sont intervenus des ingénieurs structurels d'Arup, symbolisent des nuages au sommet du Mont Fuji.

La forme architecturale lisse a été moulée à l'aide d'une structure polygonale maillée, conférant à la construction une forme organique qui rappelle un coquillage. Elle abrite les clients qui peuvent y admirer le paysage majestueux. Près de la moitié du vaste espace intérieur est occupé par la cuisine en acier inoxydable, le reste par la salle de restaurant.

La chaleur et la lumière circulent de façon naturelle par les entrées semi-circulaires, laissées ouvertes pour apprécier le paysage et permettre au brouillard et à l'air de pénétrer dans le restaurant. La pluie et la neige peuvent tomber dedans : les portes coulissantes cintrées en acrylique ne sont fermées qu'en cas de conditions climatiques extrêmes pour profiter des vues presque toute l'année.

01 Construction took three years
to complete and cost £150,000

02 Hoto Fudo is named after the
local, traditional speciality houtou
noodles, which are served here

03 Thick urethane insulation keeps
the inside temperature stable
throughout the year

Il Milione

Website	il-milione.com
Date Opened	December 2012
Designer	designLSM
Size of Build	279 m² / 3,000 ft²
Award	Shortlist 2013
Address	G16-21, Hutchinson House
	10 Harcourt Road
	Central
	Hong Kong

Michelin-starred chef Marco Gubbiotti's first Asian venture is a graceful and charismatic Umbrian restaurant transplanted to Hong Kong. Taking inspiration from Italy for both concept and form, this ground-floor interior breathes life into the past by using art deco motifs to highlight the continuing connections between Europe and Asia over the centuries.

The restaurant's name ("The Million") comes from the Italian title of *The Travels of Marco Polo*, a 13th-century account of journeys in the East which also informs the overall identity, including the illuminated graphic sign that greets diners upon arrival.

The design represents a physical fusion between East and West, with core materials and lighting being sourced from Europe, sitting alongside locally produced elements such as the glass wall opposite the kitchen.

01 Limited natural light and a low ceiling were treated with circular and square mirrors, while a large black-and-gold-framed window was installed, allowing passers-by to see into the bar area

02 Lighting by UK-based Into gives the restaurant a divine glow, while golden ropes with naked light-bulbs hang from the ceiling in the dining area

03 A striking wall of stacked hexagonal shelving units lines the back of the cocktail bar

Das erste in Asien eröffnete Lokal des mit einem Michelin-Stern ausgezeichneten Chefs Marco Gubbiotti ist ein ansprechendes und charismatisches umbrisches Restaurant, das nach Hongkong versetzt wurde. In Konzept und Design von Italien inspiriert, erweckt dieser Raum im Erdgeschoss die Vergangenheit zum Leben durch Art-déco-Motive, welche die über Jahrhunderte bestehenden Verbindungen zwischen Europa und Asien betonen.

Der Name des Restaurants („Die Million") stammt von Marco Polos Reisebericht in den Orient aus dem 13. Jahrhundert mit dem deutschen Titel *Il Milione. Die Wunder der Welt*. Er ist Ausdruck der Gesamtgestaltung des Lokals, die auch das beleuchtete Schild einschließt, welches die Gäste bei ihrer Ankunft begrüßt.

Das Design repräsentiert die physische Verbindung zwischen Ost und West auch durch aus Europa stammende Kernmaterialien und Leuchten neben vor Ort produzierten Elementen wie der gläsernen Wand gegenüber der Küche.

Marco Gubbiotti est le chef étoilé au Michelin de ce qui est sa première aventure asiatique : un restaurant élégant et charismatique de l'Ombrie transplanté à Hong Kong. Concept et agencement puisent leur inspiration en Italie, et le local au rez-de-chaussée fait revivre le passé à l'aide de motifs Art déco qui illustrent la connexion existant depuis des siècles entre l'Europe et l'Asie.

Le nom du restaurant (« Le million ») vient du titre en italien de l'œuvre *Devisement du monde*, un récit de voyages en Orient de Marco Polo au XIIIe siècle. L'influence de l'ouvrage se retrouve aussi dans l'identité globale, y compris le panneau lumineux souhaitant la bienvenue aux clients.

Le design traduit la fusion physique entre Orient et Occident. Les matériaux de base et l'éclairage proviennent d'Europe, et ils sont combinés à des éléments fabriqués en local, comme le mur vitré faisant face à la cuisine.

02

03

Johnnie Walker House Shanghai

Website	johnniewalkerhouse.com
Date Opened	May 2011
Designer	Asylum
Size of Build	517 m² / 5,550 ft²
Award	Longlist 2012
Address	Building 25, Sinan Mansions
	519 Fuxing Zhong Lu
	Shanghai
	China

01

In homage to the brand, this resplendent design creates a captivating environment in which to partake in the Johnnie Walker story. The private whisky club features unique design elements, such as pendant lights made from vintage decanters and copper lamps modelled from whisky stills.

Bathed in shades of gold and brown, visitors move through a series of interactive spaces, including a tasting-room and library, with each room designed to reflect a different aspect of the product.

To ensure that the historic building conformed with modern safety regulations, the malt and peat (used in the whisky distilling process) used to decorate the embassy's walls had to be thoroughly fireproofed.

Als Reverenz an die Marke bietet diese prächtige Ausstattung ein faszinierendes Ambiente, in dem man an der Johnnie-Walker-Story teilhaben kann. Der private Whisky-Klub zeigt einzigartige Designelemente, etwa Hängeleuchten aus Weinkaraffen und kupferne Leuchtkörper in Form von Destillierkolben für Whisky.

Die in Gold- und Brauntöne getauchten Besucher werden durch eine Folge interaktiver Bereiche geführt, zu denen eine Probierstube und eine Bibliothek gehören. Jeder Raum spiegelt in seinem Design einen anderen Aspekt des Produkts wieder.

Um im historischen Gebäude die modernen Sicherheitsvorschriften zu erfüllen, musste die Dekoration der Wände aus Malz und Torf (die für die Whisky-Produktion benötigt werden) feuerfest gemacht werden.

02

En hommage à la marque, le somptueux design d'intérieur permet de partager l'histoire de Johnnie Walker. Ce club privé de whisky possède des caractéristiques uniques, comme les lustres fabriqués avec des carafes et les luminaires en cuivre faits à partir d'alambics à whisky.

Baignés dans une lumière dorée et brune, les clients parcourent une série d'espaces interactifs, dont une salle de dégustation et une bibliothèque. Chaque pièce est conçue pour illustrer un aspect différent du produit.

Pour que le bâtiment historique soit conforme aux normes actuelles de sécurité, le malt et la tourbe, qui interviennent dans le processus de distillation du whisky et qui ont été utilisés pour décorer les murs du local, ont dû être complètement ignifugés.

01 A concave wall is lined with shelves displaying different blends of whisky

02 The copper scale model of a distillery shows the process from baked malt to where spirits are casked and aged for a minimum of three years before they can be considered whisky

03 The golden wave, made entirely from whisky glasses, forms an installation in the foyer

04 The oak floor has been laid at a 24-degree angle, to reflect the label's position on a Johnnie Walker bottle

03

04

Kismet

Website   theparkhotels.com/hyderabad/
hyderabad/kismet.html
Date Opened 2011
Designer   Blacksheep
Size of Build 1,070 m² / 11,500 ft²
Award   Longlist 2012
Address   The Park Hyderabad
22, Raj Bhavan Road
Somajiguda
Hyderabad 500082
India

As part of the high-end Park Hotel chain, this brightly coloured and glossy night-time space has been designed to attract guests with all the promise the riches of jewels can offer.

The night-club is adorned with a dizzying variety of different futuristic layers, juxtaposed to striking effect, which mix the region's traditional craft heritage with a hi-tech and cutting-edge contemporary aesthetic.

Hyderabad was known historically for its diamond and pearl trading and it was this reputation which inspired the interior's design, from the golden honeycomb hexagonal lighting to the crystal cave-spaces that glow like jewels.

Als Teil der vornehmen Park-Hotel-Kette sollte die Gestaltung dieses prächtigen Nachtlokals in leuchtenden Farben seine Gäste mit allen Versprechungen anlocken, die der Reichtum von Juwelen bieten kann.

Der Club ist mit einer schillernden Vielfalt unterschiedlicher futuristischer Elemente dekoriert, die mit überraschender Wirkung kombiniert wurden und eine Mischung aus regionaler Handwerkstradition und moderner High-Tech-Ästhetik darstellen.

Hyderabad war in der Vergangenheit berühmt für seinen Diamanten- und Perlenhandel, und dieser Ruf diente auch als Inspiration für die Innenausstattung: von den goldenen, hexagonalen Leuchten bis zu den kristallinen, höhlenartigen Bereichen, die wie Juwelen glänzen.

01 A gold fringe curtain is a
feature in one of the tucked-away
seating areas

02 80% of the materials used
in the club's design were sourced
and fabricated locally

03 The club sits directly
underneath the swimming pool
which can be seen through void
spaces in the ceiling

02

Ce club de nuit haut en couleur et étincelant appartient à la chaîne exclusive Park Hotel. Il a été conçu pour attirer les clients avec toutes les promesses que les richesses des joyaux peuvent offrir.

Le club affiche un éventail incroyable de couches futuristes juxtaposées pour un effet saisissant. Il combine l'héritage artisanal de la région à une esthétique contemporaine de pointe.

Hyderabad est historiquement connu pour le commerce de diamants et de perles, ce qui a inspiré le design d'intérieur, de l'éclairage sortant d'alvéoles dorées aux différents recoins en verre qui brillent comment des pierres précieuses.

L'Idiot Restaurant

Website	lidiotrestaurant.com
Date Opened	July 2009
Date Closed	January 2013
Designer	Ballistic Architecture Machine
Cost of Build	$$$$
Size of Build	400 m² / 4,300 ft²
Award	Longlist 2010
Address	1F, No 156 Minsheng E Rd, Sec 3
	Taipei City, 105
	Taiwan

The design of the restaurant, named in reaction to the formal dining culture found in Western restaurants throughout Taipei, is a blend of surreal ambiguity, craft traditions and the homely atmosphere of country interiors.

Two magnificent mosaic sculptures add an extravagant dimension to the light and simple interior – with its plain wooden furniture, floor and rafters, and peach walls adorned with eclectic motifs – while also embodying the food philosophy of the restaurant.

Embracing such a new and free way of working in order to construct the sculptures proved to be a learning experience for the local building team, whose creative vision was tapped to realise the designs. The result is a fascinating, shape-shifting experience, invoking a range of references and forms depending on the individual viewer.

Die Gestaltung dieses Lokals, benannt als Reaktion auf die formelle Esskultur westlicher Restaurants in ganz Taipei, ist eine Mischung aus surrealer Vieldeutigkeit, handwerklicher Tradition und der heimeligen Atmosphäre ländlicher Gasthöfe.

Zwei großartige Mosaikskulpturen verleihen dem hellen und schlichten Innenraum eine extravagante Dimension. Das einfache Mobiliar, der Fußboden und die Sparren sind aus Holz, die Wände mit eklektischen Motiven geschmückt verkörpern die Esskultur des Restaurants.

Die neuartige und offene Arbeitsweise bei der Herstellung der Skulpturen erwies sich als Lernprozess für das örtliche Team der Bauarbeiter, deren Kreativität bei der Ausführung des Entwurfs gefordert war. Das Ergebnis ist ein faszinierendes gestalterisches Erlebnis, das bei jedem Betrachter individuell unterschiedliche Bezüge und Reaktionen auslöst.

01 A sensual island curves across the main dining area, marking off space for food preparation, and features integrated shelving and a porthole fireplace that looks through to the seating area on the other side

02 Swimming in from the window-box, the first sculpture also provides the menu in the window

03 Roughly three metres in height, the sculptures were made using a high-tech rendering process, before being constructed from wood and covered with mosaic tiles

02

01

03

Le design du local, baptisé en réponse à la culture de restaurants occidentaux traditionnels à Taipei, mêle ambigüité surréaliste, traditions artisanales et atmosphère chaleureuse des intérieurs campagnards.

Deux imposantes sculptures en mosaïque ajoutent une dimension extravagante à la simplicité de l'intérieur clair (mobilier, sol et chevrons en bois, murs couleur pêche accueillant des tableaux éclectiques) et traduisent la philosophie culinaire du restaurant.

Pour construire les sculptures, l'équipe sollicitée pour sa vision créative en a tiré un apprentissage intéressant, adoptant une approche libre et inédite. Le résultat : des créations fascinantes et subjectives, qui évoquent des références et des formes différentes selon la personne les observant.

LAM Café

Date Opened   December 2011
Designer   a21studio
Cost of Build $$
Size of Build   333 m² / 3,600 ft²
Award   Longlist 2012
Address   105b Nguyen Thi Minh Khai
Nha Trang
Khanh Hoa
Vietnam

As a low-cost and flexible space which could be quickly set up and easily dismantled, owing to a temporary lease on the property, the main characteristic of this light and open café is its all-wood interior.

The design concept is related to the café's name, which means "louvres". Partitions made from vertical wooden slats are placed throughout the main hall area, providing both structural support and simply dividing the open-plan design into separate areas.

The warm climate, humidity and high rainfall determined the use of local materials in the design which ensured that light and air could circulate freely throughout the interior. The result is a big visual statement, but one with little environmental impact on the surrounding area.

Als preiswertes und flexibles Gebäude, das schnell aufgestellt und aufgrund der kurzfristigen Pachtzeiten auch leicht abmontierbar sein muss, ist die hölzerne Innenausstattung das entscheidende Charakteristikum dieses hellen und offenen Cafés.

Das Gestaltungskonzept bezieht sich auf den Namen des Lokals, der „Lamellen" bedeutet. Trennwände aus vertikal angeordneten Holzlatten sind in dem großen Raum aufgestellt, sowohl als tragende Elemente wie auch einfach zur Aufteilung des offenen Grundrisses in getrennte Bereiche.

Das warme, feuchte Klima und starke Regenfälle bestimmten die Wahl der Materialien für diesen Entwurf, der die Zirkulation von Licht und Luft durch den Innenraum garantiert. Das Ergebnis ist eine starke visuelle Aussage mit geringen ökologischen Auswirkungen auf die Umgebung.

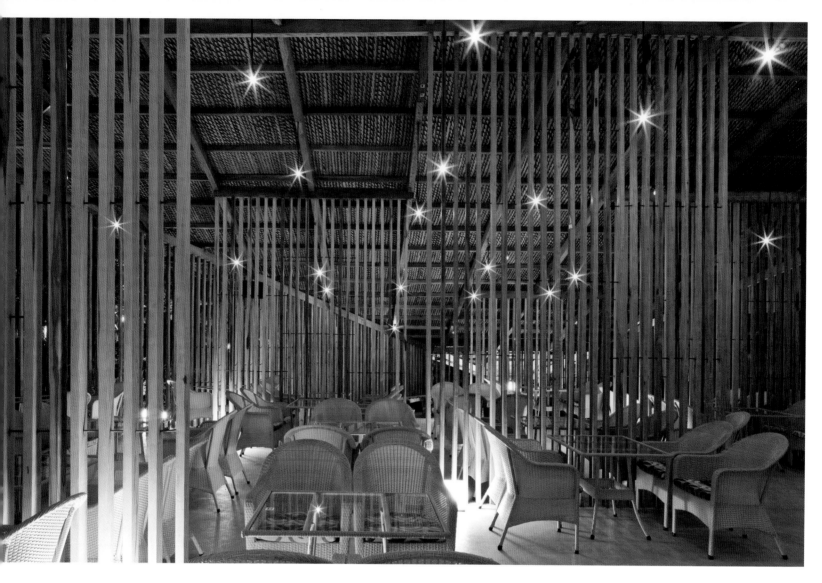

Tenu par un bail temporaire, cet espace se voulait de faible coût et flexible pour être facilement installé et démonté. La caractéristique principale de ce café ouvert est son intérieur exclusivement en bois.

Le concept derrière le design est lié au nom du café, qui peut être traduit par « persiennes ». Les séparations faites en lattes de bois verticales sont distribuées dans la salle principale. Elles servent d'éléments structurels et permettent de diviser le plan ouvert.

Le climat chaud, l'humidité et les précipitations abondantes ont imposé l'emploi de matériaux locaux. Le design garantit quant à lui que lumière et air circulent librement à l'intérieur. Le résultat est visuellement impactant, avec une empreinte minime sur l'environnement.

01 A diagonally slanting roof
means that guests' eyes
are drawn down into the space
and away from views of the
residential surroundings

02 Facilities and toilets are located
in an annexe to the rear of the
building next to a private garden

03 The roof has three layers and
is made from coconut leaves
and fishing nets

Ozone

Website ritzcarlton.com/en/properties/
hongkong/dining/ozone/default.htm
Date Opened May 2011
Designer Wonderwall
Size of Build 760 m² / 8,200 ft²
Address The Ritz-Carlton Hong Kong
Level 118 International Commerce Centre
1 Austin Road West, Kowloon
Hong Kong

Serving a mixture of Asian tapas and Japanese delicacies, this 250-seat bar with excellent views over Victoria Harbour presents a complex and astonishing interior that combines sublime elements from nature with the power of science. At 490 metres above sea level, the world's highest bar lives up to its name.

The theme, "Edenic Experiment", has evolved into an immaculate and multi-textured space which fuses cellular shapes with man-made forms. Inter-crossing throughout the space, this detailing recurs on almost every surface, from the mosaic-patterned floor, lattice-work partitions and low-relief walls to the grey veins in the marble bar.

From the futuristic entrance, guests are transported into a hyper-modern world saturated with organic honeycombs and geometric patterns in marble, glass and granite, with customised designs including a glass bauble lighting installation and asymmetrical lounge seating.

Das Angebot dieser Bar mit 250 Sitzplätzen besteht in einer Mischung aus asiatischen Vorspeisen und japanischen Delikatessen. Sie bietet einen großartigen Ausblick über den Victoria Harbour und eine komplexe und erstaunliche Innenausstattung, die wunderbare Elemente der Natur mit der Kraft der Wissenschaft verbindet. In einer Höhe von 490 Metern über dem Meeresspiegel trägt diese welthöchste Bar ihren Namen zu Recht.

Das Thema, „paradiesisches Experiment", hat zu einem makellosen, vielfach strukturierten Bereich geführt, der zellulare Formen mit von Menschen geschaffenen verbindet. Diese sich im gesamten Raum überschneidende Thematik ist fast auf jeder Fläche sichtbar, vom Mosaikfußboden über die Gitter-Abtrennungen und die Wände mit Flachrelief bis zur grauen Äderung der Marmorbar.

Vom futuristischen Eingang werden die Gäste in eine hypermoderne Welt geführt, die mit organischen Waben- und geometrischen Mustern in Marmor, Glas und Granit angefüllt ist. Speziell hierfür entworfen wurden eine verspielte gläserne Leuchteninstallation sowie die asymmetrischen Sitzgelegenheiten in der Lounge.

Pouvant accueillir jusqu'à 250 clients, ce bar propose des tapas asiatiques et des mets japonais. Outre les magnifiques vues sur Victoria Harbour, il se targue d'un intérieur surprenant et sophistiqué mariant éléments naturels et pouvoir de la science. Perché à 490 mètres au-dessus du niveau de la mer, le plus haut bar du monde porte bien son nom.

Le concept « Expérience édénique » a évolué pour donner un espace immaculé et rempli de textures, fusionnant formes cellulaires et formes artificielles. Cette fusion se retrouve sur quasiment toutes les surfaces, du motif de mosaïque au sol aux séparations en treillis, en passant par les veines grises du bar en marbre.

Après l'entrée futuriste, les clients sont transportés dans un monde ultramoderne saturé de nids d'abeille et de motifs géométriques en marbre, en verre et en granite. Ils peuvent apprécier des designs sur mesure, comme le luminaire de boules en verre et les sièges asymétriques du lounge.

"The challenge was creating a space that had never been seen before."

Wonderwall

01 Entry to the 118th floor is by elevator, which opens out on to reflective surfaces and contrasting curtain walls

02 Anatomically themed shelving has been cleverly constructed to hold bottles behind the bar

03 Curvy stacked pillars stand alongside the angular protrusions of the marbled bar and leather bar-stools

02

03

Shikata

Website	facebook.com/yakiniku.nabe.shikata
Date Opened	December 2012
Designer	Matsuya Art Works
Cost of Build	$$$
Size of Build	110 m² / 1,200 ft²
Award	Longlist 2013
Address	COMS I Nakameguro B1F 2-44-24
	Kamimeguro, Meguro-ku
	Tokyo 153-0051
	Japan

Specialising in *yakiniku*, a popular Japanese style of dining where the meat is cooked on a grill at the table, this traditional-style barbecue restaurant is located in an exclusively residential area of Tokyo.

The original partitions dividing the seating areas into separate cubicles made the restaurant's narrow space feel more cramped, but removing them made customers feel uncomfortable so they had to stay. Replacing them instead with partially mirrored screens decorated with traditional paintings transformed the space into a dynamic and visually stimulating interior that matched the food being served.

The result is a graphic explosion of mythical figures, organic motifs and red and white Koi, set against dark wooden tables and stone and concrete walls.

Dieses traditionelle Barbecue-Restaurant liegt in einem reinen Wohngebiet von Tokyo. Es hat sich auf *Yakiniku* spezialisiert, eine populäre japanische Speiseform, bei der Fleisch auf einem Grill am Tisch zubereitet wird.

Die originalen Trennwände, die den Sitzbereich in separate Kabinen teilten, ließen den engen Raum gedrängter wirken. Aber deren Entfernung machte ihn für die Gäste unbehaglicher, also mussten sie bleiben. Sie wurden ersetzt durch teils verspiegelte, mit traditionellen Malereien dekorierte Zwischenwände, die den Bereich in einen dynamischen und visuell anregenden Raum verwandelt haben, der zu den angebotenen Speisen passt.

Das Ergebnis ist eine grafische Explosion mythischer Figuren, organischer Motive sowie roter und weißer Koi-Fische im Kontrast zu dunklen Holztischen und Wänden aus Naturstein und Beton.

Ce restaurant à viande de style traditionnel est spécialisé en *yakiniku*, une technique japonaise populaire de cuisson sur une plaque chauffante. Il se trouve dans une zone résidentielle de Tokyo.

Les divisions originales des zones en cabines accentuaient l'exigüité du local, mais les clients n'ayant pas aimé qu'elles soient retirées, elles ont été conservées. Leur substitution par des panneaux semi-transparents et décorés de peintures traditionnelles a rendu l'intérieur plus dynamique et visuellement stimulant, à l'image des plats qui y sont servis.

Le résultat est une explosion graphique de personnages mythiques, de motifs organiques et de carpes koï rouges et blanches, contrastant avec les tables en bois sombre et les murs en pierre et en béton.

01   02

03

01 Specially designed grills have been built into the tables for guests to cook meat to their own taste

02 Glass partitions have been decorated with traditional graphicmotifs and paintings depicting kami spirits from the Shinto religion

03 Mirror reflection makes the room feel much more spacious

Shyo Ryu Ken

Website shoryu-ken.com
Date Opened July 2012
Designer STILE/Ietsugu Ohara
Cost of Build $$$
Size of Build 123 m² / 1,300 ft²
Award Category winner 2013
Address 1-1-1 Higashinoda
Miyakojima-ku
Osaka 534-0024
Japan

A "house within a house", this noodle and *ramen* restaurant exploits a lateral approach to create its welcoming invitation. The unusual design is in part inspired by the strict building regulations which apply under the railway pass where the building is located.

Booths inside take the form of a row of open-sided houses, modelled on a traditional type of Japanese architecture called *nagaya* and here constructed as a wooden framework using plyboard and plastering. This "open-house" set-up contributes to a communal atmosphere.

Customers enter via a sliding steel door and take up residence in their miniature homes, complete with own roof and windows. With the serving counter also being made to look like a building, and the long bar and low-hung pendant lighting, the space has a warm and homely glow.

Mit Freude am Querdenken schufen die Architekten einen freundlichen Empfang zu diesem Nudel- und *Ramen*-Restaurant: ein „Haus im Haus". Die ungewöhnliche Gestaltung wurde auch von den strengen Bauvorschriften bestimmt, die unter der Bahnüberführung gelten, wo das Gebäude liegt.

Nischen im Innenraum haben die Form aufgereihter, einseitig offener Häuser nach dem Vorbild eines traditionellen japanischen Bautyps, der *Nagaya* heißt und hier als Holzfachwerk mit Sperrholz und Verputz ausgeführt wurde. Dieser „offene" Haustyp trägt zur gemeinschaftlichen Atmosphäre bei.

Die Besucher treten durch eine stählerne Schiebetür ein und beziehen ihre Miniaturhäuser, die komplett mit eigenem Dach und Fenstern ausgestattet sind. Auch die Theke gleicht einem Haus, und die lange Bar sowie die tief hängenden Leuchten tragen zur warmen und heimeligen Atmosphäre bei.

01 Guests can sit at a long
bar which overlooks the chefs
in the kitchen

02 Continuing the element of
surprise, local building materials
and traditional techniques
were used when creating the
unconventional design

03 The lighting was designed by
Hiroyuki Nagatomi of Maxray

01

02

« Maison dans une maison », ce restaurant de *noodles* et *ramen* suit une approche latérale pour attirer la clientèle. Le design singulier tient en partie aux normes strictes de construction sous une ligne de chemin de fer, comme celle passant au-dessus du local.

À l'intérieur, des cabines forment un alignement de maisons ouvertes d'un côté. Elles ont été élaborées selon un type traditionnel d'architecture japonaise appelé *nagaya*, avec une structure en bois, contreplaqué et plâtre. Cette distribution de « maisons ouvertes » crée une atmosphère communautaire.

Les clients entrent par une porte coulissante en acier et s'installent dans une maison miniature dotée d'un toit et de fenêtres. L'espace inclut un comptoir s'apparentant lui aussi à un bâtiment, un long bar et des lustres bas qui apportent à l'ensemble une lumière chaleureuse.

03

Sound

Date Opened July 2009
Designer Inverse Lighting Design &
Orbit Design Studio
Award Category winner 2010
Address 3/F/F, Jungceylon Shopping Complex
193 Rut U Thit 200 Pi Rd.
Patong, Phuket 83150
Thailand

A sensational night-club in southern Thailand's concrete city of hedonism, this radical design is situated on the third floor of a shopping centre and entertainment complex and can accommodate up to 700 clubbers.

The concept for the design is decidedly ultra-modern, combining visions of the future with strong use of light and colour to visualise sound-waves throughout the space. Lighting plays a key role in creating a euphoric atmosphere, immersing bodies in a rich electric-blue that saturates the exposed concrete surfaces, or following the continuous curving of the walls and pulsating on the dance floor.

Special features include a sealed glass vessel for VIPs lit in complementary amber, LED lighting that responds to the rhythm of the music and a 'Wall of Sound' with LCD screens in the shape of a sound-wave.

01

01 Lighting strips embedded in the walls create continuous lines of light that react to the audio being played

02 A glass-lined VIP pod uses pinhole downlights to create a striking feature within the space

03 Rotating lights, strobes and lasers are coupled with circular seating pods for tired clubbers

Dieser radikal gestaltete, aufsehenerregende Club in Südthailands hedonistischer Betonstadt befindet sich im dritten Geschoss eines Einkaufs- und Vergnügungszentrums und kann bis zu 700 Nachtschwärmer aufnehmen.

Das Planungskonzept ist bewusst ultramodern und verbindet futuristische Visionen mit starkem Einsatz von Licht und Farbe, um Klangwellen im Raum zu visualisieren. Die Beleuchtung spielt eine wichtige Rolle um eine euphorische Atmosphäre zu erzeugen: Das Licht taucht die Besucher in ein kräftiges Elektrikblau, das auch die Sichtbetonflächen überzieht, es folgt der durchgehenden Krümmung der Wände und vibriert auf der Tanzfläche.

Zu den besonderen Elementen zählen ein bersteinfarben beleuchtetes Schiff aus Verbundglas für bevorzugte Gäste. Die LED-Beleuchtung reagiert auf den Rhythmus der Musik und eine „Schallwand" mit LED-Bildschirmen in Form einer Schallwelle.

Cette spectaculaire boîte de nuit a ouvert ses portes dans la capitale de l'hédonisme au sud de la Thaïlande. Au troisième étage d'un centre commercial et de loisirs, il peut accueillir jusqu'à 700 *clubbers* dans un design radical.

Le concept mise sans conteste sur un espace ultramoderne, avec des aspects futuristes et une utilisation soignée de la lumière et de la couleur pour représenter les ondes sonores dans l'espace. L'éclairage joue un rôle clé pour créer le sentiment d'euphorie. Les corps sont baignés dans une lumière bleu électrique saturant les surfaces en béton. Il suit aussi les murs courbes et le rythme sur la piste de danse.

Parmi les éléments caractéristiques du local, un vaisseau vitré est réservé aux VIP et éclairé d'une lumière ambre. Un éclairage de LED réagit au rythme de la musique et un « mur de son » composé d'écrans LCD épouse la forme d'une onde sonore.

03

Taiwan Noodle House

Website	dianping.com/shop/5678217
Date Opened	May 2012
Designer	Golucci International Design
Cost of Build	$$$
Size of Build	300 m² / 3,250 ft²
Award	Longlist 2013
Address	4#1F, No.789 Li Zhong Road
	Ningbo
	315177 Yinzhou
	China

In reaction to the cosmopolitan development of one of China's oldest cities, this restaurant combines traditional cultural elements with a clean and spare modern style.

Part of a larger building complex, the ground-floor space has floor-to-ceiling louvred shutter-doors which, when open, allow tables to spill out on to the street in the manner of café culture. Inside, oak grain has been used to panel the walls, a modest backdrop to the simple wooden seating and plain tables, minimalist shelving and recessed spot-lighting.

Inverted porcelain bowls suspended over a central, communal dining-table embellish the hall with an explosion of pattern and texture. The installation also complements the scatter-box storage unit and irregular window intersections that admit extra daylight, adding a quirky, domiciliary touch to this mix of ancient and modern.

Als Reaktion auf die kosmopolitische Entwicklung einer der ältesten Städte Chinas verbindet dieses Restaurant traditionelle kulturelle mit klaren und nüchternen modernen Stilelementen.

Das Lokal im Erdgeschoss ist Teil eines größeren Baukomplexes und hat raumhohe Lamellentüren, so können wie in einem Straßencafé die Tische hinausgestellt werden. Innen sind die Wände mit Eichenfaserplatten verkleidet; ein bescheidener Hintergrund für die schlichte Holzbestuhlung und einfachen Tische, minimalistischen Regale und eingebauten Strahler.

Verkehrt herum über einem zentralen, gemeinschaftlichen Esstisch aufgehängte Porzellanschüsseln schmücken den Saal mit einer Fülle von Mustern und Strukturen. Diese Installation ergänzt die Stapelregale und die unregelmäßig angeordneten Fenster, die zusätzliches Tageslicht einlassen und zur besonderen, heimischen Atmosphäre dieser Mischung aus Alt und Modern beitragen.

01 Following the lines of the wooden-clad walls, a panelled mirror creates the illusion of additional space

02 A simple grey slate staircase leads up to more seating and a private dining area

03 Traditional-style tableware on both tables and shelving creates a hybrid between a customary and contemporary aesthetic

"Chinese heritage symbols like porcelain bowls and chopsticks add a touch of nostalgia."

Golucci International Design

01

02

Pour répondre au développement cosmopolite de l'une des plus vieilles villes de Chine, ce restaurant mélange des éléments de la culture traditionnelle et un style moderne épuré.

Intégré dans un complexe immobilier, l'espace au rez-de-chaussée peut ouvrir ses portes persiennes allant du sol au plafond : les tables s'immiscent ainsi dans la rue comme une terrasse improvisée. Des panneaux en chêne recouvrent les murs intérieurs et forment une toile de fond discrète pour les sièges et les tables en bois, les étagères minimalistes et les spots encastrés.

Les bols pendus à l'envers au-dessus d'une grande table centrale ornent la salle dans une explosion de motifs et de textures. L'installation complète l'empilement irrégulier de caisses de rangement et les fenêtres de toutes tailles qui laissent entrer la lumière naturelle. La composition ajoute une touche conviviale et décalée à cette fusion d'ancien et de moderne.

03

Tazmania Ballroom

Website	tazmaniaballroom.com
Date Opened	2010
Designer	Tom Dixon
Size of Build	300 m² / 3,250 ft²
Award	Category winner 2011
Address	1/F LKF Tower
	33 Wyndham Street
	Central
	Hong Kong
	China

Awarded Best International Bar in the Restaurant & Bar Design Awards for 2011, this hyper-real grotto of irregular lines and luxurious materials evokes the decadence of another era. The spectacular design re-imagines elements from typical British games-rooms, merging them with ultra-modern forms and reflective surfaces to create an exclusive hangout.

A mirrored bronze staircase leads to the low-lit pool hall, with its multiple seating areas, long golden bar and outdoor area. Diagonally across from the hall, a black cave with irregular contours, lined with strips of white light, provides the seating area beside the DJ booth.

Aurulent tables, bronze lighting and turquoise banquettes stand out like jewels in the dark and enigmatic setting, whilst a wall of white plaster books, downlit to dramatic effect, mimics the libraries often formerly found in billiards rooms.

Diese hyperrealistische, mit unklaren Linien und luxuriösem Material ausgestattete Grotte, die 2011 als beste internationale Bar mit dem Restaurant & Bar Design Award ausgezeichnet wurde, erinnert an die Dekadenz einer vergangenen Ära. Die spektakuläre Gestaltung enthält typische Elemente aus britischen Spielkasinos und verbindet diese mit ultramodernen Formen und reflektierenden Oberflächen, wodurch ein exklusives Ambiente entstanden ist.

Ein verspiegeltes Treppenhaus führt zu dem schummerigen Billardsaal mit verschiedenen Sitzflächen, einer langen goldenen Bar und einem Außenbereich. Diagonal gegenüber bietet eine schwarze Höhle mit unregelmäßigen Konturen und weißen Lichtstreifen einen Rückzugsraum neben dem DJ-Pult.

Goldfarbene Tische, bronzene Leuchten und türkisfarbige Sitzbänke stehen wie Schmuckstücke vor dem geheimnisvollen und dunklen Hintergrund. Eine mit dramatischer Wirkung angestrahlte Wand aus weißen Gipsbüchern verweist auf die früher häufig in Billardzimmern vorhandenen Bibliotheken.

01

01 A collection of bronze and copper Dixon globes creates a stunning central lighting feature

02 Curved seating upholstered in 'chalk-blue' fabric is paired with silver and gold domed tables

03 The elevated DJ booth overlooks the plush red pool tables edged with gold

Élu « Best International Bar » lors des prix Restaurant & Bar Design Awards de 2011, cet antre aux lignes irrégulières et fait de matériaux nobles illustre la décadence d'une ère révolue. Le design spectaculaire reprend des éléments traditionnels des salles de jeux en Angleterre et les marie à des formes ultramodernes et à des surfaces brillantes pour attirer une clientèle exclusive.

Un escalier aux murs recouverts de miroirs mène à une salle de billard à l'éclairage tamisé. Des fauteuils, un long bar doré et un espace extérieur font face en diagonale à une sorte de grotte obscure : de contours irréguliers et zébrée de bandes de lumière blanche, elle permet de se détendre à côté de la cabine du DJ.

Les tables en forme de sablier, les lampes en bronze et les banquettes turquoise brillent comme des bijoux dans le décor sombre et énigmatique. Un mur de livres en plâtre, éclairé vers le bas pour plus d'effet, imite les bibliothèques souvent présentes auparavant dans les clubs de billard.

The Lookout Café

Date Opened December 2010
Designer design spirits co., ltd.
Size of Build 172 m² / 1,850 ft²
Award Category winner 2011
Address Niseko Village
atop Mount Annupuri
Abuta District
Hokkaido 048-1592
Japan

Built entirely from wood and paper, this 80-seat café won the Restaurant & Bar Design Award for Best International Restaurant in 2011. A retreat for skiers, the small and aptly named pit-stop is located at a remote point on Niseko mountain.

The wooden lattices are intended to capture a universally recognised Japanese identity, catering to the high percentage of tourists who visit the slopes. The redesigned interior of the long, narrow space features simple bench-seating partitioned off with slatted louvres to create a gentle and welcoming atmosphere.

The remote location and need to build quickly outside the skiing season meant the café could only be reached by foot or using heavy machinery to transport larger materials. Extreme conditions, including possible landslides, strong winds and minimal hours of daylight, made the project much more difficult to realise.

Dieses ganz aus Holz und Pappe erbaute Café mit 80 Sitzplätzen wurde bei den Restaurant & Bar Design Awards 2011 als bestes internationales Restaurant ausgezeichnet. Die kleine und bezeichnenderweise Gipfel-Stopp genannte Einkehr für Skifahrer befindet sich an abgelegener Stelle auf dem Berg Niseko.

Das hölzerne Gitterwerk des Gebäudes soll das weltweit anerkannte japanische Image widerspiegeln und die große Zahl von Pistenbesuchern versorgen. Der neu gestaltete lange und schmale Innenraum ist mit schlichten, durch Lattenwände voneinander getrennten Sitzbänken möbliert und empfängt die Gäste in freundlicher Atmosphäre.

Der entfernte Standort und der Zwang, kurzfristig außerhalb der Skisaison zu bauen, bedeuteten, dass das Café nur zu Fuß oder mit schwerem technischen Gerät zum Transport umfangreicherer Baustoffe erreicht werden konnte. Zusätzlich erschwerten die extremen Bedingungen, wie potenzielle Erdrutsche, starke Winde und kurzzeitiges Tageslicht, die Realisation dieses Projekts.

Ce café de 80 places a été entièrement construit à base de bois et de papier. Il a remporté le prix « Best International Restaurant » des Restaurant & Bar Design Awards de 2011. Refuge de skieurs, ce petit lieu de ravitaillement au nom pertinent est perché à l'écart sur la montagne Niseko.

Les lattes en bois permettent d'évoquer une identité japonaise universellement connue. Dans l'intérieur remodelé de ce local allongé et étroit, les touristes fréquentant les pistes prennent place sur de simples bancs séparés par des jalousies, dans une atmosphère agréable et accueillante.

De par l'isolement du café et le besoin de le construire rapidement pendant la basse saison, l'accès n'a pu se faire qu'à pied et des machines pour transporter des matériaux plus volumineux ont été utilisées. L'exécution du projet a été compliquée par les conditions extrêmes (dont de possibles glissements de terrain), des vents forts et des heures réduites de soleil.

01 Indirect lighting has been used to help combat glare from the sun and to avoid darkening shadows

02 Spruce was used for the interior and has been finished using a clear lacquer, or black gloss

03 The café was redesigned using only three materials: wood, paper and paint

The More

Date Opened	December 2012
Designer	Betwin Space Design
Cost of Build	$$
Size of Build	52 m² / 560 ft²
Award	Longlist 2013
Address	1F, U-space 1 Sampyeong-dong Bundang-gu Seongnam-si 463-400 South Korea

Inspired by the modernist mantra, "less is more", this coffee and dessert café is an exercise in understated quality design. A combination of subtle wall patterns, mirrored surfaces and simple furniture offsets the standout feature – a nest of black transparent lighting which floats above the serving counter.

In keeping with the strict design concept, all formal expression in the functional elements was reduced to the minimum, resulting in an uncomplicated, yet exquisite space.

Integrated strip-lighting was set into both walls and runs the length of the café; with its simple lines the lighting rests just above the glossy marble tabletops to create a soft ambience throughout. Furthermore, mirrors and a central-hanging mirror pendant catch the light and transform the interior dimensions, injecting energy and softening the angles.

Dieses vom modernistischen Mantra „Weniger ist mehr" inspirierte Café in großartiger Lage ist eine Übung in dezentem Qualitätsdesign. Die Kombination aus zurückhaltender Wandgestaltung, verspiegelten Flächen und schlichtem Mobiliar wird durch ein auffälliges Element aufgewogen – ein Netz aus schwarzen, transparenten Leuchten schwebt über der Theke.

In strenger Anlehnung an das Designkonzept wurde jede formale Gestaltung der funktionalen Elemente auf das Minimum reduziert. Das Resultat ist ein schlichter, aber exquisiter Raum.

Integrierte Leuchtstoffleisten an beiden Längswänden des Cafés werfen Lichtstrahlen auf die glänzenden Marmor-Tischplatten und bewirken ein durchgehend weiches Ambiente. Deckenspiegel und ein zentral angebrachte verspiegelte Hängeleuchte fangen das Licht ein und verändern die Dimensionen des Innenraums, strömen Energie aus und mildern die scharfen Kanten.

01

02

Inspiré de la célèbre devise « less is more », ce café-pâtisserie offre un exemple de design sobre de qualité. Pour mettre en valeur l'élément phare, un éclairage dans un maillage noir transparent, l'intérieur combine des motifs muraux délicats, des surfaces réfléchissantes et un mobilier simple.

Fidèle à ce concept, l'expression formelle de chaque élément fonctionnel a été réduite à son minimum pour créer un espace simple et raffiné.

Une rampe lumineuse a été intégrée aux deux murs et court sur toute la longueur. Au-dessus des plateaux en marbre, l'éclairage crée une atmosphère agréable. Des miroirs au plafond et un miroir pendu au centre captent la lumière et changent les dimensions de l'intérieur, le rendant plus dynamique tout en adoucissant les angles.

01 With a small and narrow footprint the café's amenities are located out of sight, leaving a clean and simple dining area

02 A large single pane of glass provides the frontage for the café, functioning as a door, but looking like a window

03 Walls are lacquered in white paint and feature subtle bejewelled patterns in relief

03

The Tower Kitchen

Date Opened	October 2012
Designer	Khosla Associates & tsk Design
Size of Build	450 m² / 4,850 ft²
Award	Longlist 2013
Address	24, 16th Floor, Canberra Block
	Vittal Mallya Rd
	UB City
	Bangalore 560001
	India

Located in India's hi-tech city, this fine-dining restaurant in its resplendent setting serves modern European cuisine to the local culinary-loving elite. The lavish venue on the 16th floor of the UB building features three zones: an entrance lounge, whisky bar and semi-outdoor smoking area, and main dining-room.

The guiding concept combines bold graphic designs, luxurious materials and modernist-inspired detailing to create a warm and vibrant environment. The strong typographic identity by tsk Design interconnects the menus, rotating customised screens and metal partitions, whose bright-red cut-outs of kitchen utensils are drawn from the traditional manufacturing method of model moulding.

In keeping with the affluent setting, the clad timber walls, local black cuddapah stone floor and smoked mirror accompany a 10-metre wine wall and a custom-designed light installation suspended over a water feature.

Dieses vornehme, in Indiens High-Tech-Stadt in prächtiger Umgebung gelegene Restaurant bietet der örtlichen verwöhnten Elite anspruchsvolle, moderne europäische Küche. Das luxuriöse Lokal im 16. Stock des UB Buildings besteht aus drei Zonen: einer Eingangslounge, einer Whisky-Bar mit partiell im Freien liegendem Raucherbereich und einem großen Speisesaal.

Das Leitkonzept verbindet auffällige grafische Elemente, luxuriöse Materialien und modernistisch inspirierte Detailgestaltung zu einem freundlichen und lebhaften Ambiente. Die eindrucksvolle typografische Gestaltung von tsk Design zeichnet die Speisekarten aus. Die nach Maß gefertigten rotierenden Trennelemente und metallenen Zwischenwände mit leuchtend roten Ausschnitten in Form von Küchengeräten wurden auf traditionelle Weise in Formen gegossen.

In Einklang mit der glamourösen Kulisse aus kaschierten Holzwänden, einem Boden aus regionalem schwarzen Kalkstein und dem verwendeten Milchglas, wird der Wein des Hauses in einer zehn Meter langen Wand präsentiert, und ein Wasserspiel erstrahlt unter einer extra angefertigten Lichtinstallation.

01 Concrete coffered ceilings were an original feature and have been updated using LED lighting

02 Brightly coloured red and blue chairs, inspired by Saarinen, complement lime-green and chocolate banquettes

03 Made from smoked veneer with bright-red edging, the large utensil cut-outs rotate on a pivoting base to screen off guests in the dining-room

"A grid of shapes: pots, pans, spatulas and whisks draw inspiration from nostalgic model moulds."

Khosla Associates

02

Situé dans la ville high-tech d'Inde, ce restaurant élégant au décor somptueux offre une cuisine européenne moderne à l'élite locale adepte de gastronomie. L'intérieur opulent se trouve au 16e étage du complexe UB City et compte trois zones : un *lounge* à l'entrée, un bar à whisky avec un espace fumeur semi-extérieur, et une salle de restaurant.

Le concept allie un design graphique audacieux et des détails aux allures modernistes, l'ensemble formant un environnement chaleureux et haut en couleur. La forte identité typographique signée par tsk Design assure la cohérence entre les menus, les écrans rotatifs et les séparations métalliques, dont les éléments rouge vif représentant des ustensiles de cuisine ont été obtenus selon une méthode traditionnelle de moulage.

En écho au décor faste, les murs habillés de bois, le sol en pierre à chaux noire et le miroir fumé complètent un mur de casiers à vin de 10 mètres de long et un lustre sur mesure au-dessus d'une installation d'eau.

ZENSE Gourmet Deck & Lounge Panorama

Website	zensebangkok.com
Date Opened	September 2012
Designer	Department of Architecture
Cost of Build	$$$$+
Size of Build	4,000 m² / 43,000 ft²
Award	Shortlist 2013
Address	Level 17, ZEN World
	Central World shopping complex
	4/5 Rajdamri Road
	Pathum Wan
	Bangkok 10330
	Thailand

Offering breathtaking views over the city, this re-designed popular club has been given a new lease of elegance and a brand-new identity for the future after the building was gutted by fire during recent unrest.

The huge space integrates influences from architecture, fashion and interior design, as is clear upon exiting the lift where a permanent light installation suggesting falling confetti casts dramatic shadows on the entrance walls. Dynamic steel lines thread through the club, invoking fabric pleats against a cool colour palette of greys and blacks punctuated by fuchsia-pink and deep purple.

The light installation in the reception area, black cubed frames with naked bulbs, is echoed elsewhere by standing floor-lamps and hanging lanterns. Diagonal grooves in the staircase walls are a rigged-line motif, seen also in the steel ceiling structure and rooftop pavilions.

01

Die Umgestaltung dieses beliebten Clubs mit atemberaubendem Ausblick über die Stadt hat ihm wieder Eleganz und ein brandneues, zukunftsweisendes Image verliehen, nachdem er bei kürzlich stattgefundenen Unruhen durch Feuer zerstört worden war.

Sobald man aus dem Fahrstuhl tritt wird deutlich, dass der große Raum von Architektur, Mode und Raumgestaltung bestimmt wird. Eine permanente Lichtinstallation deutet fallendes Konfetti an und wirft dramatische Schatten auf die Eingangswand. Auffällige Stahlbänder führen durch den Raum und simulieren Stofffalten auf einer kühlen Farbpalette mit fuchsiaroten und dunkelvioletten Akzenten.

Die Formen der Lichtinstallation im Empfangsbereich aus schwarzen, kubischen Fassungen mit nackten Glühbirnen werden an anderer Stelle von aufgestellten Bodenleuchten und aufgehängten Laternen aufgenommen. Diagonale Kehlen in der Wand des Treppenhauses bilden ein orthogonales Motiv, das auch in der stählernen Deckenkonstruktion und den Dachpavillons wieder auftritt.

Avec des vues à couper le souffle sur la ville, ce club populaire a été remodelé et a gagné en élégance. Son identité a aussi été repensée après que le bâtiment a été ravagé par un incendie lors de récentes émeutes.

Les influences de l'architecture, de la mode et du design d'intérieur s'apprécient dans le vaste espace. Dès la sortie de l'ascenseur, les clients peuvent admirer une installation lumineuse permanente illustrant une chute de confettis et projetant des ombres sur les murs de l'entrée. Des barres en acier tracent des lignes dynamiques à travers le club, telles les plis d'une étoffe. La palette de couleurs froides, de gris et noir, est ponctuée par des touches fuchsia et violet foncé.

À la réception, l'installation lumineuse composée d'ampoules nues et de supports cubiques noirs trouve son pendant dans les lampes sur pied et les suspensions. Dans l'escalier, des rainures diagonales forment un motif linéaire, reproduit par la structure en acier au plafond et par les tonnelles sur le toit.

02

01 Sitting on an amazing futuristic decking system, contributed by the Thai landscape architecture studio T.R.O.P., the modular steel structures form elegant outdoor pavilions, on the 18th floor overlooking the capital

02 Dogtooth patterns on the outdoor tables echo the repeating patterns found in the steel structures

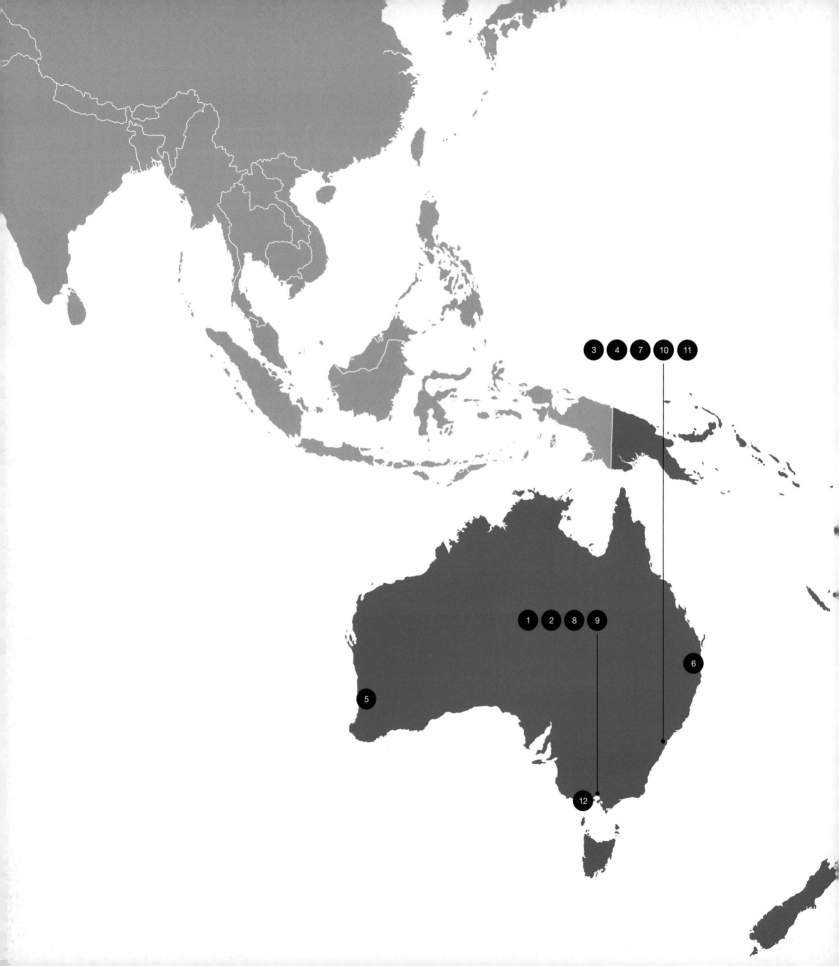

Australia

Australia

Dominic Harris
Founder and Director
Cinimod Studio

Founder and creative director of Cinimod Studio, Dominic Harris qualified as an architect at the Bartlett School of Architecture, London, where he was awarded a Distinction for his work in interactive design. His architectural experience includes work for Future Systems and Softroom. He was named Breakthrough Talent of the Year" at the FX Design Awards in 2008, and in 2009 was awarded its "Best Bar or Restaurant Design" for his work on Snog. In 2010 he won the Lighting Design Award for "Best Hotel or Restaurant Lighting Scheme".

Der Gründer und Kreativdirektor von Cinimod Studio, Dominic Harris, studierte Architektur an der Bartlett School of Architecture in London, wo er eine Auszeichnung für seine Arbeit über interaktives Design erhielt. Praktische Erfahrungen erwarb er im Architekturbüro Future Systems (Lords Media Center, Selfridges & Co Birmingham, New Look Flagship Store) und Softroom (Virgin Atlantic Upper Class Lounge in Heathrow). 2008 wurde Dominic bei den FX Design Awards zum „Breakthrough Talent of the Year" ernannt und 2009 für seine Arbeit für Snog als „Best Bar or Restaurant Design" ausgezeichnet. 2010 gewann er den Lighting Design Award für „Best Hotel or Restaurant Lighting Scheme".

Fondateur et directeur artistique de Cinimod Studio, Dominic Harris a obtenu son diplôme d'architecte de la Bartlett School of Architecture, à Londres, dont il a reçu une distinction honorifique pour son travail en design interactif. Son parcours en architecture inclut les travaux Future Systems (Lords Media Centre, Selfridges & Co Birmingham, magasin-phare New Look) et Softroom (salon Virgin Atlantic Upper Class, à Heathrow). Il a été nommé Breakthrough Talent of the Year » à l'occasion des FX Design Awards en 2008. Un an plus tard, il remportait le prix « Best Bar or Restaurant Design » pour son travail pour Snog. En 2010, il s'est vu décerner le prix « Lighting Design Award » dans la catégorie « Best Hotel or Restaurant Lighting Scheme ».

From industrial chic to rustic, modern or retro, the selection of beautiful projects here demonstrates a continuing growth of design quality emerging from Australia and South Pacific. What has always attracted me to the Restaurant & Bar Design Awards is the continued deliverance of stand-out designs, featuring intricate details within striking immersive environments.

I first met Marco Rebora, the Awards' founder, in 2009 when I created the inaugural launch event for the R&BDA. Cinimod Studio was commissioned to create an outdoor interactive lighting installation; conceived as a huge "exploded globe of light", it was suspended from the trees over London's Hoxton Square and controlled interactively by guests using special punch-cards to choreograph their own colour animations.

The project was not only a success in its own right, but for me personally it served as a real introduction into understanding the ethos of Marco and his Awards. Marco is driven by a genuine passion and belief in designers and their continuing abilities to push design boundaries as they strive to achieve the remarkable.

From a lighting and interactive perspective, I look out for the experiential aspect of design and the shortlist here exhibits an array of multi-faceted environments similar to my own interests and practice. My preferred palette of architectural elements generally consists of materials and finishes that work well with curves and can be formed. However, my main tool, used on all projects, is light. It's really important to me that the lighting design is integrated as part of the conceptual process.

A solid example is March Studios (Baker D. Chirico) and the way they combine a methodical approach with striking undulated waves that pays homage to traditional bread-making. Evident here is a real understanding of the use of the space with features that complement the type of premises, a bakery.

Similar to my own approach, it is important to take into account the underlying narrative or purpose of a space. Telling a story through design is key when creating a heightened environment in order to produce a responsive aesthetic experience.

The overall calibre of the projects in this chapter is incredible. Each excites me for different reasons. There is a trend for an almost ritualistic repetition within each case, of a form, slice or object: whether architectural slices, repeated light fixtures, or seemingly decorative elements that have become more than just that, each successfully establishes a vital sense of place that for me results in a fantastic memory of each project.

These examples push the design envelope without resulting in overly complex narratives or forms. They are projects that in my humble opinion exemplify design excellence.

Die wunderbaren Projekte in dieser Auswahl, ob industriell schick, rustikal, modern oder retro, zeugen von einer ständig zunehmenden Design-Qualität in Australien und dem Südpazifik. Schon immer habe ich bei den Restaurant & Bar Design Awards die herausragenden Entwürfe bewundert, die komplizierte Details in prächtiger, faszinierender Umgebung zeigen.

Ich traf den Preisgründer Marco Rebora erstmals 2009, als ich die Eröffnungsveranstaltung für den R&BDA ausgestaltete. Cinimod Studio war beauftragt, eine interaktive Lichtinstallation im Freien zu planen, die als riesige „explodierte Lichtkugel" konzipiert war. Sie hing an den Bäumen über dem Londoner Hoxton Square und wurde von den Gästen interaktiv kontrolliert, indem sie mit speziellen Lochkarten ihre eigenen Farbanimationen erstellen konnten.

Das Projekt wurde nicht nur zu einem Erfolg an sich, mir persönlich diente es auch als konkrete Einführung in das Verständnis der Zielsetzungen von Marco und seiner Awards. Er ist passioniert und glaubt daran, dass Designer in ihrem Streben nach Bemerkenswertem gestalterische Grenzen überschreiten können.

Aus meiner auf Licht und Interaktion ausgerichteten Perspektive suche ich nach dem experimentellen Aspekt von Gestaltung, und die hier vorliegende Auswahl zeigt eine Vielfalt von Umfeldern, die meinem eigenen Interesse und meiner Praxis entsprechen. Meine bevorzugte Palette von Architekturelementen besteht im Allgemeinen aus Materialien und Oberflächenbehandlungen, die Kurven und andere Formen ermöglichen. Mein Hauptwerkzeug bei allen Projekten ist jedoch Licht, das als wichtiger Bestandteil in den Entwurfsprozess integriert werden muss.

Ein gutes Beispiel sind die March Studios (Baker D. Chirico), die methodisches Vorgehen mit eindrucksvollen Wellenformen verbinden und damit der traditionellen Brotherstellung Respekt erweisen. Hier zeigt sich echtes Verständnis für die Nutzung des Raumes durch Elemente, die einer Bäckerei gerecht werden.

Ähnliches gilt für meine eigene Arbeitsweise: Es ist wichtig, die betreffende Aussage oder die Funktion eines Raumes zu berücksichtigen. Eine Geschichte durch Design zu erzählen ist entscheidend, um ein qualitätvolles Umfeld zu erzeugen, das entsprechende ästhetische Eindrücke vermitteln kann.

Das Gesamtniveau der Projekte ist unglaublich hoch. Jedes einzelne begeistert mich aus unterschiedlichen Gründen. Bei jedem ist ein Trend zu fast ritueller Überfülle von Formen und Objekten zu erkennen: von Architekturteilen, Leuchtkörpern oder scheinbar dekorativen Elementen, die über ihre eigentliche Funktion hinausgewachsen sind. Und alle zeigen sie erfolgreich eine starke Ortsbezogenheit, die sie für mich besonders erinnerungswürdig macht.

Diese Beispiele befördern den Fortschritt des Designs, ohne zu einem Übermaß an komplexen Aussagen oder Formen zu führen. Es sind Projekte, die meiner bescheidenen Meinung nach für gestalterische Hochleistung stehen.

Chic industriel, rustique, moderne, rétro : la sélection des superbes projets dans ces pages prouve la montée d'un design de qualité venu d'Australie et du Pacifique sud. Les Restaurant & Bar Design Awards m'ont toujours attiré pour être la vitrine de designs originaux, truffés de détails élaborés dans d'incroyables environnements immersifs.

C'est en 2009 que j'ai rencontré pour la première fois Marco Rebora, fondateur des Awards. Cinimod Studio était chargé de créer en extérieur une installation lumineuse interactive : conçue comme un énorme « globe de lumière explosé », elle pendait des arbres d'Hoxton Square, à Londres, et les invités chorégraphiaient à l'aide de cartes perforées leurs propres animations en couleur.

Ce projet a été une réussite à part entière et au niveau personnel, il m'a permis de comprendre la philosophie de Marco et de ses Awards. Marco est guidé par une véritable passion et une profonde croyance dans les designers et dans leur capacité à repousser les limites du design en quête d'excellence.

J'observe l'approche expérimentale du design du point de vue de l'éclairage et de l'interaction, et ces environnements complexes sont proches de mes propres centres d'intérêt et expériences. Mes éléments architecturaux favoris incluent normalement des matériaux et des finitions se prêtant aux formes courbes et pouvant être façonnés, mon outil fétiche restant dans tous les cas la lumière. Le design de l'éclairage doit à mon sens faire partie intégrante du processus conceptuel.

Exemple parlant de cette démarche, March Studios (Baker D. Chirico) combine une approche méthodique et de belles vagues ondulantes pour rendre hommage à la fabrication du pain. Sans conteste l'emploi de l'espace et le choix des détails ont été parfaitement dominés pour l'aménagement de cette boulangerie.

Dans la même ligne, il est important de prendre en compte l'intention sous-jacente d'un espace. Le design doit raconter une histoire en vue d'une expérience esthétique réceptive.

En général, les projets dans ce chapitre sont d'un calibre incroyable, et chacun d'eux me fascine pour des raisons différentes. Ils traduisent la tendance à une abondance presque systématique, qu'il soit question d'une forme ou d'un objet : choix architecturaux, répétition de lustres, éléments décoratifs prenant une dimension supérieure, chaque aspect communique un sentiment vital laissant un merveilleux souvenir.

Ces exemples dépassent les frontières conceptuelles sans pour autant présenter des histoires ou des formes surfaites. À mon humble avis, ils incarnent l'excellence en matière de design.

Baker D. Chirico

Website	bakerdchirico.com.au
Date Opened	September 2011
Designer	March Studio
Size of Build	150 m² / 1,600 ft²
Award	Category winner 2012
Address	178 Faraday Street
	Carlton, VIC 3053
	Australia

The winner of the Restaurant & Bar Design Awards
Australia & Pacific category in 2012, this elegant bakery
is a homage to the age-old tradition of bread-making.

The design was inspired by the methodical and
integrated chain of tasks involved, in cooling, storing
and presenting freshly baked loaves, and resulted in this
distinctive wicker-basket surround with its undulating
waves. The wooden structure stands in contrast to the
exposed concrete wall and classic harlequin-tiled floor,
while over the course of the day the slatted shelves
house the bread at different stages of production.

A traditional storefront with large window frames
the beautiful design, complete with the long wooden
'chopping board' counter which holds all the necessary
tools for slicing, packing and serving the bread, adding
a rustic, yet contemporary feel.

Diese elegante Bäckerei, 2012 Gewinner des Restaurant
& Bar Design Awards in der Kategorie „Australia &
Pacific", ist eine Hommage an die uralte Tradition
des Brotbackens.

Die Planung wurde von der methodischen und
bewährten Aufgabenkette Kühlen, Lagern und Auslegen
der frisch gebackenen Brotlaibe bestimmt und führte zu
dieser unverwechselbaren, wellenförmigen Anmutung
eines Weidenkorbs. Die Holzkonstruktion steht im
Kontrast zu der Sichtbetonwand und dem klassischen
Schachbrett-Fliesenboden. Die im Laufe des Tages
immer wieder frisch gebackenen Brote werden in
Lattenregalen präsentiert.

Eine traditionelle Ladenfront mit großen Fenstern
rahmt die ansprechende Gestaltung ein. Die Theke ist
auch ein Schneidebrett und enthält alle notwenigen
Geräte zum Aufschneiden, Verpacken und Ausliefern
des Brotes, zudem trägt sie zum rustikalen und doch
zeitgemäßen Eindruck des Lokals bei.

01 The integrated shelving system was made from CNC routed plywood

02 The long wooden counter is intended to age with use over the years

03 The striking design is perfectly framed by the traditional glass-fronted storefront

"'Just bread?', we said, and thought of containers for bread. Baskets, cooling racks, peels. A basket the size of a shop. A basket that was also a rack."

March Studio

02

03

Lauréate des Restaurant & Bar Design Awards 2012 pour la catégorie Australia & Pacific, cette élégante boulangerie rend hommage à la longue tradition de fabrication de pain.

Le design s'est inspiré de la chaîne intégrée et méthodique d'opérations pour refroidir, stocker et présenter les pains frais. Le décor est une sorte de panier en osier raffiné aux formes ondulantes. La structure en bois contraste avec le mur en béton et le sol à damiers. Les étagères à lattes accueillent les pains à différentes étapes de leur élaboration.

Avec sa grande vitrine, la devanture traditionnelle encadre l'élégant design. Elle laisse apprécier le long comptoir en bois où se trouvent tous les ustensiles nécessaires pour trancher, emballer et servir le pain. L'ensemble adopte une apparence rustique bien que contemporaine.

Bar Ampere

Website barampere.com
Date Opened November 2012
Designer BG Architecture
Cost of Build $$$$
Size of Build 118 m² / 1,250 ft²
Award Longlist 2013
Address 16 Russell Place
Melbourne, VIC 3000
Australia

Lodged between a new residential development above and an electricity substation below, this European-inspired bar in the heart of downtown Melbourne is a wonderland of industrial chic. In order to compensate for limited space, the design concentrated on making the interior as intriguing as possible.

Named after the unit of an electric current, the bar is furnished with all sorts of mechanical fixtures, glowing lamps, exposed wires and chromed fittings.

A particular source of inspiration was the Futurists, the early 20th-century Italian arts movement whose members' love of high-power machinery made them the first fanatics of industrialisation. With regard to this, each fixture and fitting used had a previous life as an element of manufacturing, such as the set of custom lights made from old hairdressing heat-lamps.

Über dieser europäisch angehauchten Bar im Herzen der Innenstadt von Melbourne liegt eine neue Wohn-anlage und darunter eine Außenstelle des Elektrizitäts-werks. Ein Wunderland aus industiellem Schick, dessen Innenausstattung als Ausgleich für den beschränkten Raum so ansprechend wie möglich gestaltet wurde.

Benannt nach der Einheit für elektrische Strom-stärke, ist das Lokal mit allen technischen Vorrichtun-gen ausgestattet: strahlenden Leuchten, frei liegenden Leitungen und verchromten Armaturen.

Eine spezielle Inspirationsquelle waren die Futuristen. Mit ihrer Vorliebe für Hochleistungstechnik gehörten die Mitglieder der italienische Kunstrichtung aus dem frühen 20. Jahrhunderts zu den ersten Fanatikern der Industrialisierung. Aus diesem Grunde hatten alle eingebauten Vorrichtungen schon ein Vorleben als Industrieprodukte, etwa die hierfür ange-fertigten Leuchten aus alten Friseursalonlampen.

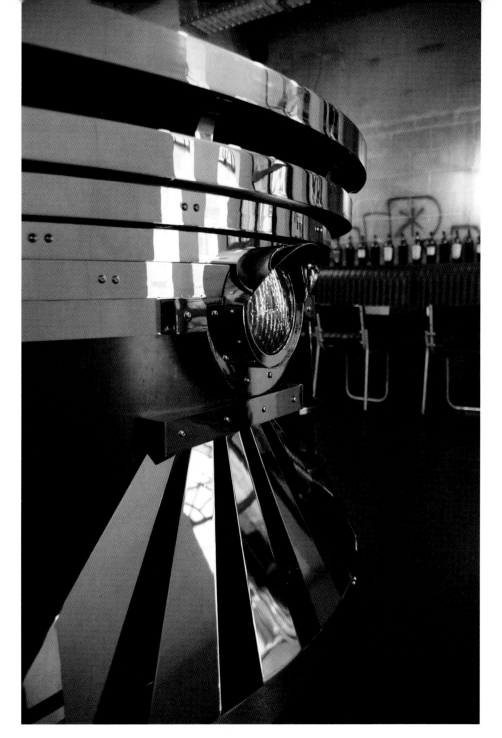

02

01 Stacked bottle-ends frame a dramatic bar that resembles a Victorian B-Class locomotive

02 Warren McArthur-designed ex-military aluminium chairs, mass-produced during the Second World War, accompany wooden tables that have also been treated with aluminium

"The high-tech kitchen was to serve 'fast' slow food, a celebration of the Machine Age."

BG Architecture

Niché sous un nouveau complexe résidentiel et au-dessus d'une sous-station électrique, ce bar aux allures européennes au cœur de Melbourne est un paradis du chic industriel. Pour pallier les limitations spatiales, le design s'est attaché à rendre l'intérieur aussi intrigant que possible.

Du même nom que l'unité de courant électrique, son mobilier inclut toutes sortes d'installations mécaniques, d'ampoules nues, de fils dénudés et de finitions chromées.

Le Futurisme, mouvement artistique né en Italie au début du XXᵉ siècle, a été une grande source d'inspiration pour ce projet. L'amour pour les machines puissantes a fait des Futuristes les premiers défenseurs de l'industrialisation. À cet égard, chaque montage, chaque revêtement a été dans une vie antérieure une pièce industrielle, comme la série de luminaires fabriqués à partir d'anciennes lampes chauffantes de coiffeur.

Cave Restaurant

Date Opened   December 2009
Designer   Koichi Takada Architects
Size of Build   70 m² / 754 ft²
Award   Category winner 2011
Address   944 Anzac Parade
   Maroubra
   Sydney, NSW 2035
   Australia

With its interior fully visible from the street thanks to the large glass façade, the series of sweeping wooden arches in this warm and inviting sushi restaurant create a cave-like atmosphere that is calm and relaxing.

A starting point in conceiving the design was the consideration to ensure that the acoustic quality was just right. To obtain the ambient noise-levels which would best suit pleasant dining conversation, 3D models of the timber profiles were made to test and refine the sound and to control the acoustic level throughout the restaurant.

Each of the curving forms was cut and installed using CNC, creating a receding series which disappears towards the back of the space and a sound quality similar to being in a recording studio.

Der dank der großen Glasfassade von der Straße voll einsehbare Innenraum dieses gemütlichen und einladenden Sushi-Restaurants bietet mit einer Reihe geschwungener Holzbögen eine ruhige und entspannende Atmosphäre.

Ausgangspunkt für die Planung war die Sicherung einer einwandfreien Akustik. Um für Unterhaltungen einen angenehmen Geräuschpegel im Raum zu erreichen, wurden 3D-Modelle der Holzprofile angefertigt. Der Schall wurde getestet und verbessert, und so konnte die Akustik im gesamten Bereich gesteuert werden.

Alle gekrümmten Formen wurden mit Hilfe von CNC geschnitten und montiert. Das Ergebnis sind eine Folge von Rücksprüngen, die im Hintergrund des Raumes verschwinden, und eine Tonqualität, die der eines Aufnahmestudios entspricht.

01

02

01 The acoustics harmonise
naturally with sounds coming
from the busy central dining-hall

02 Lights are hidden between
the wooden profiles and can be
seen only from directly beneath

03 Breaking up the simple
blonde-wood colour palette,
a canary-yellow sushi train runs
its own curves through the
central island inside

L'intérieur de ce local est entièrement visible de la rue par sa grande devanture vitrée. L'enchaînement d'arcs en bois aux lignes douces crée pour cet accueillant restaurant de sushi un cadre calme et de détente.

La conception du design est partie de la recherche d'une bonne qualité acoustique. Pour que le niveau de bruit de fond ne gêne pas les conversations des convives, des modèles 3D des profils en bois ont permis de tester et de contrôler le son et le niveau acoustique dans tout le restaurant.

Chaque forme courbe a été découpée et montée à l'aide d'une machine-outil CNC. L'enchaînement s'enfile jusqu'au fond du local et offre une qualité sonore digne d'un studio d'enregistrement.

03

ChimmiChurri

Website	chimmichurri.com.au
Date Opened	December 2011
Designer	Luchetti Krelle
Cost of Build	$$$$
Size of Build	500 m² / 5,400 ft²
Award	Longlist 2013
Address	23 Ward Avenue
	Darlinghurst, NSW 2010
	Australia

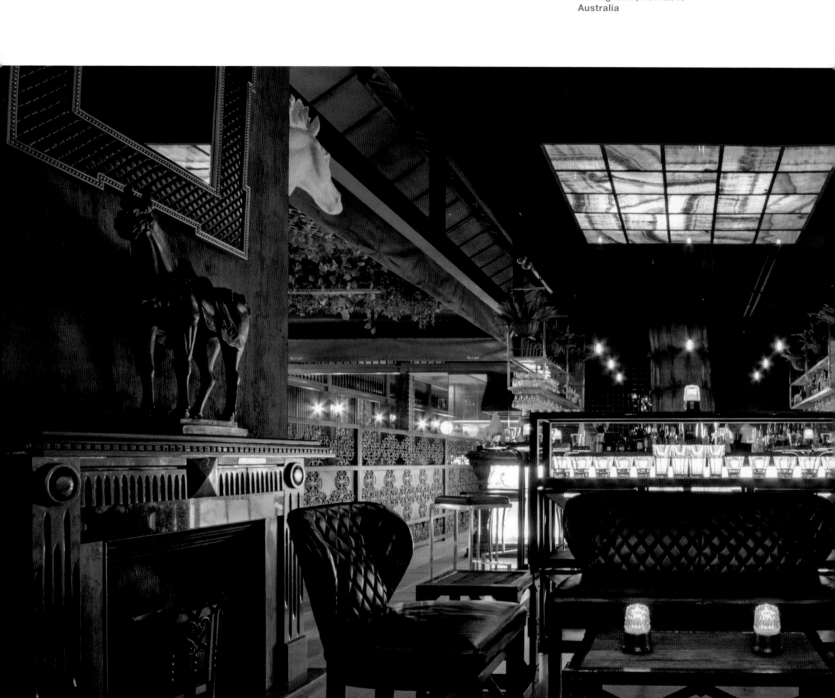

Just a few steps from the lively streets of Sydney's Kings Cross, this South American hideaway is a vibrant meat-eaters' paradise that adds a little Latin charm to the local dining culture.

The *hacienda*-themed interior is strongly reminiscent of colonial Argentinean decadence and sets the tone for an immersive yet rustic environment. Doors were constructed from reclaimed wood while the exposed concrete walls crumble on to tiled floors, the design being completed by the traditional custom-cast iron grill, called an *asador*.

Given the strong winds well known in these parts, special cares were taken to withstand the elements in the semi-outdoor dining area. Pinstriped awnings and vines offer cover, whilst other features include the wrought-iron sliding doors and a showpiece aged-sandstone fountain.

Dieses verborgene, nur wenige Schritte von den belebten Straßen in Sydneys Bezirk Kings Cross entfernte südamerikanische Lokal ist ein bevorzugtes Paradies für Fleischliebhaber, und es verleiht der lokalen Esskultur ein wenig latinischen Charme.

Der im Hazienda-Stil gestaltete Innenraum erinnert stark an die untergegangene argentinische Kolonialwelt und vermittelt den Eindruck eines versunkenen und dennoch rustikalen Umfelds. Die Türen wurden aus Altholz gefertigt, während die Sichtbetonwände auf den gefliesten Boden bröckeln. Die Ausstattung wird durch einen traditionellen, als *Asador* bezeichneten, speziell für diesen Ort angefertigten gusseisernen Grill ergänzt.

Wegen der in dieser Gegend herrschenden starken Winde wurde für den Schutz vor den Elementen im halboffenen Speisebereich besonders Sorge getragen: Gestreifte Markisen und Weinstöcke halten die Winde ab. Zu weiteren Besonderheiten zählen die Schiebetüren aus Schmiedeeisen und das Paradestück eines Brunnens aus altem Sandstein.

Tout près du quartier animé de Kings Cross à Sydney, ce refuge sud-américain est le paradis des amoureux de viande ; il ajoute un charme latin à la culture gastronomique locale.

L'intérieur de style *hacienda* incarne la décadence coloniale argentine et plante un décor immersif et rustique à la fois. Les portes ont été fabriquées avec du bois de récupération, et les murs en béton brut viennent rejoindre des sols carrelés. L'ensemble est assorti d'un grill en fonte traditionnel appelé *asador*.

En raison de vents forts fréquents dans cette région, les éléments dans l'espace semi-extérieur ont été soigneusement protégés. Des auvents rayés et de la vigne vierge y forment un abri, et l'on y trouve aussi des portes coulissantes en fer forgé et une fontaine en vieux grès.

01 Suspended trellises covered with vines create a vibrant canopy of lush greens above the diners

02 Woven wicker and white material chairs teamed with steel tables play with the various textures of Brazilian dining culture

03 Wine bottles in a glass display case combine with the marbled ceiling and deep-brown leather seating

03

Clancy's Fish Bar

Website	clancysfishpub.com.au
Date Opened	January 2012
Designer	Paul Burnham Architect
Cost of Build	$$$
Size of Build	460 m² / 4,950 ft²
Award	Longlist 2012
Address	195 Challenger Parade
	City Beach
	Perth, WA 6015
	Australia

This large and open-plan dining hall in Western Australia is awash with kaleidoscopic colours. The look is rounded out with vibrant ensembles and retro furnishings together with use of exotic materials.

The beachside location meant the design was to be attractive to families as well as other groups, resulting in a fusion between carnival and summer vibes, the standout feature being the 12 multi-coloured fabric chandeliers. As well as drawing the eye out to the beach and the sea, they add a theatrical injection of colour above the long communal tables.

Second-hand fixtures and fittings, such as '60s- and '70s-styled lampshades and stools, have been placed throughout, whilst recycled timber was used to create the candy-coloured striped and slatted wooden seating overlooking the ocean.

Dieser große Saal mit offenem Grundriss im Westen Australiens ist kaleidoskopartig mit Farbe überzogen. Der Eindruck wird verstärkt durch eindrucksvolle Ensembles und Retro-Mobiliar sowie die Verwendung exotischer Materialien.

Die Lage am Strand erforderte eine für Familien und andere Gruppen attraktive Ausstattung und führte zu einer Mischung aus karnevalesker und sommerlicher Stimmung. Besonderes Merkmal sind zwölf farbige, textile Kronleuchter. Das Auge wird also nicht nur zum Strand und zum Meer gelenkt, sondern auch über die langen, gemeinschaftlich genutzten Tische mit ihren theatralischen Farbelementen.

Überall stehen Leuchten und Einrichtungsgegenstände aus zweiter Hand, zum Beispiel Lampenschirme und Hocker im Stil der 1960er und 1970er Jahre. Von den bunt gestreiften Möbeln aus recycelten Holzlatten genießt man den Blick auf den Ozean.

Cette grande salle de restaurant ouverte en Australie occidentale est inondée de couleurs kaléidoscopiques. Le décor est complété de compositions éclatantes, d'un mobilier rétro et de matériaux exotiques.

Situé en bord de plage, son design se devait attirant pour les familles comme pour d'autres groupes. La fusion entre l'esprit carnaval et une ambiance estivale se matérialise dans les 12 chandeliers en tissu multicolore. Ils détournent l'attention de la plage et de la mer et ajoutent une dimension théâtrale au-dessus des grandes tables collectives.

Des appareils et des accessoires d'occasion, comme les abat-jours et les tabourets au look des années 60 et 70, ont été distribués dans l'espace. Faisant face à l'océan, les sièges aux couleurs acidulées ont été construits en lattes de bois recyclé.

01 Colourful replicas of the 1920s Tolix Chair in the main restaurant area stand out against the communal wooden tables and handcrafted chairs sourced from Byron Bay

02 A fun and unexpected touch – children's games and bright murals have been painted on the floor

03 Shells have been used as miniature lampshades, hanging from wicker baskets above the counter

02

Fat Noodle

Website	treasurybrisbane.com.au
Date Opened	October 2013
Designer	Luchetti Krelle
Cost of Build	$$$$+
Size of Build	500 m² / 5,400 ft²
Award	Longlist 2013
Address	130 William Street
	Brisbane, QLD 4000
	Australia

01

"Drawing inspiration from travels to Asia, everything except the chairs was custom designed."

Stuart Krelle, founder Luchetti Krelle

Blending the colonial architecture of the historic Treasury Building building with the dynamic heritage of Southeast Asian culture, this restaurant has been transformed into a treasure trove of different Asian styles in a reflection of the culinary explosion it serves.

Traditional Asian motifs and references provided the models for everything from layout and furnishings to surface detailing. From the Forbidden City to the ancient game of mah-jong, each element in the design has then been updated to give it new relevance.

The lofty ceiling features a 15m-long fire dragon light sculpture called *Kimono* (2012). Realised with the assistance of Armature Design Support, the striking installation flows through the entrance corridor and 'breathes energy' into the market-themed and open-plan kitchen area.

Dieses Restaurant, in dem sich die koloniale Architektur des historischen Treasury Buildings mit dem dynamischen Erbe südostasiatischer Kultur verbindet, wurde in eine Fundgrube unterschiedlicher asiatischer Stilformen verwandelt und spiegelt die Fülle der angebotenen kulinarischen Gerichte wider.

Traditionelle asiatische Motive und Bezüge dienten als Vorbild für alles: vom Grundriss und der Möblierung bis zur Oberflächengestaltung. Von der Verbotenen Stadt bis zum alten Mah-Jongg-Spiel wurden sämtliche Elemente mit neuer, aktueller Bedeutung versehen.

Unter der hohen Decke befindet sich die 15 Meter lange Lichtskulptur *Kimono* (2012) in Form eines feuerspeienden Drachen. Realisiert mit der Unterstützung von Armature Design Support, zieht sich die eindrucksvolle Installation durch den Eingangskorridor und „verströmt Energie" bis in den Verkaufsraum und den offenen Küchenbereich.

Ce restaurant mêle l'architecture coloniale de l'emblématique *Treasury Building* et l'héritage de la culture sud-asiatique. Il recèle les trésors de différents styles d'Asie, à l'image de l'explosion culinaire dans les plats proposés.

Des motifs et des références asiatiques traditionnels ont servi d'inspiration pour tous les aspects intérieurs, de la distribution aux meubles, en passant par le choix des surfaces. De la Cité interdite au jeu de mah-jong, chaque élément du design a été actualisé pour lui redonner une utilité.

Le plafond élevé accueille une sculpture lumineuse de dragon de feu appelée *Kimono* (2012). Réalisée avec l'aide d'Armado Design Support, cette installation surprenante serpente depuis l'entrée et dynamise la cuisine ouverte au look de marché.

01　A backlit ancient scroll wraps around the pelmet of the front bar

02　The parquet floor is intended to resemble the wicker baskets in which food is carried or served

03　The ceiling installation *Heaven & Earth* (2012) consists of 3,920 golden chopsticks, whilst six recessed lucky coin impressions are illuminated by the wok lamps beneath

03

Ippudo Sydney

Website   ippudo.com.au
Date Opened   December 2012
Designer   Koichi Takada Architects
Cost of Build $$$$+
Size of Build   240 m² / 2,600 ft²
Award   Shortlist 2013
Address   Westfield Sydney
                 Level 5, Shop 5021
                 188 Pitt Street
                 Sydney, NSW 2000
                 Australia

With the aim of enhancing the character of Japanese noodle culture as found in the city, this honey and caramel-coloured restaurant has been designed in close homage to the art of this ancient Asian cuisine.

The Ippudo chain has already made telling the history and processes behind *ramen* culture part of its signature style, so the present design is a continuing stage in that aspect of the brand's identity.

Wood is used throughout in the form of strips of timber, backlit to dazzling effect. With the word *ippudo* meaning "gust of wind", this has been given physical form in the rolling slatted wooden wave that covers the ceiling and is also intended to provide a contemplative focus into the traditions of Japanese dining.

Dieses Restaurant in Honig- und Karamellfarben hat sich zum Ziel gesetzt, der in der Stadt präsenten japanischen Nudelkultur mehr Raum zu geben. Seine Ausstattung ist eine Liebeserklärung an diese alte asiatische Kochkunst.

Markenzeichen der Ippudo-Kette ist es, die Geschichte und das Verfahren der *Ramen*-Kultur zu erzählen. Das neue Lokal ist daher im Sinne der Imagepflege des Unternehmens ein weiterer Schritt in diese Richtung.

Überall ist Holz eindrucksvoll in Form hinterleuchteter Leisten in Szene gesetzt. Das Wort *ippudo* bedeutet „Windstoß" und hat die physische Form der Wellen aus Holzlatten bestimmt, welche die Decke überziehen und auch einen kontemplativen Mittelpunkt für die Tradition japanischen Essens bilden sollen.

01

01 A traditional clay wall as found in Hakata has been used to divide the main dining space

02 Natural finishes and attention to detail can be seen in the traditional noodle bowls and spoons on the plain shelves

Visant à améliorer la perception de la culture des nouilles japonaises, ce restaurant dans des tons miel et caramel a été conçu pour rendre hommage à l'art de cette ancienne cuisine asiatique.

La chaîne Ippudo s'est déjà attachée à expliquer l'histoire et les procédés derrière la culture des nouilles *ramen*. Le design de ce local n'est qu'un chapitre de plus dans l'identité de la marque.

Le bois est omniprésent, sous la forme de bandes rétroéclairées pour un effet éblouissant. Le terme *ippudo* signifie « rafale de vent », d'où la vague en lattes de bois déferlant sur le plafond. La composition d'ensemble permet de se concentrer sur les traditions dans la cuisine japonaise.

02

"More than just a restaurant, Ippudo is a gallery of the noodle culture."

Koichi Takada Architects

Kumo Izakaya

Website kumoizakaya.com.au
Date Opened August 2011
Designer Ritchie Built
Award Longlist 2012
Address 152 Lygon Street
Brunswick, VIC 3057
Australia

Formerly a bank and now a gourmet Japanese restaurant, this stunning conversion also offers possibly the largest range of sake in Australia. *Izakaya* dining is a popular choice in Japan, serving food as an accompaniment to drink.

The clad wooden ceiling, exposed concrete walls and metal rafters underpin the sleek industrial styling, creatively paired with art deco-inspired iron framework railings. A long, central table provides communal dining alongside copper and black high-backed booth seating, whilst traditional Japanese imagery is used throughout in the form of vintage photographs and colourful graphic murals.

The restaurant is named *kumo* after the Japanese word for "cloud", and from the mezzanine floor the street can be seen outside and below through the double-height glass façade covering one side of the space.

Dieser gelungene Umbau eines Bankhauses in ein japanisches Gourmet-Restaurant bietet die wohl größte Auswahl von Sake in Australien. In *Izakaya*-Restaurants zu essen ist in Japan sehr beliebt, weil dort Speisen als Begleitung zum Getränk serviert werden.

Die holzverkleidete Decke, Sichtbetonwände und Metallträger betonen die elegante industrielle Ausstattung, die auf kreative Weise mit vom Art déco inspirierten eisernen Geländern verbunden wurde. An einem langen, zentral positionierten Tisch kann gemeinschaftlich gespeist werden wie auch individuell in Nischen auf hochlehnigen schwarz- und kupferfarbenen Stühlen. Traditionelle japanische Bildmotive sind überall in Form alter Fotografien und farbenfreudiger grafischer Wanddekorationen präsent.

Das Restaurant heißt *Kumo* nach dem japanischen Wort für „Wolke", und vom Zwischengeschoss aus ist durch die doppelgeschossige Verglasung der Fassade auf einer Seite der Blick auch nach draußen und hinunter auf die Straße gegeben.

Cette ancienne banque devenue un restaurant japonais gourmet est un exemple remarquable de transformation. Ce local offre probablement le plus grand choix de saké dans toute l'Australie : au Japon, les *izakaya* sont très populaires et servent des boissons et quelques plats.

Le plafond recouvert de bois, les murs en béton brut et la charpente métallique soulignent le style industriel élégant et astucieusement marié à des encadrements en fer aux allures art déco. Une longue table collective occupe le centre de l'espace, un côté étant aménagé avec des banquettes au dossier noir élevé. Une imagerie japonaise traditionnelle est présente sous forme de photographies *vintage* et de peintures murales.

Le restaurant se nomme *kumo*, terme japonais signifiant « nuage ». La rue est visible depuis la mezzanine et le rez-de-chaussée, à travers la façade en verre de double hauteur occupant tout un côté.

01 Seating 150, the elegant interior features a colourful Japanese-themed mural across both floors

02 For special guests: a ten-seat private dining-room with authentic tatami mats and a lowered dining table

03 Vintage photographs of Japan are a special touch and have been placed inside lightbox headboards above the booths

02

03

Mister Close

Website	misterclose.com.au
Date Opened	April 2011
Designer	Russell & George
Cost of Build	$$$$
Size of Build	130 m² / 1,400 ft²
Award	Longlist 2012
Address	Shop 13, Midtown Plaza
	246 Bourke Street
	Melbourne, VIC 3000
	Australia

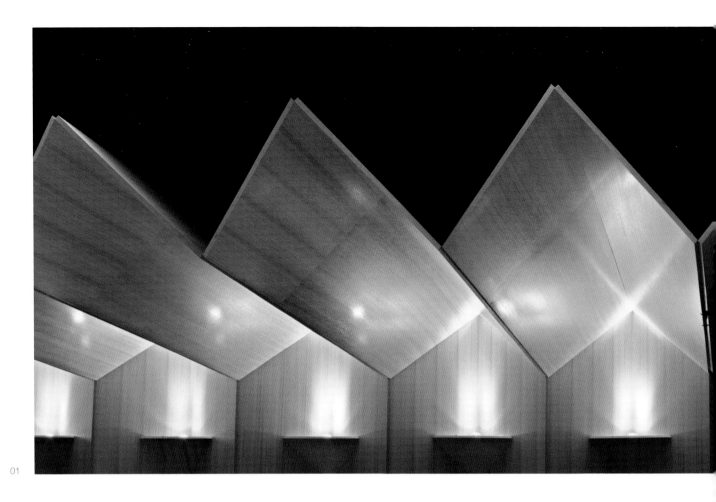

01

At the junction of two main shopping thoroughfares, this oasis of calm in the city centre offers quality food and service. Named after a geography teacher in high school in the year the two owners first met, Mister Close has a warm and inviting nature.

The design employs a decidedly back-to-school feel, featuring blonde wood against a black background to stand out in the open space. Tapered benches and tables give the feeling of extra space while creating a quirky illusion of stability.

Lacking a proper extraction system and with four-metre-high ceilings, the kitchen had to be covered to comply with health and safety regulations. A lowered ceiling was fitted to conceal the required equipment and was given form in the guise of a row of pitched roofs.

Diese Oase der Ruhe an der Kreuzung zweier belebter Geschäftsstraßen im Stadtzentrum bietet qualitätvolles Essen und entsprechenden Service. Benannt nach einem Geografielehrer im Gymnasium aus dem Jahr, als die beiden Besitzer sich zum ersten Mal begegneten, zeichnet sich Mister Close durch ein freundliches und einladendes Ambiente aus.

Die Ausstattung erweckt bewusst eine „back-to-school" Atmosphäre und Elemente aus hellem Holz heben sich von einem schwarzen Hintergrund ab.

Platzsparende abgeschrägte Bänke und Tische erzeugen eine illusionäre Vorstellung von Stabilität.

Mangels eines entsprechenden Lüftungssystems musste die vier Meter hohen Decke über der Küche abgehängt werden, um Hygiene und Sicherheitsstandards zu entsprechen. Unter den aufgereihten Satteldächern konnten die technischen Einrichtungen verborgen werden.

À la croisée de deux artères commerçantes, cette oasis de calme en centre-ville offre une cuisine et un service de qualité. Elle porte le nom du professeur de géographie que les deux propriétaires ont eu l'année du lycée où ils se sont rencontrés. Mister Close est un local chaleureux et accueillant.

Le design crée une atmosphère résolument scolaire, avec du bois blond contrastant sur un fond noir dans cet espace ouvert. Les bancs et les tables au profil conique augmentent la sensation d'espace et crée une étrange illusion de stabilité.

En l'absence d'un système d'extraction et avec quatre mètres de hauteur sous plafond, la cuisine devait être couverte pour être conforme aux normes d'hygiène et de sécurité. Un plafond abaissé permet de dissimuler l'équipement nécessaire et imite les toits à versants.

02

03

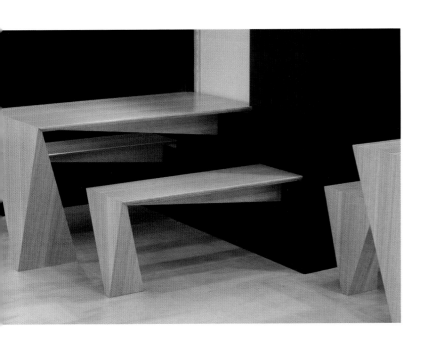

Neild Avenue

Date Opened	December 2011
Date Closed	July 2013
Designer	Lazzarini Pickering Architetti
Cost of Build	$$$$+
Size of Build	700 m² / 7,550 ft²
Award	Shortlist 2012
Address	10 Neild Avenue
	Rushcutters Bay
	Sydney, NSW 2011
	Australia

A former tyre factory has here been dramatically converted into a theatrical stage with an ever-evolving scenography. Five houses "inhabit" the space and contain the entrance, bar, kitchen and two dining-rooms. Taking advantage of the 12.5m-high space, two of the stage-set houses have been suspended from the ceiling – connected by iron chains, they can be lowered for an intimate dining experience, or kept raised, depending on the desired atmosphere.

Built from canvas and timber, the interior surfaces of these movable units are decorated by a changing roster of artists who are invited to paint their own designs, thereby creating a new and entirely different setting every six months.

Seating is organised to give great flexibility to grouping the tables in the dining-rooms for communal eating, a design feature that reflects the sharing nature of the Mediterranean-style menu.

Eine frühere Reifenfabrik wurde eindrucksvoll in eine Theaterbühne mit ständig veränderbarer Ausstattung umgebaut. Fünf „Häuser", in denen Eingang, Bar, Küche und zwei Essbereiche untergebracht sind, stehen in dem Raum. Dank der 12,5 Meter hohen Decke konnten zwei der Kulissenhäuser aufgehängt werden. Sie sind mit eisernen Ketten verbunden und können für eine vertraulichere Stimmung herabgelassen werden, oder sie bleiben hochgezogen, je nach gewünschter Atmosphäre.

Die Innenseiten dieser beweglichen, aus Leinen und Holz erbauten Einheiten werden von wechselnden Künstlern dekoriert, die sie nach ihren eigenen Entwürfen bemalen, wodurch alle sechs Monate eine neue und vollkommen andere Szene entsteht.

Tische und Stühle sind flexibel arrangiert, so können sie zu größeren Essbereichen gruppiert werden, ein Gestaltungselement, das den Gedanken vom gemeinschaftlichen Essen der mediterranen Küche reflektiert.

01

02

01 The simple wooden structures, made from timber and canvas, help absorb noise inside the space and feature the art work of Sydney-based artist Anthony Lister

02 The black colour scheme can be seen in the upholstered banquettes and industrial bar-stools, with the fittings and adornments continuing the stage-set theme

03 Exposed brick walls and wooden beams and rafters create the impression of a large and spacious hall, with diners being given a clear view of the whole interior when the crates are raised

Une ancienne usine de pneus a été totalement transformée pour devenir une scène de théâtre à la scénographie changeant constamment. Cinq maisons sont aménagées à l'intérieur, avec entrée, bar, cuisine et deux salles de restaurant. Grâce à une hauteur de 12,5 m, deux de ces décors ont été suspendus du plafond : connectés par des chaînes en fer, ils peuvent être descendus pour donner un espace plus intime, ou laissés en hauteur, selon l'atmosphère recherchée.

Faites de toile et de bois, les surfaces intérieures de ces panneaux mobiles sont décorées par différents artistes invités à peindre leurs propres créations ; tous les six mois, le décor est ainsi complètement renouvelé.

Les sièges ont été distribués pour permettre de regrouper facilement les tables et accueillir des groupes, à l'image du menu de style méditerranéen invitant au partage.

03

Ocean Room

Website	oceanroomsydney.com
Date Opened	June 2007
Designer	Glamorous co., ltd.
Cost of Build	$$$$
Size of Build	536 m² / 5,750 ft²
Award	Shortlist 2010
Address	Ground Level
	Overseas Passenger Terminal
	Circular Quay West
	The Rocks
	Sydney, NSW 2000
	Australia

Blessed with a world-famous view overlooking the Sydney Opera House, this exclusive restaurant expertly makes use of simplicity in its breath-taking design to create a modern expression of timeless elegance.

Atmosphere was the key note in responding to the location and the restaurant's already established reputation. This became crystallised as representing the premises as the point where the winds of Sydney and Japan meet.

A wide glass entrance shows off the beautiful wave chandelier that dominates the space. Rolling out across the ceiling and above the seated diners, the installation is made of more than 40,000 individual wooden elements which together form a sensuous and almost introspective texture.

Dieses exklusive Restaurant mit dem Vorzug der weltberühmten Aussicht auf das Opernhaus von Sydney nutzt bewusst die Schlichtheit seiner atemberaubenden Gestaltung für ein modernes Ambiente in zeitloser Eleganz.

Die Atmosphäre war der wichtigste Aspekt beim Bezug auf den Standort und das bereits etablierte Ansehen dieses Restaurants. Dies betraf aber auch die Bewältigung der Tatsache, dass hier die Winde von Sydney und Japan aufeinandertreffen.

Bereits am großen gläsernen Eingang kommt der prächtige, wellenförmige Kronleuchter zur Geltung, der den großen Raum beherrscht. Er füllt die gesamte Decke aus und erstreckt sich über den Sitzbereich. Diese Installation besteht aus 40.000 einzelnen Holz-elementen, die zusammen eine die Sinne ansprechende und fast introspektive Struktur bilden.

01

01 Long suspended pendants provide ambient lighting in an extension of the chandelier installation, which separates the main dining area from the bar, allowing for different atmospheres in each part of the restaurant

02 The monumental chandelier comes to a point connecting to the central island of the bar

Bénéficiant d'une vue mondialement connue de l'Opéra de Sydney, ce restaurant exclusif fait preuve d'une brillante simplicité. Son design remarquable est l'expression moderne d'une élégance intemporelle.

La priorité a été donnée à l'atmosphère, pour qu'elle soit en harmonie avec l'emplacement et la réputation de l'établissement. L'idée s'est concrétisée en symbolisant le point de rencontre entre les vents de Sydney et ceux du Japon.

Une grande entrée vitrée expose le magnifique lustre ondulant qui occupe l'espace. En se déployant sur tout le plafond, l'installation comptant plus de 40 000 pièces de bois forme une texture sensuelle, presque introspective.

Third Wave Kiosk

Website	thirdwavekiosk.com.au
Date Opened	November 2011
Designer	Tony Hobba Architects
Cost of Build	$$$$
Size of Build	110 m² / 1,200 ft²
Award	Category winner 2013
Address	The Esplanade
	Torquay, VIC 3228
	Australia

An extension of the ragged coastline where it is located, this bold design is as tough as it is beautiful in adding to the stunning natural environment.

With a small site footprint and restrictions arising from its sensitive coastal location, the finished structure had to be hardy enough to withstand the climate and have an appearance that would fit in with the surroundings.

Serving refreshments and snacks to beach-goers at Torquay Surf Beach all year round, the kiosk's rusting façade is a canvas of tonal browns across a series of grooves rising up out of the ground. The recycled steel piles are purposely intended to integrate into the landscape, as if it was a sculpture made from the jetsam washed up on the shore.

Wie ein Ausläufer der zerklüfteten Küstenlinie, ist dieses kühne Design eine ebenso robuste wie ansprechende Ergänzung der fantastischen natürlichen Umgebung.

Bei einem kleinen Grundriss und Einschränkungen durch den sensiblen Küstenstandort musste das fertige Gebäude robust genug sein, um den klimatischen Bedingungen zu widerstehen, und sich mit seinem Erscheinungsbild in die Umgebung einfügen.

Die rostfarbene Fassade des Kiosks, der ganzjährig den Besuchern der Torquay Surf Beach Erfrischungen und Snacks anbietet, gleicht einer Leinwand voll von Brauntönen zwischen einer Reihe von Stützen, die aus dem Boden wachsen. Die recycelten Stahlpfähle sollen sich bewusst in die Landschaft einfügen, als handele es sich um eine Skulptur, entstanden aus dem Strandgut, das ans Ufer gespült wurde.

Tel le prolongement du littoral irrégulier où il se trouve, ce design audacieux est aussi résistant que beau, planté au milieu d'un superbe environnement naturel.

La construction devait laisser une empreinte minime sur la nature et respecter les restrictions liées à l'emplacement côtier. Elle devait résister aux conditions climatiques tout en se fondant dans le paysage.

Toute l'année, ce local sert des boissons et des collations aux visiteurs de Torquay Surf Beach. Sa façade rouillée affiche un camaïeu de tons bruns et une série de rainures s'élevant du sol. Les palplanches en acier recyclé sont pensées pour s'intégrer dans le paysage, telles une sculpture faite d'épaves rejetées par la mer.

02

03

01 Simple outdoor stools and
tables let people gather beside the
kiosk and watch the tide

02 A barred gate is used as
shutters for the hatch and as the
door when the kiosk is unoccupied

03 A modest serving-hatch for
snacks and refreshments

Europe

Europe

Nicholas Oakwell
Founder and Creative Director NOUniform

Originally trained at Epsom School of Art and Design in fashion design, Nicholas Oakwell worked in the fashion industry for 15 years before he founded NOUniform in 2002, to bring luxury brand-aware uniforms to an underserved market. His background in fashion design has helped him create one of the world's most sought after uniform solutions. The company has brought his custom award-winning designs around the world to such prestigious properties as Claridge's, The Connaught, Rosewood, BBR, The Address and The Wolseley, to name a few.

Nicholas Oakwell studierte Mode-design an der Epsom School of Art and Design und arbeitete danach 15 Jahre in der Modeindustrie, bevor er 2002 die Firma NOUniform gründete, die einen unterversorgten Markt mit luxuriösen Uniformen für Marken-bewusste beliefert. Seine Erfahrung im Modedesign hat dazu beigetragen, dass seine Firma zu einem der gefrag-testen Unternehmen dieser Sparte geworden ist. Die maßgefertigten, preisgekrönten Entwürfe sind weltweit bekannt bis hin bei so renommierten Institutionen wie Claridge's, The Connaught, Rosewood, BBR, The Address und The Wolseley, um nur einige zu nennen.

Diplômé de l'Epsom School of Art and Design en design de mode, Nicholas Oakwell a travaillé dans le monde de la mode pendant 15 ans avant de fonder NOUniform en 2002, pour couvrir le créneau des uniformes de luxe. Sa formation en design de mode lui a permis de développer l'une des marques d'uniformes les plus prisées au monde. Ses créations ont été primées et sont présentes dans des établissements prestigieux comme Claridge's, The Connaught, Rosewood, BBR, The Address et The Wolseley, entre autres.

Since the dawn of the Modern Age, Europe has been the heart of international commerce, and as such, for centuries, has itself been subject to so many influences from around the world. In shaping several nations, each country within the growing European continent acquired a wealth of diversity and culture to draw upon.

It is this broad cultural base that has led to some of the best design work in the world, born of a fusion of creative ideas. While a number of brands have been slow to come to terms with the increasing expectations and education of their customers, over the past decade many European cities have realised and embraced the importance of design for both its aesthetic and branding benefits. Companies now invest into the experience of their customers. Since Jonathan Ive and the Apple team revolution, design has even become one of the most important factors in our selection process of products and experiences.

Design itself is a cyclical process, and is evident in the trends of restaurant and bar spaces, which by their very nature need to maintain an appearance of being 'current'. Phases of inspiration can be discerned in the UK, for example, with the rise and fall of the 'Shoreditch Distressed' spaces, to Parisian Chic, the Best of British, modern concrete shells or simple refined luxury. In recent years though there has been a rebellion against such repetitive trends, with venues developing their own unique DNA and because of this we are starting to see completely different spaces, with new and innovative designs, that have transformed Europe into one of the most diverse regions with regard to design. While thematic spaces are in decline, sub-trends are now emerging, in the form of geometric and repeating patterns, the use of natural, recycled and tactile materials, and using local craftsmanship to forge identities.

The examples here showcase some of the very best Europe has to offer, in my personal experience, and it's interesting that a majority of them are independent establishments, and have invested so heavily in creating distinctive and beautiful environments. When talking about designing, it's also important to point out this isn't just the space, but an entire experience. Design is now more than ever about every touch-point, from uniforms to service standards, interwoven into the brand itself.

Some of these interiors are housed in original pre-existing structures, both new and ancient, and it's nice to see a sympathetic appreciation of the standing structures, such as Archangel and Galvin La Chapelle. Other establishments such as The Crescent Inn and Searcys St. Pancras Grand or the brasserie Oriel in Heathrow give the illusion of a space that has existed for years and should be commended for making design appear so effortless. The element of fun can't be ignored, and playful spaces such as Rocambolesc, Phill and Snog Soho offer such wonderful contrasts to the unashamedly beautiful design of spaces such as the Atrium Champagne Bar and Bravo 24.

Seit Anbruch der Moderne ist Europa zum Zentrum des internationalen Handels geworden und ist selbst vielen Einflüssen aus aller Welt ausgesetzt. Mit der Entstehung der Nationen hat jedes Land dieses wachsenden Kontinents einen Reichtum an kultureller Vielfalt erworben, aus dem es schöpfen kann.

Auf dieser starken kulturellen Basis sind durch das Zusammentreffen kreativer Ideen einige der weltbesten gestalterischen Entwürfe entstanden. Während manche Unternehmen nur zögerlich den steigenden Erwartungen und dem neuen Bildungsstand ihrer Klientel gerecht werden, haben viele europäische Städte in den vergangenen Jahrzehnten aus ästhetischen wie auch wirtschaftlichen Gründen die Bedeutung von Design erkannt. Firmen investieren heute in das Erlebnispotenzial ihrer Kundschaft. Seit den revolutionären Entwürfen von Jonathan Ive und dem Apple-Team ist Design sogar zu einem der wichtigsten Faktoren in unseren Auswahlkriterien für Produkte und Erlebnisse geworden.

Gestaltung ist ein zyklischer Prozess, der sich auch in Trends für Restaurants zeigt, die ihrer Bestimmung nach „aktuell" erscheinen müssen. England etwa fand Anregungen phasenweise wechselnd beim Londoner East-End-Stil, beim Pariser Chic, dem Lifestyle Best of British, bei modernen Betonschalen oder einfach dem Wunsch nach raffiniertem Luxus. In den letzten Jahren gab es Widerstände gegen solche sich wiederholenden Trends und Lokale entwickeln ihre eigene, spezifische DNA. Daher entstehen jetzt völlig unterschiedliche Räume mit innovativem Design, wodurch Europa zu einer der vielfältigsten Regionen auf diesem Gebiet geworden ist. Während die Themenbereiche abgenommen haben, bilden sich jetzt Nebenrichtungen in Form geometrischer, sich wiederholender Dekors unter Verwendung natürlicher, recycelter und haptisch erlebbarer Materialien sowie unter Beteiligung des örtlichen Handwerks, um Identität herzustellen.

Die hier gezeigten Beispiele gehören meiner persönlichen Erfahrung nach zu den besten, die Europa zu bieten hat, und interessanterweise sind es in der Mehrzahl unabhängige Unternehmen, die viel in die Gestaltung einer unverwechselbaren Umgebung investiert haben. Das Thema Design betrifft auch nicht nur den Raum an sich, sondern das Gesamterlebnis. Gestaltung gilt heute mehr denn je für jeden Aspekt, von den Uniformen bis zum Service, und all das wird mit dem Ruf des Unternehmens verbunden.

Einige Lokale befinden sich in bestehenden Alt- oder Neubauten und lassen erfreulicherweise eine Wertschätzung ihrer Originalstruktur erkennen, zum Beispiel Archangel oder Galvin La Chapelle. Andere, etwa The Crescent Inn, Searcys St. Pancras Grand oder die Brasserie Oriel in Heathrow, vermitteln die Illusion eines Raumes, der schon jahrelang existiert, was das Design hier so mühelos wirken lässt. Auch das heitere Element ist nicht zu übersehen, und verspielte Bereiche wie Rocambolesc, Phill und Snog bieten wunderbare Kontraste zu den so unglaublich schönen Raumgestaltungen wie der Atrium Champagne Bar oder dem Bravo 24.

L'Europe est au cœur du commerce international depuis l'aube des temps modernes, des siècles passés à recevoir de nombreuses influences du monde entier. En cela, lors de la naissance de nations sur ce continent en pleine croissance, chaque pays a acquis un socle de diversité et de culture.

Grâce à cette ample base culturelle, certains des meilleurs designs au monde ont vu le jour, fruits de la fusion d'idées créatives. Alors que des marques ont tardé à répondre aux attentes croissantes de clients chaque fois plus éduqués, nombre de villes européennes ont compris pendant la dernière décennie l'importance du design en matière d'esthétique et d'image de marque. Elles ont su être à la hauteur, et des entreprises investissent à présent dans l'expérience de leurs clients. Depuis Jonathan Ive et la révolution au sein d'Apple, le design est devenu l'un des facteurs clés dans notre processus de sélection de produits et d'expériences.

En soi, le design est un processus cyclique ; preuve en sont les tendances des restaurants et des bars, dont la nature même oblige à conserver une apparence « actuelle ». Au Royaume-Uni par exemple, les vagues d'inspiration sont clairement associables à la naissance et la chute d'espaces « Shoreditch Distressed », « Parisian Chic » ou « Best of British », coquilles de béton modernes ou créations d'un luxe simple et raffiné. Ces dernières années néanmoins, ces tendances répétitives sont combattues et des locaux développent leur propre ADN : l'avènement d'espaces inédits, au design nouveau et innovant, ont fait de l'Europe l'une des régions les plus hétérogènes en terme de design. Les espaces thématiques sont en plein déclin, et des sous-tendances émergent avec des schémas géométriques et répétés, l'emploi de matériaux naturels, recyclés et tactiles, ainsi que le recours à l'artisanat local pour forger des identités.

Les exemples dans ces pages illustrent à mon sens ce que l'Europe a en partie de mieux à offrir. De façon intéressante, ces établissements sont pour la plupart indépendants et ont investi massivement dans des environnements aussi beaux que distinctifs. Quand nous parlons de design, n'oublions pas que l'espace n'est pas tout, que l'expérience globale compte. Plus que jamais, le design est présent dans tous les points de contact avec le client, des uniformes aux règles de service, qui ensemble forment la marque.

Certains intérieurs se logent dans des structures d'origine anciennes ou nouvelles. Des projets comme Archangel et Galvin La Chapelle mettent un point d'honneur à respecter les structures porteuses. D'autres établissements, comme The Crescent Inn, Searcys St. Pancras Grand ou la brasserie Oriel à Heathrow, laissent penser qu'ils ont une longue histoire et doivent être salués pour afficher un design faussement aisé. Une touche amusante est toujours bienvenue, et des espaces ludiques comme Rocambolesc, Phill et Snog contrastent merveilleusement avec le design somptueux de locaux comme Atrium Champagne Bar et Bravo 24.

A Cantina

Date Opened July 2011
Designer Estudio Nomada
Cost of Build $$
Size of Build 277 m² / 3,000 ft²
Award Overall winner 2012
Address Monte Gaias
15707 Santiago de Compostela
Spain

Architect José Antonio Vázquez Martín and interior designer Enrique de Santiago chose furniture-based elements rather than architectural overhaul to realise this bright and open space.

A Cantina is housed in the Archive of Galicia, one of six buildings constituting the City of Culture in Galicia, northern Spain. The design conveys a contemporary vision of cultural identity, drawing on both folk art and local village canteens.

The main restaurant area is dominated by a tree installation that rises from the tables' feet to form a frame-like canopy overhead. Guests gather to eat under the branches, which cast shadows and invoke the oak trees at Galicia's summer festivals.

The cavern-like opening in the thick wall, following local design, allows access to both café and museum-shop, linked by a vividly tiled central bar.

Zur Gestaltung dieses hellen und offenen Raumes entschieden sich der Architekt José Antonio Vázquez Martín und der Innenarchitekt Enrique de Santiago anstelle architektonischer Eingriffe für den Einbau von Möbelelementen.

A Cantina befindet sich im Archiv von Galicien, einem der sechs Gebäude, aus denen sich die City of Culture im nordspanischen Galicien zusammensetzt. Der Entwurf entspricht einer zeitgenössischen Vorstellung von kultureller Identität und orientiert sich an Volkskunst wie auch an örtlichen Dorfgasthöfen.

Der große Restaurantbereich wird von Baumstützen beherrscht, die von den Tischbeinen ausgehend zu einer Art Baldachin aufsteigen. Zum Essen versammeln sich die Gäste unter den Zweigen, die Schatten spenden und an die Eichen an den Sommerfesten in Galicien erinnern.

Die lokalen Bauten nachgebildete höhlenartige Öffnung in der dicken Mauer erschließt sowohl das Café als auch den Museumsshop, die eine in fröhlichen Farben geflieste, zentral gelegene Bar miteinander verbindet.

01 Awarded 'Best Restaurant'
by the Restaurant & Bar Design
Awards 2012, A Cantina's central
tree structure is made from blonde
oak reinforced by aluminium poles

02 The tall bookcases are simple
and functional and have adjustable
shelving to house the different-
sized items on sale

03 A free-standing white circular
structure and round table provide
an additional discrete area for the
bar and kitchen staff to use

04 The colour palette of geometric
tiles captures the cultural spirit of
Spain and lines the whole of the
elongated bar, which runs through
the entire space

Pour cet espace ouvert et épuré, l'architecte José Antonio Vázquez Martín et le décorateur d'intérieur Enrique de Santiago ont travaillé sur le mobilier plutôt que d'entreprendre une refonte architecturale.

A Cantina est logé dans l'Archive de Galice, l'un des six bâtiments formant la Cité de la Culture de Galice, dans le nord de l'Espagne. Le design transmet une vision contemporaine de l'identité culturelle, s'inspirant à la fois de l'art populaire et du concept de cantine.

La partie principale du restaurant est surplombée d'une sorte de plantation s'élevant depuis les pieds des tables pour former une canopée en hauteur. Les clients mangent sous les branches, qui projettent des ombres et rappellent les soirées sous les chênes lors des festivals d'été.

Telle l'entrée d'une caverne, l'ouverture dans le mur épais respecte le design et conduit au café et au musée-boutique, connectés par un bar central en mosaïque de couleur.

03

04

237

Archangel

Website archangelfrome.com
Date Opened June 2010
Designer Mitchell Taylor Workshop
Cost of Build $$$$+
Size of Build 737 m² / 7,900 ft²
Award Shortlist 2011
Address 1 King Street
Frome BA11 1BH
UK

Once a coaching inn for weary travellers, and mentioned as long ago as the Domesday Book, this historic public house in England's West Country has been transformed into a faithfully renovated boutique hotel and restaurant for the 21st century.

The building was derelict when work began and clearly all design and reconstruction had to respect both the site and the tradition of neighbouring architecture. Early work included stripping back the walls, removing 50 years of renovations and decoration to reveal the mottled and textured brickwork beneath.

The new inn operates across three levels, following the original layout while incorporating expressive materials such as zinc for the bar and a steel staircase leading up to a floating mezzanine. The additional floor makes use of the double-height ceiling and offers secluded seating.

Dieses öffentliche historische Gebäude in Englands West Country, schon zu Zeiten des Domesday Book aus dem 11. Jahrhundert als Pferdestation erwähnt, wurde zu einem authentisch restaurierten Boutique-Hotel und Restaurant für das 21. Jahrhundert umgestaltet.

Das Gebäude war vor Beginn der Bauarbeiten völlig heruntergekommen. Entwurf und Rekonstruktion hatten sowohl die Lage als auch die traditionelle Nachbarbebauung zu respektieren. Dafür mussten zuerst die Wände von allen Spuren verschiedener Renovierungen und Dekorationen aus den letzten 50 Jahren befreit und der darunter liegende gesprenkelte, strukturierte Backstein freigelegt werden.

Der neue Gasthof erstreckt sich, der ursprünglichen Architektur folgend, über drei Geschosse und beinhaltet ausdrucksvolle Materialien wie Zink in der Bar und eine stählerne Treppe, die zu einem frei schwebenden Zwischengeschoss führt. Diese zusätzliche Ebene macht von der doppelten Geschosshöhe Gebrauch und bietet separate Sitzplätze.

01 The renovated coaching inn is now a hotel and restaurant split over three levels

02 A steel staircase leads up to the floating mezzanine

03 Yellow leather seating offers a soft counterpoint to the strong materials used in the renovation

Ancien relais pour voyageurs fatigués déjà en activité
au moment de la publication du Domesday Book,
ce bâtiment public historique dans le West Country
(Angleterre) a été aménagé en un hôtel boutique et
restaurant à l'image du XXIᵉ siècle.

Au moment des travaux, l'édifice était abandonné.
Tous les efforts de design et de reconstruction ont dû
respecter le site et la tradition de l'architecture voisine.
En premier lieu, les murs ont dû être décapés pour
effacer 50 années de rénovations et de décorations
et pour révéler les briques patinées et texturées qui
étaient camouflées.

Fidèle à la distribution d'origine, la nouvelle
auberge fonctionne sur trois niveaux, mais en incor-
porant des matériaux expressifs comme le zinc pour
le bar et l'acier pour les escaliers menant à une
mezzanine flottante. L'étage rajouté profite de la
hauteur de plafond et offre un espace isolé.

Arrop

Website	almadeltemple.com
Date Opened	September 2010
Designer	Francesc Rifé Studio
Size of Build	635 m² / 3,900 ft²
Award	Shortlist 2011
Address	Calle del Almirante, 14
	46003 Valencia
	Spain

02

Combining the ultra-modern with the splendour of antiquity, the Arrop restaurant is part of the Hotel Palacio Marqués de Caro, in Valencia.

The architectural engineering was tasked with preserving three original features: a 17th-century Gothic arch, part of the Almohad city wall that dates back to the 16th century (unearthed when the building was being renovated), and an *aljibe*, the Arabic name for a water-storage tank – duly encased in tinted translucent glass to house the toilets and a wine cellar.

A large single skylight admits shafts of natural light into the partially subterranean space, with mirrored surfaces used to augment the illumination. An intuitive use of materials ensures the evocative contrast of old and new, sharp lines framing the richly textured surfaces of the historic structural elements.

Das Restaurant Arrop, Bestandteil des Hotels Palacio Marqués de Caro in Valencia, verbindet ultramoderne Architektur mit dem Prunk der Vergangenheit.

Architekten und Ingenieure hatten die Aufgabe, drei originale Bauelemente zu bewahren: einen gotischen Torbogen aus dem 17. Jahrhundert, einen (bei der Renovierung des Gebäudes zutage geförderten) Teil der aus dem 16. Jahrhundert stammenden almohadischen Stadtmauer sowie ein *Aljibe* (eine arabische Bezeich-nung für einen Wassertank) – geschützt durch getöntes, durchscheinendes Glas –, wo auch die Toiletten und ein Weinkeller untergebracht sind.

Ein einzelnes großes Oberlicht lässt Tageslicht in den zum Teil tiefer liegenden Raum ein; spiegelnde Oberflächen verstärken die Belichtung. Die einfühlsame Anwendung der Materialien bildet einen sinnvollen Kontrast zwischen Alt und Neu; scharfe Linien rahmen die stark strukturierten Oberflächen der historischen Bauteile ein.

03

01 The ancient wall stands out
against the poured-resin floor and
carpet whilst bespoke furniture adds
to the space's unique character

02 The restaurant is located
under the main area of the hotel
and also functions independently

03 Renovated to house the
bathrooms, the water-storage tank
is surrounded by a glass volume,
which separates the entrance from
the dining area and accommodates
the restaurant's wine cellar

Mariant l'ultra moderne à la splendeur de l'antiquité, le restaurant Arrop se trouve dans l'hôtel Palacio Marqués de Caro, à Valence.

Les architectes ont dû conserver trois éléments d'origine : un arc gothique du XVIIe siècle, une partie de la muraille almohade remontant au XVIe siècle (et découverte lors des travaux de rénovation du bâtiment) et un *aljibe* (nom arabe pour désigner une citerne d'eau), protégé par une gaine en verre teinté translucide pour accueillir les toilettes et le cellier.

Une grande verrière laisse passer des rais de lumière naturelle dans l'espace semi sous-terrain, des miroirs venant amplifier encore l'éclairage. L'emploi intuitif des matériaux crée un contraste évocateur entre ancien et nouveau. Des lignes pures encadrent les surfaces très texturées des éléments structurels historiques.

Atrium Champagne Bar

Website	melia.com/hotels/united-kingdom/london/me-london/index.html
Date Opened	March 2013
Designer	Foster + Partners
Award	Overall winner 2013
Address	ME London
	336–337 The Strand
	London WC2R 1HA
	UK

A stone's throw from the river Thames and overlooking the Strand, the Atrium Champagne Bar is part of the newly redeveloped ME Hotel, which incorporates a breathtaking triangular prism that serves as the spine of the building.

The bar, for hotel guests only, is an awe-inspiring atrium which extends upwards for 25 metres (the equivalent of nine floors) and stops at a triangular skylight at the summit. From the lobby entrance guests enter the minimalist lounge, clad throughout in white marble to convey a spirit of opulence and futuristic style.

The dominating geometry of the interior meant that furniture had to be especially designed to fit, such as a 30-metre white leather curved lounge.

Nur einen Steinwurf von der Themse entfernt, mit Ausblick auf den Londoner Straßenzug The Strand, gehört die Atrium Champagne Bar zum kürzlich umgestalteten ME Hotel, das ein atemberaubendes dreieckiges Prisma enthält, welches das Rückgrat des Gebäudes bildet.

Die nur für Hotelgäste zugängliche Bar ist ein höchst eindrucksvolles Atrium, das sich 25 Meter in die Höhe erstreckt (was neun Geschossen entspricht) und oben in einem dreieckigen Oberlicht endet. Von der Eingangslobby gelangen die Gäste in eine minimalistische, ringsum mit weißem Marmor verkleidete Lounge mit opulentem und futuristischem Ambiente.

Die beherrschende Geometrie des Innenraums erforderte eine maßgeschneiderte Möblierung, wie zum Beispiel das 30 Meter lange, geschwungene Sofa aus weißem Leder.

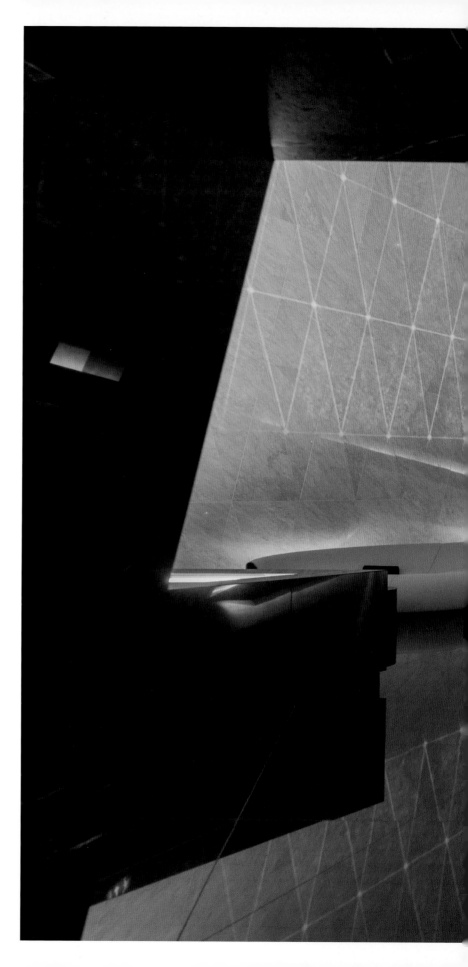

À quelques pas de la Tamise et surplombant The Strand, l'Atrium Champagne Bar trouve sa place dans le flambant hôtel ME, avec un prisme triangulaire vertigineux comme colonne vertébrale de l'édifice.

Réservé aux clients de l'hôtel, le bar est un atrium grandiose s'élevant sur 25 mètres (la hauteur de neuf étages) et se termine par une verrière triangulaire au sommet. L'entrée du lobby conduit les clients au salon minimaliste intégralement revêtu de marbre blanc pour transmettre une idée d'opulence et de style futuriste.

En raison de la géométrie dominante de l'intérieur, le mobilier a dû être conçu sur mesure, comme le banc courbe en cuir blanc long de 30 mètres.

01 Large digital projections are displayed on the walls to create atmosphere and may also be used for special events

Bangalore Express

Website	bangaloreuk.com
Date Opened	December 2007
Date Closed	December 2012
Designer	Outline
Cost of Build	$$$
Size of Build	234 m² / 2,500 ft²
Award	Shortlist 2010
Address	103-105 Waterloo Road
	London SE1 8UL
	UK

A sense of fun permeates every inch of this complete reinterpretation of a very British, 20th-century institution: the curry house. The dynamic and vibrant design not only complements the modern Indian cooking but is also composed of distinctive elements which may readily be transposed to other outlets that may open in the future.

To provide additional seating within the space available the design cutely makes use of stacked booths, like decks on an ocean liner, complete with ladders for access. A unique focal point for the rest of the design, these tiers are a playful addition to the dining experience, even if they do require some acrobatic skills for staff and customers alike.

Ein gewisser Sinn für Humor durchdringt jeden Zoll dieser komplett umgestalteten, sehr britischen Einrichtung des 20. Jahrhunderts: des „Curry House". Die dynamische und lebendige Gestaltung passt nicht nur zur modernen indischen Küche, sondern setzt sich auch aus unterschiedlichen Elementen zusammen, die sich auf mögliche zukünftige Lokale übertragen lassen.

Um auf der verfügbaren Fläche zusätzliche Sitzmöglichkeiten zu gewinnen, wurden Nischen ähnlich wie Decks auf einem Überseedampfer übereinander gestapelt, die über Leitern erreichbar sind. Sie bilden ein ganz besonderes Element im gesamten Entwurf und eine spielerische Ergänzung zum Erlebnis des Speisens, auch wenn dafür gewisse akrobatische Fähigkeiten vom Personal wie auch von den Gästen verlangt werden.

01

01 The ladders and handrails for the upstairs seating are fashioned from hollow tubing

02 The simple sheet material used for the wallpaper was installed with lines already scored into the surface, making it easy for the different colours to be painted directly on to the walls

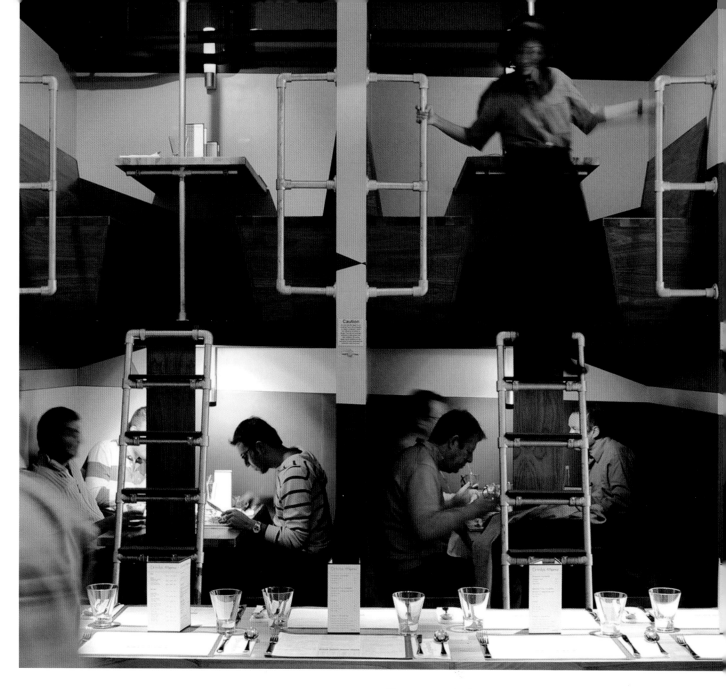

Chaque centimètre de cette réinterprétation du restaurant indien populaire, véritable institution britannique du XXe siècle, offre une note amusante. Le design dynamique et vibrant se conjugue à une cuisine indienne moderne. Il compte aussi des touches distinctives directement transposables à d'autres locaux amenés à s'ouvrir à l'avenir.

Pour installer plus de tables dans l'espace disponible, le design intègre avec grâce des cabines superposées, à l'image des ponts dans un paquebot ; des échelles permettent d'accéder au niveau supérieur. Point de mire de l'agencement du local, ces niveaux viennent enrichir l'expérience gastronomique, même s'ils demandent quelques acrobaties du personnel et des clients.

"We wanted a fun solution that customers would remember."

Outline

02

Barbican Lounge

Website	barbican.org.uk
Date Opened	September 2010
Designer	SHH
Lighting	.PSLAB
Cost of Build	$$$$+
Size of Build	250 m² / 2,700 ft²
Award	Category winner 2011
Address	Silk Street
	London EC2Y 8DS
	UK

The Barbican Lounge is one of two interconnected eateries in one of London's most well-known architectural and cultural complexes, the Barbican Centre.

Located directly above its sister venue, the Barbican Foodhall, the Barbican Lounge is more of a formal restaurant than the self-service canteen downstairs. Whilst retaining a close aesthetic link to the Brutalist architecture of the original Grade II-listed building, striking colours and various bespoke design details add extra layers and textures to the original space.

SHH joined forces with furniture designer Stefan Bench to create three different types of Scandinavian-inspired seating, while the distinctive poured-concrete ceilings and 14-metre bar have specially tailored lighting by .PSLAB. With the bar running from inside the restaurant out on to the terrace, visitors can relax *al fresco* on parasol seating.

Die Barbican Lounge ist eines von zwei miteinander verbundenen Lokalen in einem der bekanntesten Londoner Architektur- und Kulturkomplexe, dem Barbican Centre.

Die direkt über der dazugehörigen Barbican Foodhall gelegene Barbican Lounge ist ein formelleres Restaurant als das darunter befindliche Selbstbedienungslokal. Zwar kommt sie der brutalistischen Architekturästhetik des als Denkmal eingetragenen Gebäudes nahe, doch wurden dem ursprünglichen Raum durch leuchtende Farben und verschiedene, speziell maßgeschneiderte Gestaltungselemente zusätzliche Ebenen und Strukturen hinzugefügt.

SHH schloss sich mit Möbeldesigner Stefan Bench zusammen, um drei unterschiedliche Typen skandinavisch inspirierter Stühle zu entwerfen, und für die charakteristischen Gussbetondecken und die 14 Meter lange Bar gestaltete .PSLAB besondere Leuchten. Da die Bar durch das Restaurant bis auf die Terrasse führt, können die Besucher sich dort unter Sonnenschirmen auch im Freien aufhalten.

01

03

Le Barbican Lounge est l'un des deux restaurants interconnectés au sein du Barbican Centre, l'un des complexes architecturaux et culturels les plus renommés de Londres.

Juste au-dessus du Barbican Foodhall, son pendant, le Barbican Lounge est plus formel que la cafétéria libre-service à l'étage inférieur. Il conserve une esthétique proche de l'architecture brutaliste qu'affichait le monument classé d'origine (Grade II). Des couleurs vives et divers détails sur mesure dans le design rajoutent des couches et des textures à l'espace.

SSH s'est associé au designer de meubles Stefan Bench pour créer trois types de chaises d'inspiration scandinave. Les plafonds en béton coulé et le bar long de 14 mètres sont dotés d'un éclairage personnalisé signé .PSLAB. Le bar se prolonge du restaurant à une terrasse, permettant aux clients de se détendre en plein air sous un parasol.

04

01 Bespoke wooden seating with huge 'urban trees' and planting by Kate Gould, twice winner of the RHS Chelsea Flower Show, connect the terraces of Lounge and Foodhall, with notable features being the black *Polo Chairs* by Robin Day, the original art director of the Barbican

02 The turquoise-blue banquette is upholstered with vintage buttons and textile from Bute Fabrics

03 The custom *BH01* chairs are made from red lacquer while the two siblings *BH01 Low* and *BH01 High* are used instead in the Foodhall

04 The new design involved de-cladding the wood on site to reveal the pre-existing Barbican's signature aggregate walls, then pouring a Peacock Green resin floor, colour-matched to a summer photo of the Barbican outdoor lake

05 Vintage furniture includes this 1960s table with murano glass top and bespoke round black Nanna Ditzel *Trissen* tables

Barbouni

Date Opened	July 2011
Designer	k-studio
Size of Build	300 m² / 3,250 ft²
Award	Shortlist 2012
Address	Navarino Dunes
	24001 Costa Navarino
	Greece

01

On a kilometre-stretch of sandy beach at Costa Navarino, Barbouni is part of a sustainably built luxury resort in southern Greece overlooking the Ionian Sea. Wood has been used in every part of the building process so that the finished result is in close harmony with the responsibly managed landscape.

Built on a raised platform, so that high tide laps at the restaurant floor, this tranquil place is a spot where guests can while away the hours. Essentially open plan, the whole structure is built on a wooden grid, with the defining feature being a ceiling canopy of interspersed sheeting which suggests the crests of the waves. The sheets also constitute an awning, keeping visitors relaxed in dappled sunlight, and letting the air circulate naturally to alleviate the Mediterranean heat.

Das am kilometerlangen Strand der Costa Navarino gelegene Barbouni ist Teil eines nachhaltig errichteten Luxusresorts im Süden Griechenlands mit Ausblick auf das Ionische Meer. Für alle Bauten wurde Holz verwendet, sodass sich die Anlage harmonisch in die verantwortungsvoll gestaltete Landschaft der Umgebung einfügt. An diesem ruhigen Ort, der auf einer erhöhten Plattform errichtet wurde, auf der das Wasser bei Flut fast den Boden des Restaurants berührt, können die Gäste stundenlang verweilen. Der Bau ist eine Holzkonstruktion mit überwiegend offenem Grundriss, besonderes Merkmal ein mit Stoff verkleideter Baldachin, der die Bewegung der Wellen andeuten soll. Die Stoffbahnen dienen auch als Markisen, damit die Besucher im Halbschatten sitzen können und die mediterrane Hitze durch die Luftzirkulation gemildert wird.

Sur une bande de plage de sable à Costa Navarino, Barbouni fait partie d'un complexe de luxe de construction durable au sud de la Grèce, sur la mer ionienne. Le bois est le matériau omniprésent pour que le résultat final soit le plus harmonieux possible avec le paysage protégé.

Construit sur une plate-forme surélevée pour que l'eau clapote sous le sol du restaurant par marée haute, cet espace paisible permet aux clients de s'y attarder. Presque entièrement ouverte, la structure repose sur une grille en bois. En hauteur, une alternance de bandes évoque la crête des vagues. Les bandes forment également un auvent sous lequel les clients se détendent dans une lumière filtrée ; l'air circule naturellement pour atténuer la chaleur méditerranéenne.

03

01 Barbouni is situated in the Navarino Dunes and is part of the Romanos resort at Costa Navarino, in Messenia, in southern Greece

02 Hanging baskets act as pendants disguising the 'unnatural' electric lighting otherwise at odds with the restaurant's sustainable aesthetic

03 Carved driftwood doubles up as seating in the entrance and dining area

Bond & Brook

Website   fenwick.co.uk
Date Opened   August 2010
Designer   d-raw
Size of Build 250 m² / 2,700 ft²
Award   Shortlist 2011
Address   Fenwick, 63 New Bond Street
                   London W1A 3BS
                   UK

Housed on the second floor of Fenwick's flagship store in London's exclusive Mayfair, this sparkling and multi-functional daytime restaurant and café was a co-commission between the family-owned business and the hospitality consultancy of esteemed restaurant critic Fay Maschler and journalist Simon Davis.

The immaculate and uplifting design fuses retail with hospitality, in reference to the chic setting. Matching the elegance of the store's new makeover, the design sought to establish a stunning food and drink destination, in which the marbled floor and specially created designs impress opulence upon the space. Key to the layout is the central 'sculpted' pewter bar with *Ribbon* bar-stools by Cappellini.

Guests enter through two walls of asymmetrical glass panels, a partially reflective curtain overlooking the rest of the floor which lets them see out but with a degree of seclusion.

Dieses lebendige und multifunktionale Tagesrestaurant mit Café liegt im Obergeschoss des Nobelgeschäfts Fenwick's im exklusiven Londoner Bezirk Mayfair. Die Einrichtung ist das Ergebnis einer Zusammenarbeit der Eigentümerfamilie mit der Beratungsagentur der angesehenen Restaurantkritikerin Fay Maschler und dem Journalisten Simon Davis.

Das sehr tadelose und vornehme Design verbindet Einkaufen mit Bewirtung und entspricht dem anspruchs-vollen Umfeld. Passend zur eleganten Neugestaltung des Geschäfts sollte hier ein prächtiger Ort zum Essen und Trinken entstehen, an dem der Marmorboden und speziell gestaltete Elemente den eindrucksvollen Raum prägen. Ein Blickfang ist die zentrale, „plastisch" geformte, mit Zinn verkleidete Bar mit den Cappellini *Ribbon*-Hockern.

Die Gäste betreten den Raum durch zwei Wände aus asymmetrisch angeordneten Glastafeln. Ein teilre-flektierender Vorhang bietet Ausblick aus dem übrigen Raum und doch ein gewisses Maß an Abschirmung.

01

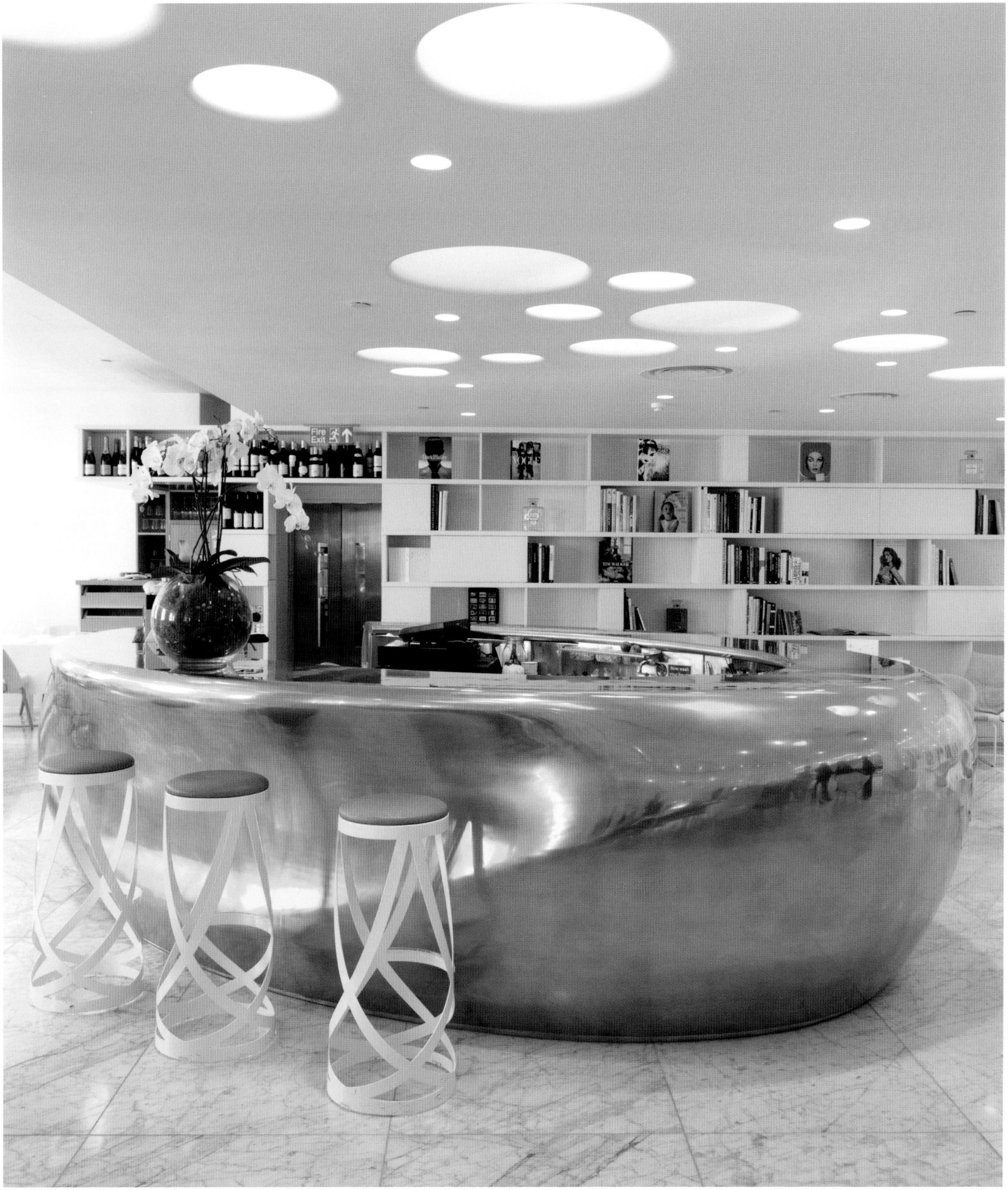

"Fay and I would go to
parties where the canapés
were better than the dinner.
We wondered whether we
could create a restaurant
for oversized appetisers."

Simon Davis, co-founder Bond & Brook, *Vogue*

02

01 A floor-to-ceiling bookcase
lines one of the walls and is
home to a fashion library, adding
another element to the design
and offering customers a selection
of reading material

02 Three areas, booth, café
and restaurant seating, cater for
the array of light food, snacks
and cocktails on offer during the
department store's opening hours

03 Verner Panton's *C1* chairs for
Vitra have been upholstered with
fabric from textile company Kvadrat

03

Au deuxième étage du magasin phare Fenwick dans l'exclusif Mayfair londonien, ce restaurant et café de jour, polyvalent et étincelant, est le fruit d'une commande conjointe de ce commerce familial et de l'agence de design de Fay Maschler, critique gastronomique distinguée, et du journaliste Simon Davis.

Le design immaculé et inspirant marie service et hospitalité à la hauteur de l'environnement chic. Pour égaler l'élégance du magasin au visage nouveau, le design a cherché à créer un espace de restauration impactant, dont le sol en marbre et les éléments sur mesure dégagent un sentiment d'opulence. Le point fort de l'agencement est le bar central en étain sculpté, assorti de tabourets *Ribbon* signés Cappellini.

Pour entrer, les clients passent entre deux murs faits de panneaux de verre asymétriques. Ce rideau reflète en partie l'espace ; il laisse entrevoir la salle tout en offrant un certain isolement.

Bravo 24

Website	projectes24.com/bravo24
Date Opened	November 2010
Designer	Isabel López Vilalta + Asociados
Size of Build	831 m² / 9,000 ft²
Award	Shortlist 2010
Address	Placa de la Rosa dels Vents, 1
	08039 Barcelona
	Spain

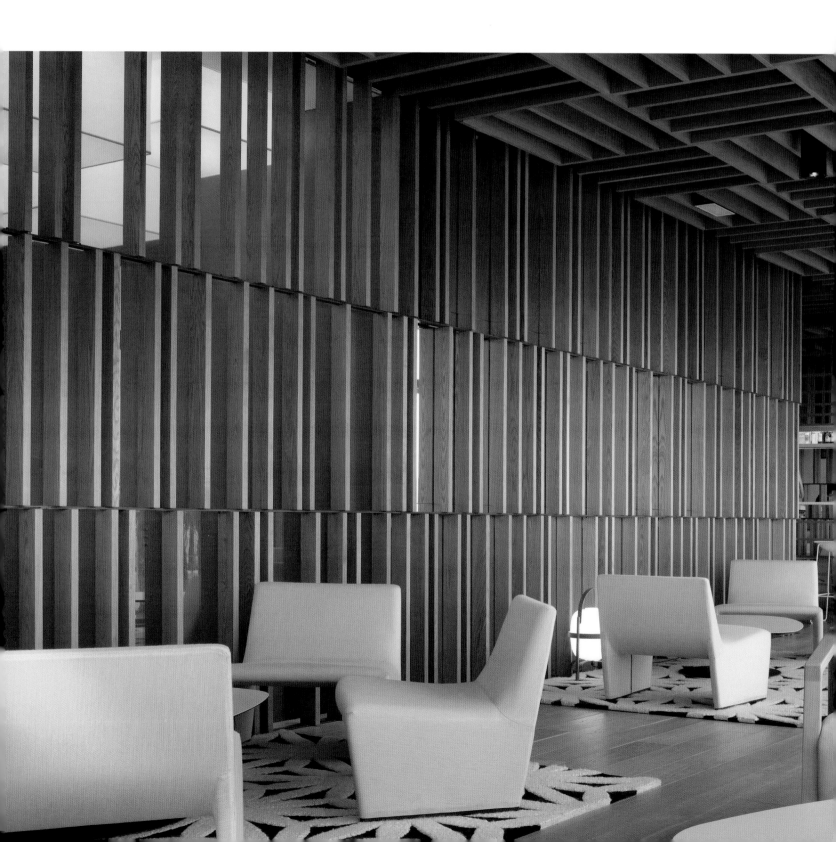

Located in the picturesque Barceloneta boardwalk and part of the international five-star chain W Hotels, the redesigned Bravo 24 is intended to epitomise the Mediterranean spirit of the city in the way the choice of materials, iron and especially wood, have been put to use.

The difficult floor-plan of the original space was controlled by the use of wood, to striking effect, and this helped unify the individual zones of the new design, including the area for guests to relax in as well as the main dining-space. Perpendicularly alternating boxes create an eye-catching ceiling, while similar vertical sections form the simple geometric partitions that divide the dining floor into more intimate cubed spaces, at the same time letting guests catch a glimpse of what is happening elsewhere in the restaurant.

Das an der pittoresken Strandpromenade Barceloneta gelegene, neu gestaltete Bravo 24 gehört zur internationalen 5-Sterne-Kette der W Hotels und soll durch die Wahl und Anwendung der Materialien – Eisen und vor allem Holz – das mediterrane Flair der Stadt verkörpern.

Der problematische Grundriss des ursprünglichen Raumes wurde mit erstaunlicher Wirkung durch die Verwendung von Holz verändert. Dadurch ließen sich die individuellen Bereiche der Neugestaltung vereinheitlichen: sowohl der Aufenthaltsbereich für die Gäste als auch der große Speiseraum. In wechselnder Richtung angebrachte Kastenelemente bilden eine auffällige Decke und ähnliche, senkrecht angeordnete Bauelemente einfache geometrische Trennwände, die das Speisegeschoss in intimere kubische Bereiche aufteilen. Die Gäste können gleichzeitig einen Blick davon erhaschen, was im übrigen Restaurant passiert.

Sur la promenade de la pittoresque Barceloneta,
le nouveau Bravo 24 de la chaîne d'hôtels cinq étoiles
W cherche à incarner l'esprit méditerranéen de la ville
grâce à des matériaux comme le fer et surtout le bois.

    Le plan complexe de l'espace initial a été structuré
à l'aide de bois pour donner un résultat imposant et
unifier les zones individuelles, dont le salon et la salle
de restaurant principale. L'alternance perpendiculaire de
caisses forme un plafond original alors que des sections
verticales semblables composent des espaces géométriques divisant la salle à manger en cubes plus intimes,
desquels les convives peuvent observer le
reste du local.

01 Welcoming banquette seating
lines the inside perimeter of the
dining areas, making for a more
intimate dining experience

02 Run by Michelin-starred Catalan
chef, Carles Abellán, and serving
traditional Barcelonan cuisine from
several periods in history, Bravo 24
has dishes on the menu originating
as far back as the 15th century

Byron Haymarket

Website byronhamburgers.com
Date Opened April 2011
Designer Michaelis Boyd Associates & Clare Nash
Cost of Build $$$$+
Size of Build 180 m² / 1,900 ft²
Award Shortlist 2012
Address 11 Haymarket
London SW1Y 4BP
UK

02

"We were asked to provide a destination restaurant that celebrated London."

Michaelis Boyd Associates & Clare Nash

Whereas many chain restaurants opt for at least a partially uniform identity, each of the Byron locations closely tailors the design to the architecture. For the Haymarket site, this meant transforming an impressive historic building in the heart of London's West End.

Inside, the space was fitted out as an eclectic and playful restaurant, with features derived from distinctive aspects of city life: accents of bright red, long associated with London buses and phone-boxes, are used in both main rooms, along with reclaimed furnishings and royal memorabilia.

To add character to the back room, a neon lighting sculpture was installed representing the different-coloured lines of the Tube map, together with additional touches, such as the metal racks above the banquette seating similar to those found on English trains and a bar lined with 10,000 mother of pearl buttons, as traditionally worn by Cockney Pearly Kings and Queens.

Während viele Restaurantketten sich für eine zumindest fast gleichartige Gestaltung entscheiden, wird bei Byron jedes Lokal seiner Architektur genau angepasst. Für den Standort Haymarket bedeutete dies die Umgestaltung eines eindrucksvollen historischen Gebäudes im Herzen des Londoner West End.

Der Innenbereich wurde zu einem eklektischen und verspielten Restaurant umgestaltet, mit Elementen, die Aspekte des städtischen Lebens entsprechen: In beiden Sälen wurden Akzente in leuchtendem Rot gesetzt, das über lange Zeit mit den Londoner Bussen und Telefonzellen verbunden war, zusammen mit restauriertem Mobiliar und royalen Erinnerungsstücken.

Um dem hinteren Raum Charakter zu verleihen, wurde eine Neonleuchte installiert, die die Farben der verschiedenen U-Bahn-Linien darstellt. Über den Sitzbänken sind Ablagen aus Metall angebracht, ähnlich denen in englischen Eisenbahnzügen und die Bar ist mit 10.000 Perlmutt Knöpfen besetzt, genau wie sie die Cockney Pearly Kings und Queens auf ihren Anzügen tragen.

01 Booth seating is upholstered with a textile design based on that used on the London Underground in the 1950s

02 Children's book illustrator Tor Freeman designed and drew the specially commissioned wallpaper

Souvent, les chaînes de restaurants préfèrent une certaine cohérence dans leur identité. Chaque local Byron en revanche adapte totalement le design à l'architecture. Pour celui de Haymarket, un bâtiment historique imposant en plein cœur du West End de Londres s'est vu métamorphosé.

L'espace intérieur a été aménagé en restaurant éclectique et détonant, avec des éléments rappelant des aspects clés de la ville : des touches de rouge vif, en hommage aux bus et cabines téléphoniques, sont présentes dans les deux salles principales, ainsi que des meubles récupérés et des articles-souvenirs de la famille royale.

Pour donner plus de caractère à l'arrière-salle, une sculpture en néons symbolise les différentes lignes de couleur du métro. Des supports en métal au-dessus des banquettes rappellent ceux des trains anglais. Le bar a été décoré avec 10 000 boutons de nacre, identiques à ceux portés par les Pearly Kings and Queens de Cockney.

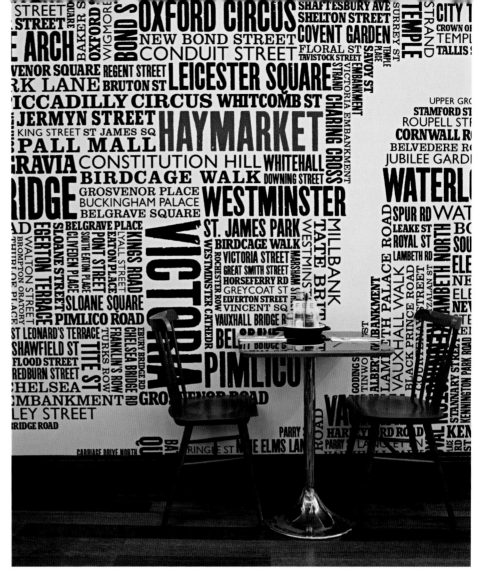

Carbon Bar

Website	carbonbar.co.uk
Date Opened	April 2007
Designer	B3 Designers
Size of Build	409 m² / 4,400 ft²
Award	Overall winner 2009
Address	Old Quebec Street
	London W1C 1LZ
	UK

In a part of the capital where many high-class hotels may be found, the design concept for a new destination night-club has to be certain of distinguishing the venue from an ordinary hotel bar.

Taking inspiration from both New York's meat-packing district and London's Shoreditch, the décor employs materials such as metal, leather, concrete and wood for a strong, sleek look to conjure a post-industrial and urban context. A 'chain-room' curtain offers a certain privacy by creating a partial divide from the main space.

The imposing 14-metre bar has a custom-built back-wall mural, and a suspended mezzanine floor serves for the champagne bar. Since the building's structure could not accommodate a poured-concrete floor, a thin top layer was used instead, referred to in the industry as a 'top screed'.

In einem Gebiet der Hauptstadt mit vielen erstklassigen Hotels muss sich das Entwurfskonzept für ein neues Lokal von einer gewöhnlichen Hotelbar unterscheiden.

Das vom New Yorker Meatpacking District wie auch vom Londoner Bezirk Shoreditch inspirierte Design verwendet Materialien wie Metall, Leder, Beton und Holz für ein eindrucksvolles, elegantes Ambiente, das einem postindustriellen und urbanen Kontext entspricht. Ein Trennvorhang bietet eine gewisse Abgeschlossenheit, indem er Bereiche vom großen Raum abschirmt.

An der Rückwand der beeindruckenden, 14 Meter langen Bar befindet sich ein extra dafür angefertigtes Wandbild. Eine aufgehängtes Zwischengeschoss dient als Champagnerbar. Da das Tragwerk des Gebäudes keine Gussbetondecke aufnehmen konnte, wurde stattdessen eine dünne Deckschicht aufgebracht, die von der Industrie als „Aufbeton" bezeichnet wird.

"We explored industrial glamour to develop a bar that was as unlike the typical hotel bar as possible."

B3 Designers

01 Modular cubed units and leather-upholstered benches provide flexible seating choices within the space

02 To reduce noise levels, neoprene fixings were used on the ceiling to make it soundproof

Dans une partie de la capitale comptant déjà bon nombre d'hôtels de catégorie, le design d'une nouvelle discothèque doit démarquer ce local des bars d'hôtel ordinaires.

Inspiré du Meatpacking District de New York et du Shoreditch de Londres, le décor fait intervenir des matériaux comme le métal, le cuir, le béton et le bois ; ensemble, ils donnent un résultat puissant et raffiné venant conjurer l'environnement urbain postindustriel. Un rideau fait de chaînes offre une certaine intimité tout en créant une division partielle de l'espace principal.

Long de 14 mètres, l'imposant bar s'étire devant un mural sur mesure ; sur la mezzanine suspendue se trouve le bar à champagne. Comme la structure du bâtiment ne pouvait pas accueillir un sol en béton coulé, une fine couche supérieure (techniquement, une « chape ») a été appliquée.

02

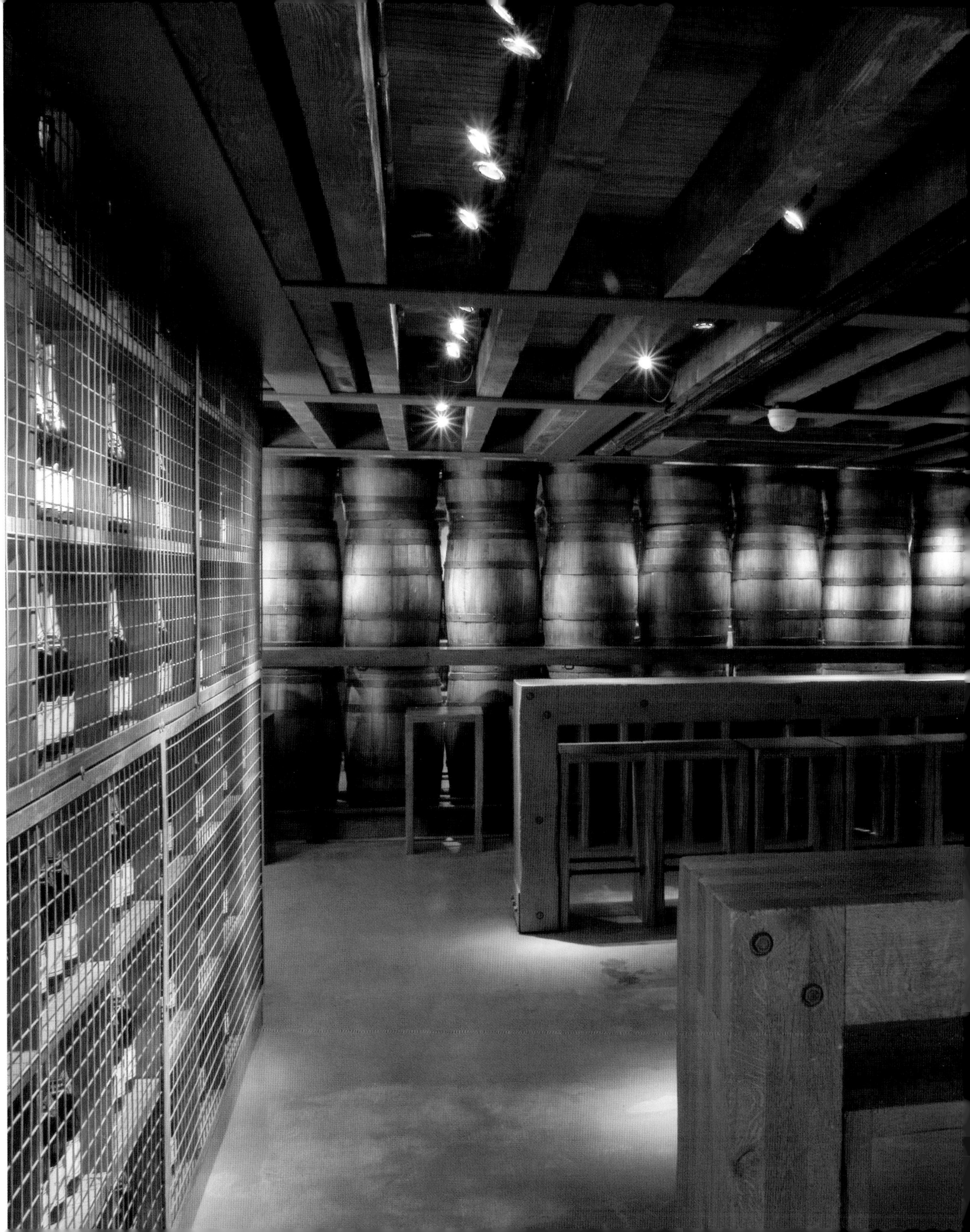

Dishoom Chowpatty Beach

Website	dishoom.com
Date Opened	May 2011
Date Closed	October 2011
Designer	Honest Entertainment
Size of Build	140 m² / 1,500 ft²
Award	Shortlist 2012
Address	Southbank Centre
	London SE1 8XX
	UK

A temporary incarnation of the Bombay-style café, Dishoom, this bold and bright pop-up ran for ten weeks during the summer of 2011.

In the spirit of the Hindu word *jugaad* ('making do'), a kaleidoscopic array of colours and a vibrant mix of patterns, textures and surfaces formed a contemporary backdrop to this space modelled on the bustling all-day traditional cafés founded by Persian immigrants in India.

The main construction element was conjoined wooden pallets, graduating from fiery red to canary-yellow outside and balanced by a fresher interior of white and pastels. An assortment of one-off and reclaimed items was used to fit out the inside, with notable features including up-cycled Brentwood bar-stools, rolled-up newspapers stacked to make walls, and jam jars converted into lamps for lighting.

Dishoom, dieses lebhafte und fröhliche Pop-up-Lokal, eine temporäre Inkarnation des Bombay-Stils, existierte für zehn Wochen im Sommer 2011.

Im Sinne des Hindu-Begriffs *jugaad* („Behelf") bildeten ein kaleidoskopisches Farbenspiel und eine Mischung aus Mustern, Strukturen und Flächen einen zeitgenössischen Hintergrund für dieses den traditionellen belebten Ganztagscafés nachgebildete Lokal, welche die persischen Einwanderer in Indien gründeten.

Das wichtigste Bauelement waren Holzpaletten, außen feuerrot bis kanariengelb gestrichen und als Ausgleich in Weiß und Pastellfarben im Innenraum. Die Einrichtung wurde aus wiederverwerteten und für den einmaligen Gebrauch bestimmten Gegenständen zusammengestellt, auch mit so bemerkenswerten Elementen wie restaurierten Brentwood-Barhockern, aufgerollten Zeitungen als Wänden und in Leuchten umgewandelten Marmeladegläsern.

02

Incarnation temporaire d'un café au style de Bombay, Dishoom est une installation haute en couleurs qui a fonctionné dix semaines pendant l'été 2011.

Dans l'esprit du mot hindou *jugaad* (« solution ingénieuse »), une composition kaléidoscopique de couleurs et un ensemble vif de motifs, de textures et de surfaces créent un décor contemporain pour cet espace construit à l'image des cafés traditionnels de jour que fondaient les immigrants perses en Inde.

Des palettes en bois, principal élément de construction, vont du rouge vif au jaune canari à l'extérieur et contraste avec l'intérieur plus frais dans les tons blanc et pastels. L'intérieur est décoré d'un assortiment d'éléments exclusifs et récupérés, notamment des tabourets de bar Brentwood recyclés, des journaux roulés et empilés pour former des murs, et des pots de confiture transformés en lampes.

01   Over 5,000 newspapers were recycled in creating the walls, tightly rolled up and stacked to form a multi-coloured textured surface

02   A portrait of two gentlemen at one end of the bar was actually a clock, their moustaches being the hands which told the time in London and in Bombay

03   Upcycled Brentwood bar-stools complement the optical illusion of painted floorboards

03

East Beach Cafe

Website eastbeachcafe.co.uk
Date Opened June 2007
Designer Heatherwick Studio
Size of Build 280 m² / 3,000 ft²
Award Category winner 2009
Address Littlehampton
West Sussex BN17 5NZ
UK

The site for this eye-catching organic design presented various difficulties, with the unsheltered location requiring protection from the weather and a restriction on permitted building materials having the potential to hamper the intended impact. From these constraints was born a form that resembles layers of bedrock, or a prehistoric exoskeleton.

Rather than disguise the shutters that protect the rear glass façade overlooking the sea, they were made into a feature. Steel ribbons make up the patinated shell which also forms the dominant structural support, each layer being arranged in step formation to enhance the café's silhouette.

Simple seating lets the undulating surface of the interior stand out; fashioned out of insulating spray-on foam, the cave-like appearance is made dramatic at night by up-lighting and candles.

Das Grundstück für diesen beeindruckenden organischen Entwurf verursachte verschiedene Probleme, da der exponierte Standort Schutz vor dem Wetter erforderte und die Beschränkung auf zugelassene Baustoffe den erwünschten Eindruck zu behindern drohte. Aus diesen Einschränkungen wurde eine Form geboren, die gewachsenen Felsschichten oder einem prähistorischen Ektoskelett ähnelt.

Anstatt die schützenden Läden an der rückwärtigen, zur See orientierten Glasfassade zu verbergen, wurden sie zu einem gestalterischen Element gemacht. Die Schale aus patinierten Stahlbändern bildet auch das dominante Tragwerk. Alle Ebenen sind gestuft angeordnet, um die Silhouette des Cafés zu betonen.

Die schlichte Möblierung lässt die gewellte Fläche hervortreten. Angestrahlt und in Kerzenlicht entfaltet das höhlenartige Erscheinungsbild, gebildet aus aufgesprühtem Isolierschaum, bei Nacht seine dramatische Wirkung.

"The British seaside did not conjure up images of twinkling sea, golden sand and blue skies. Our associations were with stumbling around on damp brown shingle and spotting magically eroded objects."

Heatherwick Studio

283

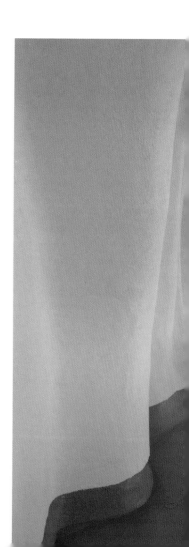

01 Fabricated by local workers, the exterior was constructed by welding together steel ribbons the same width as the shutters to form the voluptuous curved café

02 The new architectural addition to Littlehampton replaces the kiosk that originally stood on the narrow plot and spans a total 40 metres in length

Le lieu de cet original design organique présentait plusieurs difficultés. L'emplacement exposé demandait une protection face aux intempéries, et la restriction quant aux matériaux de construction pouvait nuire à l'impact recherché. De ces contraintes a émergé une forme évoquant des strates rocheuses ou un squelette préhistorique.

Au lieu d'être camouflés, les volets qui protègent la façade vitrée face à la mer sont une caractéristique en soi. Des rubans en acier forment une carapace patinée qui sert d'appui structurel. Chaque couche est disposée en retrait des autres pour souligner la silhouette du café.

La simplicité des chaises permet à la surface ondulante de l'intérieur de se démarquer. Fait de mousse soufflée isolante, l'espace-caverne gagne de l'effet à la nuit tombée grâce à l'éclairage vertical et aux bougies.

Galvin La Chapelle

Website	galvinrestaurants.com
Date Opened	November 2010
Designer	designLSM
Cost of Build	$$$$+
Size of Build	100 m² / 1,100 ft²
Award	Overall winner 2010
Address	35 Spital Square
	London E1 6DY
	UK

A stunning, vaulted space for diners to lose themselves in, this Paris-style bistro is housed in St. Botolph's Hall, a former girls' school and grade II-listed building in Spitalfields.

First built as a church, many of the original features have survived, such as the limestone walls, granite pillars and arched windows, so that much of the conversion work had to comply with strict planning regulations.

One such consideration involved installing a specially designed free-standing heating and cooling system under the fixed seating, so as not to interfere with the historic structure.

Also noteworthy is the addition of the mezzanine floor, the glass-banistered staircase to which connects the two levels of the 30-metre-high space while accentuating the aristocratic feel of the design.

01 The pewter bar was reclaimed from the Aurora Bar at the nearby Great Eastern Hotel

02 A glass walkway links the restaurant to the more informal daytime space, the Café de Luxe

Im fantastischen, gewölbten Raum dieses Bistros im Pariser Stil, das in St. Botolph's Hall, einer früheren, unter Denkmalschutz stehenden Mädchenschule in Spitalfields, untergebracht ist, können Gäste die Welt vergessen.

Vom ursprünglich als Kirche errichteten Gebäude sind viele der originalen Merkmale erhalten geblieben, zum Beispiel die Kalksteinmauern, Granitsäulen und Bogenfenster. Beim Umbau mussten strenge Planungsvorschriften beachtet werden. Dies galt auch für den Einbau eines speziellen, frei stehenden Heiz- und Kühlsystems unter der feststehenden Bestuhlung, damit das historische Bauwerk nicht beeinträchtigt wurde.

Bemerkenswert ist auch das Zwischengeschoss, das zur aristokratischen Wirkung der Gestaltung beiträgt, sowie die Treppe mit gläsernem Geländer, die beide Ebenen des 30 Meter hohen Raumes verbindet.

À Spitalfields, ce bistro de style parisien, espace voûté imposant dans lequel les convives se perdent, est logé dans le St. Botolph's Hall, une ancienne école de filles et un édifice classé (Grade II).

Le bâtiment a d'abord été construit comme une église, et la plupart des éléments d'origine ont survécu (murs en pierre calcaire, piliers de granite, fenêtres en ogive) ; une bonne partie de l'effort de transformation a donc été soumis à des règles strictes. Entre autres, un système de chauffage et de refroidissement autonome a dû être spécialement conçu sous les sièges fixes pour ne pas nuire à la structure historique.

Autre rajout notable dans cet espace de 30 mètres de hauteur, la mezzanine est connectée à l'étage inférieur par une rampe d'escaliers en verre qui accentue le caractère aristocratique du design.

01

02

Germain

Date Opened	June 2009
Designer	India Mahdavi
Cost of Build	$$$$
Size of Build	370 m² / 4,000 ft²
Award	Longlist 2010
Address	25 Rue de Buci
	75006 Paris
	France

The surprising disjunctions of modern art meet the familiar bistro in this bar and restaurant spread over two floors in the French capital.

The huge woman in heels and raincoat is 'Sophie', a bright yellow sculpture by Xavier Veilhan made from lacquered resin polyurethane. With one half of her body situated on each floor it is as if the restaurant has been built around her, as she stands on the ground floor while her top half emerges into the more exclusive first floor.

The upstairs 'billiard room' has a flourish of Sixties-inspired furnishings that include houndstooth upholstered stools. The grey textured walls of the more sober ground-floor café contrast with the orange banquette and monochrome-chequered vinyl floor, while the 'trim bar' has outsized chess pawns for stools.

Einer erstaunlichen Diskrepanz zwischen moderner Kunst und einem vertrauten Bistro begegnet man in dieser auf zwei Geschossen untergebrachten Bar mit Restaurant in der französischen Hauptstadt.

Die gewaltige Frauenfigur mit hohen Absätzen und Regenmantel ist „Sophie", eine leuchtend gelbe Skulptur von Xavier Veilhan aus lackiertem Polyurethan-harz. Mit je einer Hälfte ihres Körpers auf einem anderen Geschoss, wirkt es, als sei das Restaurant um sie herum gebaut worden, als stünde sie im Erdgeschoss, während ihre obere Hälfte in das exklusivere Obergeschoss hinaufragt.

Der „Billardsaal" im Obergeschoss wurde im Stil der sechziger Jahre möbliert, zum Beispiel mit gepolsterten Hockern aus Hahnentrittstoff. Die grauen, strukturierten Wände des nüchterneren Cafés im Erdgeschoss bilden einen Kontrast zu den orangefarbenen Bänken und dem Schachbrett-Vinylboden, während die „Trim Bar" mit Hockern in Form übergroßer Schachfiguren ausgestattet ist.

02

01 'Sophie' was modelled and named after one of the artist Xavier Veilhan's close friends

02 Attention to detail was paramount, and the corridor walls were repainted three times before the right shade of blue was found

03 A 1970s pop palette is continued in the vintage-style furniture sporting geometric patterns, bold colours and zebra print

La surprenante dichotomie entre art moderne et ambiance de bistrot s'apprécie aux deux étages de ce bar/restaurant parisien.

L'énorme femme en talons et imperméable se nomme Sophie, une sculpture jaune vif de Xavier Veilhan faite en résine polyuréthane laquée. À chaque étage est visible une moitié de son corps, comme si le restaurant avait été construit autour d'elle : ses pieds reposent sur le sol du rez-de-chaussée, alors que son buste émerge à l'espace supérieur plus exclusif.

La salle de billard à l'étage affiche un mobilier inspiré des années 60, dont des tabourets rembourrés au motif pied de poule. Les murs texturés de couleur grise du café plus sobre à l'étage inférieur contrastent avec la banquette orange et le sol en vinyle à damiers. Le bar abaissé compte des énormes pièces de jeu d'échecs en guise de tabourets.

Graffiti Café

Website	graffiti-cafe.com
Date Opened	January 2011
Designer	Studio Mode
Cost of Build	$$$$
Size of Build	300 m² / 3,200 ft²
Award	Overall winner 2012
Address	25 Tzar Osvoboditel Blvd
	9000 Varna
	Bulgaria

01

Undulating lines and repeating geometric shapes prevail in this café set within the ground-floor unit of a development that also houses apartments and a gallery. The space is always on display – thanks to a panoramic glass façade – and to give the site a sense of cohesion the transition from exterior to interior was blurred by continuing the paving-slabs in front of the café inside for the internal flooring.

The form of the columns, suggested by lathe-turned table legs, was constructed from poplar laths that ribbon across the ceiling and down to floor level, fanning out like paper decorations. The hard materials and flat surfaces resulted in unforgiving acoustics which required a special foam to reduce noise levels, housed along with the ventilation pipes in the ceiling, painted black so as not to distract from the design.

Gekrümmte Linien und sich wiederholende geometrische Formen dominieren in diesem Café im Erdgeschoss eines Baukomplexes, der auch Wohnungen und eine Galerie enthält. Der Raum ist – dank einer gläsernen Panoramafassade – einsehbar, und um dem Bereich eine einheitliche Wirkung zu verleihen, hat man den Übergang von außen nach innen verwischt, indem die Außenpflasterung im Inneren weitergeführt wurde.

Die von gedrechselten Tischbeinen inspirierten Säulen wurden aus Pappelholzlatten gefertigt, die sich über die Decke und bis zum Boden entlangziehen und sich wie Papierschmuck auffächern. Die harten Materialien und ebenen Flächen führten zu einer untragbaren Akustik, was einen besonderen Schaum zur Lärmreduktion erforderlich machte. Dieser wurde mit der Lüftungsvorrichtung an der Decke angebracht und schwarz gestrichen, um die Gestaltung nicht zu beeinträchtigen.

Les lignes ondulées et la répétition de formes géométriques caractérisent l'intérieur de ce café logé au rez-de-chaussée d'un complexe comptant aussi des appartements et une galerie.

L'espace est visible de toutes parts grâce à une façade panoramique en verre. Pour donner une sensation de cohésion, la transition entre extérieur et intérieur a été estompée en prolongeant le dallage du devant au revêtement intérieur.

Les colonnes, inspirées des pieds des tables en bois tourné, ont été fabriquées à partir de lattes de peuplier ornant tout le plafond et se déployant jusqu'au sol comme des décorations en papier. Les matériaux durs et les surfaces plates offrent une acoustique remarquable. Pour ce faire, une mousse spéciale réduisant le niveau de bruit a été placée le long des conduits de ventilation dans le plafond, peint en noir pour ne pas détourner l'attention du design.

01 Pleats in the floor-to-ceiling white curtains echo the different folds and repetitions in the space while also providing a softness to balance the hard surfaces and glass wall

02 A crystal lattice of geometric 'flowers' lines the back wall, made from pieces of polyurethane-painted MDF, prefabricated and assembled on site, which continues on to the white engineered stone floor

03 The tables are designed by Studio Mode, which was awarded European and International Best Bar at the R&BDA in 2012

Hashi Mori

Website hashi-kitchen.de
Date Opened March 2012
Designer Affect Studio
Cost of Build $
Size of Build 175 m² / 1,900 ft²
Award Longlist 2013
Address Rosenthaler Straße 63
10119 Berlin
Germany

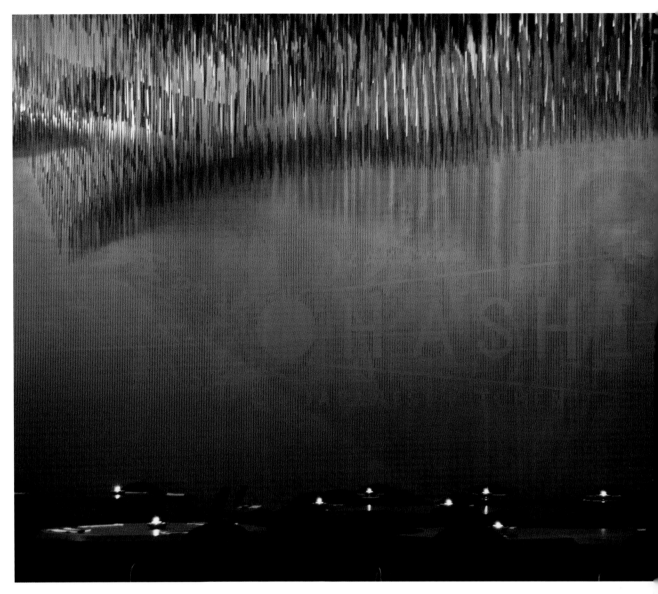

01

This Japanese *izakaya* restaurant offers a clever example of how subverting tradition through design techniques can lead to new ways of experiencing a fusion of cultures. From a new design process, combining hand-crafted traditional Japanese materials with 3D-modelling and cutting-edge computing, the shifting and immersive ceiling structure was created: the name Hashi Mori translates as 'chopstick forest'.

Two exterior glass walls are part-concealed by the wooden back-lit installation that doubles up as signage to attract customers. Half a ton of rice was also employed, diffusing the light and flooding the street with a warm glow.

Once inside, the entire forest comes into view. Across 56 m² of ceiling, the 13,454 hand-dyed chopsticks were meticulously shaped and hung with nylon string to create a wavy, semi-translucent canopy above the diners' heads.

Dieses japanische *Izakaya*-Restaurant ist ein intelligentes Beispiel dafür, wie der Umbruch von Traditionen durch bautechnische Maßnahmen zu neuen Formen der Vereinigung von Kulturen führen kann. In einem neuen Entwurfsprozess entstand durch Verbindung traditioneller japanischer Baustoffe mit Hilfe von 3D-Gestaltung und modernster Computertechnik diese bewegte und verwirrende Deckenstruktur. Der Name Hashi Mori bedeutet „Wald aus Essstäbchen".

Zwei verglaste Außenwände sind teilweise verdeckt durch die hölzerne, hinterleuchtete Installation, die auch als Markenzeichen dient, um Besucher anzulocken. Auch wurde eine halbe Tonne Reis dazu verwendet, um das Licht zu dämpfen und die Straße mit warmem Glanz zu überziehen.

Im Innern wird der ganze Wald sichtbar. Über 56 m² Deckenfläche wurden die 13.454 handgefärbten Essstäbchen sorgfältig verteilt und an Nylonschnüren aufgehängt. Dadurch entstand ein gewellter, durchscheinender Baldachin über den Köpfen der Gäste.

"The first challenge we faced was how to convince the client to hang 13,454 chopsticks from his ceiling, leading to the next challenge of gauging the timing of such an analogue process."

Affect Studio

Ce restaurant *izakaya* japonais illustre parfaitement comment revisiter la tradition avec des techniques de design et trouver une nouvelle forme de fusion de cultures. D'un procédé inédit de design, mêlant des matériaux japonais traditionnels et une modélisation 3D de pointe, est né le plafond changeant et immersif. Le nom Hashi Mori signifie « forêts de baguettes ».

Deux murs vitrés extérieurs sont un peu dissimulés par l'installation en bois rétro-éclairée, une signalisation pour attirer les clients. La demi-tonne de riz employée diffuse la lumière et inonde la rue d'une chaude lueur.

À l'intérieur, la forêt retient le regard. Sur 56 m² de plafond, les 13 454 baguettes peintes à la main ont été élaborées avec soin et pendues à des fils de nylon pour créer un auvent ondulé et semi-translucide au-dessus des convives.

01 Hand-drawn graphics, made with the aid of a computer program and processed by a customised script, were used to create the image of the forest which lines the walls of the space

02 The chopstick installation used 20 km of nylon and took a team of 14 people three weeks to complete

Höst

Website	cofoco.dk/hoest
Date Opened	November 2012
Designer	Norm Architects
Cost of Build	$$$
Size of Build	300 m² / 3,200 ft²
Award	Overall winner 2013
Address	Nørre Farimagsgade 41
	1364 Copenhagen
	Denmark

Beautiful simplicity and a bucolic lifestyle, a combination that has become synonymous with Scandinavian design, are the traits of a style here blending a utilitarian industrial aesthetic with the honest and natural principles of rustic interiors.

Danish design and architecture studio, Norm Architects, has created in Höst a simple restaurant which relies on exquisite craftsmanship, reclaimed materials and custom-made tableware to make its impact.

Salvaged wood, granite and zinc sit alongside whitewashed walls. Carefully selected products adorn the minimal space, including *Raft Barstool NA4* from &tradition and the *New Norm Dinnerware* launched by Menu, both designed by Norm, or a range of industrially themed lighting, giving a timeless feel and immersing guests in a contemporary yet rural dining experience.

Ansprechende Schlichtheit, verbunden mit einer bukolischen Lebensform, die zum Synonym für skandinavisches Design geworden sind, wurden hier zu einem Stil verarbeitet, der eine utilistaristische, industrielle Ästhetik mit den ehrlichen und natürlichen Formen bäuerlicher Innenräume vereint.

Das dänische Architektur- und Designbüro Norm Architects hat mit Höst ein einfaches Restaurant geschaffen, das durch exquisite Handwerksarbeit, recyceltes Material und speziell hierfür entworfenes Geschirr und Besteck beeindruckt.

Altholz, Granit und Zink stehen an verputzten Wänden. Sorgfältig ausgewählte Produkte schmücken den kleinen Raum. Unter anderem haben der *Raft Barstool NA4* von &tradition und das von Menu vertriebene Geschirr *New Norm Dinnerware*, jeweils von Norm gestaltet, sowie verschiedene industriell gefertigte Leuchten eine zeitlose Wirkung und vermitteln den Gästen ein modernes und doch ländliches Speiseerlebnis.

"The theme has been
to transform the feeling
of eating outside in a
Scandinavian farmyard in
rural settings to an urban
and more minimalist
indoor context."

Jonas Bjerre-Poulsen, co-founder Norm,
Dezeen magazine

01

Beauté de la simplicité, style de vie bucolique :
cette combinaison, devenue synonyme de design
scandinave, marque ici la volonté d'allier une
esthétique industrielle pratique et les principes
naturels des intérieurs rustiques.

Le studio de design et d'architecture danois
Norm Architects est l'auteur de Höst, un restaurant
simple dont l'impact tient aux pièces d'artisanat
raffinées, aux matériaux récupérés et à la vaisselle
personnalisée.

Du bois récupéré, du granit et du zinc viennent
orner les murs blanchis, alors que les peaux d'agneau
sur les chaises donnent une touche de douceur et
de délicatesse. Des éléments choisis avec soin
décorent l'espace minimaliste (comme les tabourets
Raft Barstool N4 de &tradition et la vaisselle *New
Norm Dinnerware* lancée par Menu, tous deux signés
par Norm) et toute une gamme de lampes de style
industriel pour créer un ensemble intemporel
et plonger les clients dans une expérience gastronomique contemporaine et rurale.

01 Low-hung black scissor-spring hanging lamps, by collaborator Menu, update the concept of the chandelier

02 A wall break leads to the conservatory, lined by windows from an old hospital

03 Throughout the restaurant, modern elements, such as the high-backed *J110* chair by Jørgen Baekmark for manufacturer Hay, are set against rustic, natural and reclaimed materials

02

03

Inamo

Website   inamo-restaurant.com
Date Opened December 2008
Designer   Blacksheep
Size of Build 310 m² / 3,350 ft²
Award   Longlist 2009
Address   134-136 Wardour Street
                 London W1F 8ZP
                 UK

Culinary and design experience collides in this pan-Asian restaurant which hosts the world's first interactive ordering system.

A central entrance invites diners into a small lobby introducing the colour scheme of the overall identity. Origami designs in gloss black, deep reds, oranges and white create a kaleidoscopic patterning extending from bold wallpaper graphics to wall-mounted mirrors.

Large white 'cocoons' suspended from the ceiling house projector and motion-sensor equipment for the restaurant's 'e-tables'. The virtual tablecloths enable diners to place their food and drink orders, and to play games, search their current location or even design their own screensavers while they wait. The illuminated interface even lets diners see their meals being prepared via a live 'chef-cam', adapting surveillance to restaurant culture.

In diesem pan-asiatischen Restaurant kann man Kulinarisches und Gestalterisches gleichermaßen erleben, außerdem bietet es das erste interaktive Bestellsystem der Welt.

Ein zentraler Eingang führt die Gäste in eine kleine Lobby, die das Farbsystem des gesamten Erscheinungsbilds vorstellt. Origami-Entwürfe in glänzendem Schwarz, tiefem Rot, Orange und Weiß erzeugen eine kaleidoskopische Musterung, die von eindrucksvoller Tapetengrafik bis zu Wandspiegeln reicht.

Große, weiße, an der Decke aufgehängte „Kokons" enthalten Projektoren und Bewegungsmelder für die „E-Tische" des Restaurants. Auf dem virtuellen Tischtuch können die Gäste Speisen und Getränke bestellen und während der Wartezeit Spiele spielen, ihren gegenwärtigen Standort erkunden oder sogar ihre eigenen Bildschirmschoner gestalten. Auf der beleuchteten Fläche lässt sich sogar live die Vorbereitung der Mahlzeiten über ein „Chef-Cam" verfolgen und dabei das Niveau des Restaurants überprüfen.

01

02

01 The restaurant's graphic interior style and exterior signage derive from traditional South East Asian print design

02 Ideal lighting conditions to make diners feel both comfortable and entertained

03 Seating in monochrome colours by Protocol

Ce restaurant panasiatique offre une expérience sur le plan gastronomique, mais aussi en termes de design avec le premier système interactif de commandes au monde.

Une entrée centrale conduit les clients à un petit hall qui annonce la gamme de couleurs de l'identité. Des designs d'origami brillants en noir, rouge sombre, orange et blanc créent des motifs kaléidoscopiques, des graphismes des papiers peints aux miroirs muraux.

De grands « cocons » blancs suspendus renferment des projecteurs et des capteurs de mouvement pour les « e-tables » du restaurant. Les nappes virtuelles permettent aux clients de commander les plats et les boissons, ainsi que de jouer à des jeux, rechercher leur emplacement actuel ou encore créer leurs propres économiseurs d'écran pendant qu'ils attendent.

L'interface éclairée leur permet même de suivre en
direct la préparation des plats grâce à une caméra
en cuisine ; le processus de surveillance vidéo
se fait ainsi une place dans la restauration.

Le Sergent Recruteur

Website	lesergentrecruteur.fr
Date Opened	October 2012
Designer	Hayonstudio
Cost of Build	$$$$
Size of Build	200 m² / 2,150 ft²
Award	Shortlist 2013
Address	41 Rue Saint-Louis-en-l'Isle
	75004 Paris
	France

Named after a 16th-century brasserie formerly on the site, this narrow space beside the Seine extends over two levels, ground and basement. The site's medieval origins served as design inspiration, reinvigorated with a fresh and contemporary perspective through hand-made ceramics, masks, paintings and other artworks.

The complexities of the architecture set various restrictions that had to be negotiated in creating an environment in which art, conversation and dining could be balanced. Similarly, the poor condition of many of the original features encouraged the opening-up of the space to make a warmer and more relaxing atmosphere.

Removing a *faux*-medieval wall separating the bar from the dining area created new space, a thick glass door with angled cuts in its place forming a newly functional feature decorated with honeycombs.

01

Dieses schmale, nach einer früher auf diesem Gelände bestehenden Brasserie aus dem 16. Jahrhundert benannte Lokal an der Seine liegt im Erd- und im Untergeschoss. Die mittelalterliche Vergangenheit des Gebäudes diente als Inspiration für das Design und wurde aus einem frischen, zeitgemäßen Blickwinkel durch handgefertigte Keramik, Masken, Gemälde und andere Kunstwerke wiederbelebt.

Die vielschichtige Architektur verursachte diverse Einschränkungen, die bei der Planung eines Umfelds, in dem Kunst, Konversation und Speisen gleichermaßen ihren Platz haben sollten, zu berücksichtigen waren. Auch legte der schlechte Zustand der originalen Bausubstanz nahe, den Raum weiter zu öffnen, um ihm eine wärmere und entspanntere Atmosphäre zu verleihen.

Durch Entfernung einer nicht-mittelalterlichen Wand, welche die Bar vom Essbereich abtrennte, wurde neuer Raum gewonnen. Eine schwere, im Waffelmuster dekorierte Glastür mit großen Einschnitten bildet ein neues funktionales Element.

Du même nom que la brasserie du XVIᵉ siècle qui l'a précédé, cet espace étroit près de la Seine se distribue sur deux niveaux (rez-de-chaussée et sous-sol). Les origines médiévales du lieu ont inspiré le projet de design et reçu une touche de fraîcheur et de contemporain au travers de céramiques artisanales, de masques et de tableaux, entre autres œuvres d'art.

Les difficultés architecturales ont imposé plusieurs restrictions. Pour y remédier, l'environnement créé permet l'équilibre entre art, conversations et gastronomie. Nombre éléments d'origine étant endommagés, l'espace a été ouvert pour rendre l'atmosphère plus chaleureuse et agréable.

Grâce à la suppression d'un faux mur médiéval entre le bar et la salle, un nouvel espace a été dégagé. Une épaisse porte en verre taillé et aux ornements alvéolaires forme un nouvel élément fonctionnel.

01 Upholstered green fabric, golds and marble top surfaces feature throughout

02 A series of lights and tinted mirrors were used to open up the otherwise narrow space

03 A modern take on a medieval theme – a large panelled Venetian mirror hangs on one wall

Les Grandes Tables

Website	lesgrandestables.com/de-l-ile-seguin
Date Opened	2011
Designer	1024 architecture
Size of Build	300 m² / 3,250 ft²
Award	Category winner 2012
Address	Île Seguin
	92100 Boulogne-Billancourt
	France

On a small island on the outskirts of Paris, this temporary building is home to a bar and *al fresco* café. Set in what is also a temporary garden, the raw materials of the building's structure acknowledge its short life-span with a novel innovation.

Scaffolding suspends the single-floored structure a few metres above the ground, with access via steel stairways or a lift offering an elevated view of the surrounding area. The industrial theme continues inside, where the large dining area is fitted with wood-fibre panels and lines of canteen-style tables and chairs with simple indoor lighting fixtures.

Illumination at night is a special focus of attention. With lighting effects that can be programmed and changed as desired, the basic structural materials are transformed into a radically eye-catching design.

Auf einer kleinen Insel außerhalb von Paris befinden sich in diesem temporären Bau eine Bar und ein *Al-fresco*-Café. Die unbehandelten Materialien des Gebäudes in dem ebenfalls zeitweiligen Garten sind auf ganz neue, ungewohnte Weise Ausdruck seiner kurzen Lebensdauer.

Ein Gerüst trägt den eingeschossigen Bau, der einige Meter über Geländehöhe steht. Der Zugang erfolgt über Stahltreppen oder einen Aufzug, von oben erschließt sich der Blick über die Umgebung. Das industriell gefertigte Material setzt sich im Innern fort, wo der große Essbereich mit Holzfaserplatten verkleidet und im Kantinenstil mit aufgereihten Tischen und Stühlen sowie schlichter Beleuchtung ausgestattet ist.

Die nächtliche Illuminationn ist ein besonderer Attraktionspunkt. Lichteffekte, die sich nach Belieben programmieren und verändern lassen, verwandeln die einfachen Baustoffe in ein eindrucksvolles Ensemble.

01

Sur une petite île en périphérie de Paris, ce bâtiment temporaire héberge un bar et un café avec terrasse. Le jardin qui l'entoure est aussi temporaire, et les matières premières employées pour sa structure dénotent de façon innovante qu'il n'est pas amené à durer.

Des échafaudages soutiennent à quelques mètres du sol la structure sur un niveau, auquel conduisent un escalier en acier et un ascenseur avec vue sur les environs. Le décor industriel se prolonge à l'intérieur : les murs de l'immense salle de restaurant sont recouverts de panneaux en fibre de bois, et les rangées de tables et de chaises dignes d'un réfectoire sont éclairées par des lampes simples.

La nuit, l'éclairage retient toute l'attention. Des effets de lumière peuvent être programmés et changés à souhait, et ils transforment les matériaux basiques en une installation très attrayante.

01 Red freight containers have been hung from the scaffolding to create extra space

02 The café can accommodate 120 seated diners

"An architecture which must be able to disappear without leaving any traces."

1024 architecture

02

Minibar

Date Opened	March 2009
Date Closed	September 2011
Designer	Concrete
Size of Build	120 m² / 1,300 ft²
Award	Longlist 2010
Address	Prinsengracht 478
	1017 KG Amsterdam
	Netherlands

01

The aim of three Dutch friends wanting to open a bar near the Prinsengracht canal was to eliminate queuing, bringing the convenience of having a fridge at home to a night out in the city.

Visitors collect a key to their own minbar for the evening at the reception desk and then have a choice of either champagne, beer or combination bars. Three large fridges, each with 15 separate doors, cater for the guests while a security system indicates when a fridge has been opened so that staff may restock from the back of house, thereby not intruding in the main room.

The long and narrow 1960s building was formerly a timber workshop. A glass door set back within the entrance forms a small area for smokers and is equipped with a vintage cigarette-machine, also from the 1960s.

Drei Freunde in Holland hatten das Ziel, an der Prinsengracht eine Bar zu eröffnen, in der es keine Warteschlangen gibt und die Annehmlichkeit eines heimischen Kühlschranks auf einen nächtlichen Aufenthaltsort in der Stadt übertragen werden kann.

Die Besucher erhalten an der Rezeption einen Schlüssel zu ihrer eigenen Minibar für den Abend und haben dann die Wahl zwischen einer Champagner-, Bier- oder kombinierten Bar. Drei große Kühleinheiten mit jeweils 15 Türen versorgen die Gäste, wobei ein Sicherheitssystem wahrnimmt, sobald einer davon geöffnet wird, sodass das Personal ihn von hinten auffüllen kann, ohne den Speiseraum zu betreten.

Das lange, schmale Gebäude aus den 1960er Jahren war früher eine Holzwerkstatt. Eine Glastür im Eingangsbereich trennt einen kleinen Raum für die Raucher ab, der mit einem alten Zigarettenautomaten aus derselben Zeit ausgestattet ist.

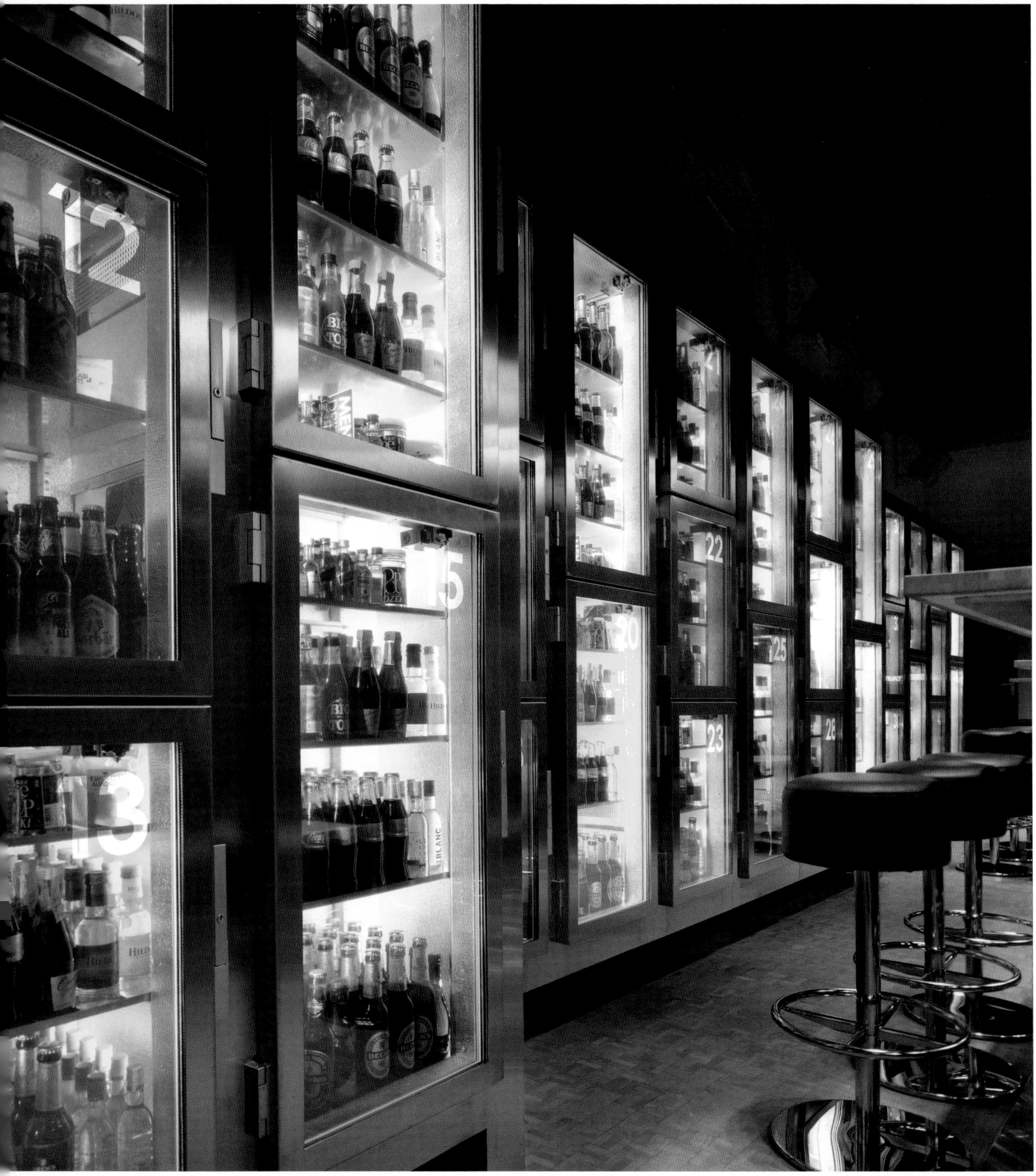

02

Pour ouvrir ce bar près du canal Prinsengracht, l'objectif de trois amis hollandais était d'éliminer les files d'attente en offrant l'aspect pratique d'un réfrigérateur lors d'une virée en ville.

Les clients se procurent à la réception la clé de leur propre minibar, où ils trouvent du champagne, des bières ou un assortiment de boissons. Trois grands réfrigérateurs, chacun comptant 15 portes, sont destinés au public. Un système de sécurité signale quand l'un d'eux est ouvert pour que le personnel le réapprovisionne depuis l'arrière, sans devoir passer par la salle.

Ce bâtiment long et étroit datant des années 60 est un ancien atelier de menuiserie. Une porte en verre en retrait dans l'entrée libère un petit espace fumeur doté d'un distributeur de cigarettes vintage, également des années 60.

01 The low side-tables and central bars are made from oak on steel frames, set beside leather-upholstered banquette and bar-stools designed by Pedrali

02 The fridges were installed at an angle, allowing them all to be viewed at the same time

03 Cylindrical lights designed by Tom Dixon dangle from the ceiling, their anodised-gold inner finish refracting the light across the room

03

Mirage Dance-hall

Website	falsterbostrandbad.se
Date Opened	2009
Designer	Kjellgren Kaminsky Architecture
Size of Build	1,600 m² / 17,200 ft²
Award	Longlist 2010
Address	Strandbadsvagen 30
	239 21 Falsterbo
	Sweden

After a fire in 2006 destroyed a much-cherished 1930s dance-hall in the historic town of Falsterbo, a high-profile competition was established to build a new one and once again attract young visitors in the summer.

On the same site as its predecessor, the new hall was installed using prefabricated concrete to minimise ecological impact on the surrounding nature reserve. An entrance staircase runs diagonally across the two-storey complex, which houses a dance floor, two restaurants, kitchen, bar and veranda.

Soundproofing was essential, to stop noise ricocheting inside and leaking outdoors. An acoustics engineer helped design the 'damping walls', realised in the form of a forest pattern which matches the surrounding pines and was inexpensively made using white wooden boards overlaid on black acoustic felt.

Nachdem ein Feuer 2006 einen beliebten Tanzsaal aus den 1930er Jahren in der historischen Stadt Falsterbo zerstört hatte, wurde ein öffentlicher Wettbewerb ausgeschrieben für einen Neubau, der wieder für junge Menschen im Sommer attraktiv sein sollte.

Auf dem Gelände ihres Vorgängerbaus wurde die neue Halle aus vorgefertigtem Beton errichtet, um die ökologischen Auswirkungen auf das umgebende Naturreservat gering zu halten. Eine Treppe führt diagonal durch den zweigeschossigen Komplex, der einen Tanzsaal, zwei Restaurants, Küche, Bar und Veranda umfasst.

Entscheidend war der Schallschutz, um den Lärm nach innen wie nach außen zu reduzieren. Ein Akustikingenieur war an der Planung der „schalldämpfenden Wände" beteiligt, die nach dem System eines Waldes errichtet wurden, das zu den Kiefern in der Umgebung passt und preiswert aus weißen, mit schwarzem Akustikfilz überzogenen Holzbrettern hergestellt werden konnte.

01 Steps in forest green mimic the surrounding foliage

02 Grey fibre cement boards clad to the outside walls also help reduce noise levels, while mirrored glass dotted on its surface evokes a certain mirage, inspired from photos of the original 1930s dance-hall

03 The new dance-hall can host up to 1,500 people

03

Après l'incendie ayant détruit en 2006 une salle de danse très populaire des années 30 dans la ville historique de Falsterbo, un concours de grande envergure a été lancé pour en construire une nouvelle et attirer la jeune clientèle en été.

Au même endroit que celle d'avant, la nouvelle salle de danse a été érigée en béton préfabriqué pour réduire l'impact écologique sur la réserve naturelle environnante. Un escalier d'accès monte en diagonale dans le complexe de deux étages, qui renferme une salle de danse, deux restaurants, une cafétéria, un bar et une véranda.

L'insonorisation était essentielle pour empêcher le bruit de résonner et de se propager à l'extérieur. Un ingénieur en acoustique a aidé à concevoir des « murs amortisseurs » bon marché : le motif rappelle une forêt à l'image des pins au dehors, grâce à des planches de bois recouvrant une toile acoustique noire.

"When designing we always work with our manifesto which puts focus on people, needs and context."

Kjellgren Kaminsky Architecture, World Buildings Directory

Oriel

Website	orielbrasserie.co.uk
Date Opened	December 2011
Designer	Afroditi Krassa
Cost of Build	$$$$+
Size of Build	355 m² / 3,800 ft²
Award	Shortlist 2012
Address	Heathrow Terminal 3, Unit R3017
	Hounslow TW6 1QG
	UK

A nostalgic haven bringing a touch of the golden age of travel to today's Heathrow airport, Oriel is at the same time a reincarnation of the celebrated brasserie of that name in Sloane Square that welcomed customers for over 25 years.

In researching the design in a number of Europe's smartest cafés, it became apparent that stylised art deco interiors were as important in making each place a success as creating a space in which customers felt perfectly at ease.

Classical proportions were used to set the geometry of the space, then furnished with vintage details such as the art deco-style motifs and photographs of early explorers. Mirrors, green-veined marble and dark wood offset the herringbone-tiled floor, with the theme extending also to the design of the signage.

Als nostalgischer Zufluchtsort verleiht Oriel dem heutigen Flughafen Heathrow ein Flair aus dem goldenen Zeitalter des Reisens. Das Lokal ist zugleich eine Reinkarnation der berühmten Brasserie dieses Namens am Sloane Square, die über 25 Jahre Gäste empfing.

Bei der Untersuchung einer Reihe von Europas beliebtesten Cafés wurde deutlich, dass Ausstattungen im Stil des Art déco stets jedes dieser Lokale erfolgreich und zu einem Ort gemacht haben, an dem sich die Besucher absolut wohlfühlen.

Klassische Proportionen bestimmen die Geometrie des Raumes, der mit Retro-Details wie Motiven im Art-déco-Stil und Fotografien von frühen Entdeckern ausgestattet wurde. Spiegel, grün geäderter Marmor und dunkles Holz kontrastieren mit dem im Fischgrätenmuster gefliesten Boden. Das Thema setzt sich bis in die Gestaltung der Beschilderung fort.

Ce refuge nostalgique fait revivre l'âge d'or des voyages à l'aéroport d'Heathrow. Oriel est aussi la réincarnation de la célèbre brasserie du même nom à Sloane Square, qui a accueilli des clients pendant plus de 25 ans.

Lors de l'étude du design des cafés les mieux conçus d'Europe, il s'est avéré que les intérieurs de style art déco cherchent un agencement pratique dans lequel les clients se sentent tout à fait à leur aise.

Les proportions classiques ont été appliquées pour définir la géométrie de l'espace. Le mobilier a été assorti de détails vintage, comme des motifs art déco et des photographies des premiers explorateurs. Des miroirs, du marbre vert veiné et du bois sombre créent l'équilibre avec le sol au motif en épi, tout comme la signalétique.

01 The restaurant is named after a style of bay window, found throughout history and across the world from France to India

02 The slightly raised booths have parquet floors and green leather seats, continuing the feel of quality throughout the restaurant

02

"Oriel, by the way, is a type of window, hence the prominent, elongated feature windows alongside the booth seating."

Afroditi Krassa

Paramount

Website	paramount.uk.net
Date Opened	May 2010
Designer	Tom Dixon
Cost of Build	$$$$
Size of Build	1,356 m² / 14,600 ft²
Award	Shortlist 2009
Address	Centre Point, 101-103 New Oxford Street
	London WC1A 1DD
	UK

More than 30 floors up in the Centre Point building, this sumptuously laid-out restaurant, bar and events space stretches over two high-rise levels. A robust interior design was influenced by the breathtaking views and brutalist architecture of the office block designed by Richard Seifert, which opened to the public in 1966.

A large shaped-copper bar, stretching ten metres in length, has been built from protruding polyhedral forms. Its dominating futuristic tone likewise mimics the V-shaped concrete windows that run the height of the tower block.

The seating, a combination of bright red and muted retro styles, was similarly chosen to fit with the Modernist aesthetic, and has been twinned with low lighting to encourage guests to relax and drink in the view.

Dieses über 30 Geschosse hoch im Centre-Point-Building liegende, prächtig ausgestattete Restaurant mit Bar und Veranstaltungsbereich erstreckt sich über zwei Stockwerke. Die robuste Innenausstattung wurde von den atemberaubenden Ausblicken und der brutalistischen Architektur des von Richard Seifert geplanten Bürogebäudes bestimmt, das 1966 fertiggestellt wurde.

Eine große, zehn Meter lange Bar aus Kupferblech bildet auskragende vielflächige Formen. In ihrer dominanten, futuristischen Wirkung entspricht dies in gewissem Sinne den v-förmigen Betonfenstern an der gesamten Fassade des Hochhauses.

Auch die Bestuhlung, eine Kombination aus leuchtendem Rot und reduziertem Retro-Stil, wurde gewählt, um der modernen Ästhetik gerecht zu werden, und lädt die Gäste bei gedämpfter Beleuchtung ein, sich zu entspannen und zu genießen.

01 Dixon worked in conjunction with GIA Equation to conceive and design the special lighting

02 Norman Cherner's plywood stools line the bar and allow guests to look out over views of London from the 33rd floor

03 Luscious red sculpturally shaped *Organic Chairs* by Charles Eames & Eero Saarinen for Vitra line the tables

04 A semi-transparent partitioning wall carries a geometric design complemented by a selection of turquoise *Cone Chairs* by Verner Panton in the foreground

Plus de 30 étages en haut de l'édifice Centre Point, ce restaurant, bar et lieu d'événements au décor somptueux se distribue sur deux niveaux élevés. Le design d'intérieur est robuste et s'inspire des vues imprenables et de l'architecture brutaliste de l'immeuble de bureaux conçu par Richard Seifert, ouvert au public en 1966.

Long de dix mètres, un bar généreux et géométrique en cuivre a été construit à base de formes polyédriques saillantes. Sa touche futuriste imite la forme en V des fenêtres en béton alignées sur la façade de la tour.

Les chaises combinent le rouge vif et des styles rétro neutres. Elles ont été choisies pour se fondre dans l'esthétique moderniste et mariées à un éclairage faible permettant aux clients de se détendre et d'admirer la vue.

04

03

Paul Hamlyn Hall Champagne Bar

Website	roh.org.uk
Date Opened	September 2011
Designer	B3 Designers
Size of Build	830 m² / 8,900 ft²
Award	Shortlist 2012
Address	Royal Opera House, Bow Street
	London WC2E 9DD
	UK

This curved iron and glass atrium is located within the Royal Opera House in Covent Garden. The completed building in 1870 was originally used as an exotic flower market – now transformed into a champagne bar with an upper-level restaurant.

The redesigned hall features a cantilever bar which may be removed for special functions, a smoothly curved oval with an illuminated bar-top which forms a radiant centrepiece in the impressive space. The bar is wrapped in Scottish quilted leather with a harlequin pattern, offset by down-lighting.

Given the large swells of people that descend on the bar during intervals, making use of the space was a key consideration. By siting attractive table-lamps on the far walls visitors are drawn to the less-crowded perimeter of the hall to enjoy their drinks.

Dieses überwölbte Atrium aus Eisen und Glas befindet sich im Royal Opera House in Covent Garden. Das 1870 fertiggestellte Gebäude wurde ursprünglich als exotischer Blumenmarkt genutzt – jetzt wurde dort eine Champagnerbar mit einem Restaurant auf der oberen Ebene eingerichtet.

Im Zentrum der umgestalteten Halle befindet sich eine frei stehende Bar, die für spezielle Veranstaltungen abgebaut werden kann. Das flach abgerundete Oval hat einen beleuchteten Aufsatz und bildet einen strahlenden Mittelpunkt im dem eindrucksvollen Raum. Die Bar ist mit schottischem Lederquilt verkleidet und mit Deckenstrahlern ausgeleuchtet.

Der große Personenandrang während der Pausen stellte ein besonderes Problem dar. Tischlampen an den entfernteren Wänden locken die Besucher an den weniger bevölkerten Rand der Halle, wo sie ihren Drink genießen können.

01

03   Cet atrium voûté en fer et en verre se loge à l'intérieur du Royal Opera House, à Covent Garden. Achevé en 1870, le bâtiment servait à l'origine de marché aux fleurs exotiques ; il est aujourd'hui un bar à champagne avec un restaurant au niveau supérieur.

Après sa rénovation, le hall présente un bar en porte-à-faux pouvant être retiré pour des occasions spéciales ; de forme ovale, son comptoir est éclairé, devenant ainsi la pièce maîtresse de cet espace spectaculaire. Le bar est recouvert de cuir matelassé au motif arlequin, avec un éclairage vers le bas.

Il était déterminant de bien penser l'usage de l'espace en raison des flots de gens qui accèdent au bar à certains moments. L'installation de lampes de table attrayantes le long des murs les plus éloignés évite l'accumulation des clients et les conduit à un périmètre plus calme pour prendre un verre.

01 Quality materials used throughout include Hungarian wooden flooring and upholstered *Domus* chairs by Finnish brand, Artek

02 A mirror on the rear wall was extended so that it now runs floor to ceiling, further dramatising the hall's proportions

03 A reception held in the hall, named after the generous donation of the Paul Hamlyn Foundation, can accommodate up to 1,000 guests

04 The 13.5-metre bar can be arranged in three different ways, in accordance with the size of the crowd, and is equipped with 16 serving points

Phill

Website	facebook.com/phill.restaurant
Date Opened	October 2011
Designer	Nuca Studio
Cost of Build	$$$$
Size of Build	600 m² / 6,450 ft²
Award	Longlist 2012
Address	120 Drumul Potcoavei, Pipera
	77191 Bucharest
	Romania

01

Catering for theatre-lovers and puppet-show fans, this bright and open family-friendly restaurant serves modern cuisine from all across the globe. Customers themselves were involved in the planning stage by expressing the ideal features they would look for.

The overall design, from wall and floor graphics to tiling and decoration, pays homage to Japanese anime and manga. An outsized music-loving white elephant has painted-on headphones and an MP3-player, and the staircase that skirts it connects the ground-floor restaurant to a playground and theatre space in the basement below.

The air-duct system is concealed by making the interior work around the operational features. Moulding techniques produced geometric shapes and contours which created a world of appealing curves and smooth surfaces.

In diesem hellen, offenen und familienfreundlichen Restaurant werden Liebhaber von Schauspiel und Puppentheater aus aller Welt mit moderner Küche bewirtet. Die Besucher waren selbst in den Planungsprozess einbezogen und konnten ihnen wichtig erscheinende Merkmale zur Diskussion stellen.

Die Gesamtgestaltung, von der Grafik auf Boden und Wänden bis zu den Fliesen und der Dekoration, ist eine Hommage an japanische Zeichentrickfilme und Mangas. Einem übergroßen, musikliebenden weißen Elefanten wurden Kopfhörer und ein MP3-Player aufgemalt. Die um ihn herumführende Treppe verbindet das Restaurant im Erdgeschoss mit einem Spiel- und einem Theaterraum im Untergeschoss.

Das Lüftungssystem ist hinter den funktionalen Einrichtungen verborgen. Gegossene geometrische Formen erzeugen ein Umfeld aus ansprechenden Kurven und glatten Oberflächen.

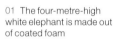

02

01 The four-metre-high
white elephant is made out
of coated foam

02 A vivid colour palette of
purple, green, yellow and red
graphics emphasises the
circular interior windows cut
into the walls which allow dining
parents to keep an eye on
their children whilst they play

03 Fun and airy, the restaurant
combines classic design with
playful tactility as in the
kaleidoscopic *DSW* chairs by
Charles & Ray Eames

03

Ce restaurant clair et ouvert, d'ambiance familiale, offre une cuisine moderne du monde entier aux amoureux du théâtre et aux fans de spectacles de marionnettes. Les propres clients ont été impliqués dans l'étape de planification en faisant part des caractéristiques idéales qu'ils aimeraient y trouver.

Tout le design, des graphismes sur les murs et le sol au carrelage et à la décoration, rend hommage aux dessins animés et mangas japonais. Sur un gigantesque éléphant blanc sont peints un casque et un lecteur MP3, comme si l'animal écoutait de la musique, alors que l'escalier qui le contourne relie le restaurant au rez-de-chaussée à une aire de jeu et à la salle de théâtre au sous-sol.

Le système de conduits d'air est caché, l'intérieur enveloppant les éléments fonctionnels. Grâce à des techniques de moulure, des formes et des contours géométriques donnent vie à un monde attrayant de courbes et de surfaces lisses.

Rocambolesc Gelateria

Website	rocambolesc.com
Date Opened	April 2012
Designer	Sandra Tarruella Interioristas
Cost of Build	$
Size of Build	64,5 m² / 690 ft²
Award	Category winner 2013
Address	Calle Santa Clara, 50
	17001 Girona
	Spain

A small ice-cream parlour which harks back to days of old, when ice-cream making used all-natural ingredients.

Seeking a new approach to an old concept, the design conjures up a place that combines childhood fantasy with eccentric machines. Inspired by the gadgets of Heath Robinson and the illustrations of *Charlie and the Chocolate Factory*, the playful interior is a wonderful world of levers and strange gizmos.

Brightly striped pipes run across the space and are used for dispensing napkins, spoons or bags. A bicycle-cart is parked inside the parlour while the big serving-counter takes the form of an ice-cream trolley, nods to the past when ice-cream sellers would cycle through the streets with their wares.

Eine kleine Eisdiele wie in alten Tagen, als das Eis nur aus natürlichen Zutaten hergestellt wurde.

Der Entwurf, eine neue Lösung für ein altes Konzept, beschwört einen Ort, der Kinderfantasien mit ausgefallenen Maschinen verbindet. Inspiriert von den Geräten von Heath Robinson und den Illustrationen zu Roald Dahls Buch *Charlie und die Schokoladenfabrik*, ist der verspielte Innenraum eine wundervolle Welt voller Schalter und anderen kuriosen Dingen.

Bunt gestreifte Rohre führen durch den Raum und dienen zum Entsorgen von Servietten, Löffeln und Tüten. Ein Fahrradkarren ist in der Eisdiele geparkt, und die große Theke hat die Form eines Eiswagens – ein Hinweis auf die Zeit, als die Eisverkäufer noch mit ihrer Ware durch die Straßen fuhren.

01

> ## "The wall represents a fantastical industrial ice-cream machine; it has movement, lights and even sound."
>
> **Sandra Tarruella Interioristas**

02

03

Ce petit glacier nous renvoie d'antan, quand la fabrication des glaces était à base d'ingrédients naturels.

Recherchant une approche nouvelle pour un concept ancien, le design plante un lieu mêlant rêves d'enfant et machines excentriques. Inspiré des gadgets de Heath Robinson et des illustrations de *Charlie et la fabrique de chocolat*, l'intérieur ludique est un monde merveilleux de leviers et d'objets bizarres.

Des tuyaux rayés de couleur vive circulent dans l'espace et servent de distributeurs de serviettes, de cuillères ou de sachets. Un vélo avec une remorque avant est garé à l'intérieur, alors que le grand comptoir a la forme d'un chariot à glaces. Tout évoque le temps où les vendeurs de glaces circulaient à vélo dans les rues pour vendre leur marchandise.

01 Door handles take the form of
levers for the glass-door entrance

02 Ice-cream cups are dispensed
from a slatted rack made of oak,
a reference to the materials used in
the sister venue, El Celler de Can
Roca restaurant

03 Suspended boxes provide
additional storage and display
space, hanging from scissor
mechanisms in keeping with
the magical setting

04 A candy-floss machine helps
make a wide range of toppings to
accompany the various ice-cream
flavours available, which are written
up on the glass frontage and
mirrored wall

Searcys St. Pancras Grand

Website	searcys.co.uk
Date Opened	September 2008
Designer	Martin Brudnizki Design Studio
Award	Shortlist 2009
Address	Grand Terrace St. Pancras International Station London N1C 4QL UK

Set within the hyper-modern redevelopment of King's Cross St. Pancras railway station, the interior design here gestures to a far-away nostalgic world, inspired by the classic style of railway décor of yesteryear. Up to 200 guests can be accommodated, amongst the Oyster Bar, Whisky Bar and Betjeman Room for private dining.

The romance of rail travel is evoked through the use of seductive features and quality materials, such as the herringbone laid-oak floor which runs throughout the interior. Brass fittings and mirror-lined walls reflect a golden hue which softens the opaline glass lighting.

The dining area is fitted out with tables set with crisp white tablecloths coupled with stylish blue and brown leather banquettes and separated by custom-made screens with transparent art deco graphics.

In die hypermoderne Umgestaltung des Bahnhofs King's Cross St. Pancras integriert, simuliert die Innenarchitektur dieses Lokals eine weit zurückliegende, nostalgische Welt im Stil des klassischen Bahndekors der Vergangenheit. Bis zu 200 Gäste können hier bewirtet werden: in der Oyster Bar, der Whisky Bar und dem Betjeman Room für private Veranstaltungen.

Die Romantik des Eisenbahnfahrens wird durch verführerische Elemente und qualitätvolle Materialien heraufbeschworen, zum Beispiel das im Fischgräten-muster verlegte Eichenparkett im gesamten Innenbereich. Messinginstallationen und Spiegelwände reflektieren einen goldenen Farbton, der die Beleuchtung aus Opalglas dämpft.

Der Essbereich ist mit weiß gedeckten Tischen und eleganten blauen und braunen Lederbänken ausgestattet und mit transparenten, maßgefertigten Zwischenwänden in Art-déco-Musterung abgeteilt.

En parallèle du réaménagement ultramoderne de
la gare de King's Cross St. Pancras, ce design
d'intérieur renvoie à un monde nostalgique inspiré du
style classique des trains d'antan. Le Oyster Bar,
le Whisky Bar et la salle Betjeman peuvent accueillir
à eux trois jusqu'à 200 convives.

Le romantisme des voyages en train est palpable
dans le choix des éléments séduisants et des matériaux
de qualité, comme le sol en chêne en épi qui orne
les salles. Les ferrures en laiton et les murs recouverts
de miroirs renvoient une teinte blonde adoucissant
l'éclairage en verre opalin.

La salle de restaurant est meublée de tables aux
nappes d'un blanc éclatant, de banquettes stylisées
de couleur bleu et marron, ainsi que de panneaux transparents sur mesure aux motifs art déco pour séparer
les espaces.

01 With references to classic elements such as the station clock, a balance was found between the old and new, a spirit Head Chef Chris Dines continues in his menu combining old favourites with modern dishes

02 Awarded the Imbibe Seal of fine Whisky, Searcys St. Pancras Grand offers over 50 varieties, whilst opposite on the Grand Terrace is the Searcys Champagne Bar

02

Sketch

Website	sketch.uk.com
Date Opened	March 2012
Designer	Martin Creed
Award	Shortlist 2013
Address	9 Conduit Street
	London W1S 2XG
	UK

To mark their 10th anniversary and reaffirm their innovative outlook, Sketch invited Turner Prize-winning artist Martin Creed to reconsider one of their dining-spaces. The Gallery is an open-plan, ground-floor 'gastro-brasserie', a less formal space where art, food and design commingle.

Creed's is the first of a new long-term programme of artist-conceived interiors here. Exploring the relationship between art and functionality, he used a combination of ready-made objects and his own works. By treating floor, walls and furniture, he created a vibrant scene of colour, texture and form.

In the installation *Work No.1343*, mass-produced items sit beside specially handcrafted classic and antique pieces. No two objects are the same, whether cutlery, glassware, tables or chairs, while this eclectic array has been set against an ordered pattern of repeating graphics on the walls and floor, creating an energetic explosion of visual stimuli.

Zur Feier seines zehnten Jahrestags und Bestätigung seiner innovativen Ausrichtung lud Sketch den Künstler und Turner-Preisträger Martin Creed ein, einen der Speisesäle neu zu gestalten. Die Gallery ist eine „Gastro-Brasserie" im Erdgeschoss mit offenem Grundriss, ein eher informeller Raum, in dem Kunst, Essen und Design zusammentreffen.

Creeds hier realisierte Gestaltung ist die erste von einem langfristig angesetzten Programm für von Künstlern gestaltete Räume. Er kombiniert Gebrauchsgegenstände mit eigenen Kunstwerken, und setzt sich so mit der Beziehung von Kunst und Funktionalität auseinander. Creed bezieht Boden, Wände und die Einrichtung mit ein und kreiert eine lebendige Szenerie aus Farbe, Struktur und Form.

In der Rauminstallation *Work No.1343* stehen industriell produzierte neben speziell handgefertigten klassischen Objekten und Antiquitäten. Keine zwei Stücke sind gleich, weder Bestecke, Gläser, Tische oder Stühle, wobei dieses eklektische Aufgebot im Kontrast zu einem geordneten System aus sich wiederholenden grafischen Elementen gesetzt ist, was zu einer kraftvollen Entladung visueller Anreize führt.

01

01 The series of 4 canvases, *Work No. 1100* (2011), is part of the 18 paintings by Creed which overlay his wall designs

02 *Work No. 1347* is a floor made from 96 different types of marble laid in a repeating zigzag pattern

03 Creed wanted "the whole world to be in it", his installation *Work No. 1343,* which was especially made for Sketch and comprises more than a thousand different items

02

À l'occasion de son 10ᵉ anniversaire et pour réaffirmer sa vision innovante, Sketch a demandé à Martin Creed, vainqueur du prix Turner, de repenser l'un de ses restaurants. En rez-de-chaussée, The Gallery est une brasserie gastronomique moins formelle où art, restauration et design ne font qu'un.

Le projet de Creed inaugure un nouveau programme à long terme d'intérieurs conçus par des artistes. Explorant la relation entre l'art et le fonctionnel, il associe des objets aux œuvres des artistes. Son travail sur le sol, les murs et le mobilier lui a permis d'obtenir un décor dynamique de couleurs, textures et formes.

Dans son installation *Work No. 1343*, des objets fabriqués en série cohabitent avec des antiquités et des pièces artisanales. Couverts, verres, tables, chaises, il n'y a pas deux objets identiques. L'ensemble éclectique a été installé sur fond de graphismes récurrents sur les murs et au sol pour une stimulation visuelle explosive.

03

Snog Soho

Website	ifancyasnog.com
Date Opened	March 2009
Designer	Cinimod Studio
Cost of Build	$$$
Size of Build	15 m² / 160 ft²
Award	Shortlist 2010
Address	9 Brewer Street
	London W1F 0RG
	UK

This branch of the frozen-yoghurt bar chain attracts passers-by with its polychromatic ceiling lighting installation. Spilling out on to the street, a spectrum of evolving colours bathes customers inside in bright pinks, intense fuchsias and golden yellows.

The design had to complement the brand's bright identity and it was this which resulted in a space that conjured up the illusive and tantalising experience of a 'never-ending summer'.

The main feature is the 'bubbling globe ceiling', made from 700 glass globes suspended above the long white counter and seating area to suggest the nostalgic warmth and festival vibes of the summer months. The same spirit is also reflected in the photographic grass floor.

Diese Filiale einer Frozen-Yoghurt-Kette lockt Passanten durch ihre vielfarbige Lichtinstallation an der Decke heran. Ein Spektrum sich verändernder Farben fällt auf die Straße und taucht die Besucher im Innern in leuchtendes Rosa, Purpurrot und Goldgelb.

Das Design sollte das erfolgreiche Image der Firma hervorheben und hat zu einem Interieur geführt, welches das illusionistische und verlockende Erlebnis eines „nie endenden Sommers" heraufbeschwört.

Hauptmerkmal ist die „wogende Kugeldecke" aus 700 über der langen weißen Theke und dem Sitzbereich aufgehängten Glaskugeln, um die nostalgische Wärme und eine festliche Atmosphäre der Sommermonate anzudeuten. Die gleiche Stimmung spiegelt der fotografisch reproduzierte Grasboden.

02

01 Made with rotational moulding, the irregular surface of the *Shitake* seats designed by Marcel Wanders adds to the playful environment

02 At the far end of the space a wall is dedicated to murals, which are changed each season

03 The ceiling required a special lighting system whose design and manufacture had to be closely overseen

03

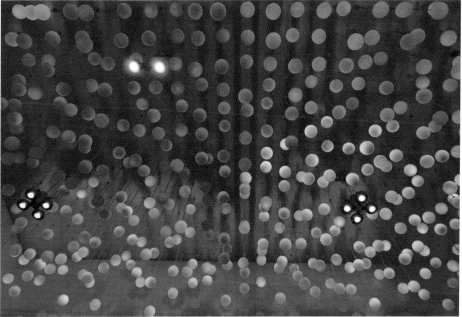

Cette filiale d'une chaîne de vente de yaourts glacés attire les passants grâce à son éclairage polychromatique au plafond. Se prolongeant dans la rue, un spectre de couleurs changeantes baigne les clients de lumière rose vif, fuchsia intense et jaune doré.

Le design devait respecter l'identité éclatante de la marque. Le résultat est un espace qui évoque la douce illusion d'un été sans fin.

L'élément principal est un plafond « bouillonnant », avec 700 globes de verre suspendus au-dessus du long comptoir blanc et des sièges. L'idée étant d'évoquer la chaleur et l'ambiance des festivals pendant les mois d'été, une photo de gazon a aussi été choisie comme revêtement au sol.

The Crescent Inn

Website	thecrescentinn.co.uk
Date Opened	June 2011
Designer	Robert Angell Design Studio
Cost of Build	$$
Size of Build	75 m² / 750 ft²
Award	Longlist 2012
Address	Brook Street
	Ilkley
	West Yorkshire LS29 8DG
	UK

In refurbishing the original 1861 stone building's interior, this former hotel in the market town of Ilkley has been transformed into a traditional-style public house attracting locals and visitors alike.

As most of the original features had been replaced with the different functions the building had served, it was the structure's basic proportions which determined how it was to be refitted. A stone-pillared entrance leads to an authentic curved bar serving real ales, with bright-blue walls offsetting the dark-wood furnishings which continue up and out into the guest rooms.

The moorland landscape and local wool factories helped inspire the design concept. Specially sourced antique town-hall benches, copper-topped tables and solid oak chairs upholstered with locally produced cloth are all redolent of the rich heritage of the surrounding area.

Bei der Modernisierung der Innenräume dieses Natursteingebäudes von 1861 wurde das frühere Hotel im Marktflecken Ilkley in eine für Einheimische und Besucher gleichermaßen attraktive öffentliche Einrichtung im traditionellen Stil umgewandelt.

Da die meisten originalen Elemente wegen der veränderten Funktion des Gebäudes ersetzt werden mussten, konnten bei diesem Umbau lediglich die originalen Grundproportionen beibehalten werden. Der Eingang zwischen steinernen Pfeilern führt zu einer stilgerechten Bar, in der echtes Ale ausgeschenkt wird. Die leuchtend blauen Wände bilden einen Kontrast zur dunklen Holzmöblierung, die sich bis in die Gästezimmer fortsetzt.

Das Entwurfskonzept wurde von der Moorlandschaft und den örtlichen Wollfabriken inspiriert. Gezielt dafür gesuchte alte Rathausbänke, mit Kupfer überzogene Tische und solide, mit lokal produziertem Stoff bezogene Eichenstühle zeugen alle vom reichen Erbe dieser Region.

01

02

01 New skirting, wall panelling and cornices have been fitted to bring out the atmosphere of the original architecture

02 Carved, high-backed benches and ram's horn carver chairs were re-upholstered with local Yorkshire tweeds

03 Locally made bespoke brass lighting lines the Inn's interior walls, creating a warm comforting glow in the bar and dining areas

"The colours were inspired by the Yorkshire landscape and beautiful skies."

Robert Angell Design Studio

La rénovation de l'intérieur de cet immeuble en pierre datant de 1861 a transformé cet ancien hôtel dans le bourg d'Ilkley en brasserie de style traditionnel qui attire locaux et visiteurs.

L'aménagement n'a été conditionné que par les proportions de base de la structure, sachant que la plupart des éléments d'origine ont été remplacés à chaque fonction remplie par l'immeuble. L'entrée avec ses piliers en pierre mène à un bar courbe authentique auquel il est possible de commander une véritable ale. Les murs bleu clair contrastent avec le mobilier en bois sombre dans toutes les salles.

Le paysage marécageux et les usines de laines locales ont motivé le concept esthétique. De vieux bancs qui appartenaient à la mairie, des tables au plateau de cuivre, des chaises robustes en chêne tapissées d'un tissu fabriqué aux alentours : tous ces éléments évoquent le riche héritage de la région.

The Havana Club Mojito Embassy

Website	mojito-embassy.com
Date Opened	May 2012
Date Closed	May 2012
Designer	Campaign
Cost of Build	$$$$
Size of Build	440 m² / 4,750 ft²
Award	Shortlist 2013
Address	La Posteria, Via Giuseppe Sacchi 5/7
	20121 Milan
	Italy

Inspiration for this themed pop-up came from the colonial architecture and vibrant atmosphere of Havana's long coastal esplanade, and from Cuba's rum cocktail, the Mojito, whose different elements were deconstructed to create a multi-sensory environment for this touring project.

Illuminated signs and hand-painted graphics established an authentic atmosphere, where guests buy drinks at a saloon-bar modelled on a Cuban original, with dark-wood counter and mirrored walls. Chequered flooring and furniture made from reclaimed materials add to the ambience.

Accompanying the bar is a playful marketplace where trays of fresh mint, limes and rum provide all that's needed for making a Mojito. Scaffolding façades not only functioned as a trolley system to hold the ingredients, but could easily be reconfigured to suit each new location as the project toured.

Die Anregungen zu diesem Pop-up-Erlebnisrestaurant entstammten der kolonialen Architektur und der lebendigen Atmosphäre der langen Strandesplanade in Havanna sowie Kubas Rumcocktail, dem Mojito. Für diese mobile Einrichtung wurden unterschiedliche Elemente in einer die Sinne ansprechenden Umgebung zusammengefasst.

Beleuchtete Schilder und handgefertigte Grafiken erzeugen eine authentische Atmosphäre, in der die Gäste in einer Saloon-Bar nach original kubanischem Vorbild mit einer dunklen Holztheke und verspiegelten Wänden Getränke konsumieren können. Ein Fußboden mit Schachbrettmuster und Möbel aus wiederverwendetem Material ergänzen das Ambiente.

Zur Bar gehört auch eine Verkaufsstätte, wo man alles erwerben kann, was man zur Herstellung von Mojito braucht: frische Minze, Limonen und Rum. Regalwände funktionieren nicht nur als fahrbares Behältersystem, sondern können auch für jeden neuen Standort umgebaut werden.

01

02

01 Walls and furniture are plastered in a red and yellow collage, with slogans and newspaper cuttings relating to Cuban culture

02 Seating is made from salvaged materials and re-purposed furniture

03 The Havana Club Mojito Embassy, a pop-up bar concept devised by M&C Saatchi Sport & Entertainment, travelled around Europe from 2012 to 2013

Ce local thématique a puisé son inspiration dans l'architecture coloniale et l'ambiance animée du passage maritime de La Havane. Il affiche aussi les couleurs du Mojito, le célèbre cocktail cubain dont les ingrédients sont présentés séparément pour que ce projet itinérant se fasse dans un environnement multisensoriel.

   Des panneaux éclairés et des graphismes peints à la main apportent une touche d'authenticité. Les clients prennent un verre dans un salon-bar à l'image d'un local cubain, avec un comptoir en bois sombre et des murs recouverts de miroirs.

   Adjacent au bar, un marché coloré compte des stands de menthe fraîche, de citrons verts et de rhum pour faire le Mojito parfait. Les échafaudages servent de chariots pour ranger les ingrédients ; ils peuvent aussi être adaptés aux autres lieux que le projet visitera.

03

The Movement Café

Website	themovementgreenwich.com/mvmnt-cafe
Date Opened	July 2012
Date Closed	MAy 2013
Designer	Morag Myerscough
Cost of Build	$$$
Size of Build	140 m² / 1,500 ft²
Award	Shortlist 2013
Address	Waller Way, Greenwich London SE10 8JA UK

A witty combination of art, design and functionality, this pop-up space was a regeneration project set to coincide with the 2012 Olympic Games, and was put together in only 16 days. The aim was to create a social space to showcase a series of performances within a relaxed café environment.

The wooden structure required only shallow foundations to be dug, and housed a café, outside seating and small tiered-amphitheatre. An edible garden along the edge of the site was designed and maintained by Growing Greenwich volunteers and café staff.

The Official Poet of the Games, Lemn Sissay, worked with the designer to reconsider his poem, "Shipping Good". Bold colours illustrated the poem across 34 pieces of plywood attached to the café's scaffold tower, with the same hand-painted geometric forms also decorating other areas of the café.

Dieses Pop-up-Lokal, eine witzige Kombination aus Kunst, Design und Funktionalität, war ein anlässlich der Olympischen Spiele von 2012 wieder aufgegriffenes Projekt und wurde in nur 16 Tagen errichtet. Ein gemeinschaftlicher Bereich als Schauplatz für verschiedene Veranstaltungen in entspannter Café-Atmosphäre sollte geschaffen werden.

Die Holzkonstruktion benötigte nur eine flache Gründung und umfasste ein Café, Sitzflächen im Freien und ein kleines Amphitheater. Am Rande des Geländes wurde ein Nutzgarten angelegt, der von Freiwilligen des Projekts Growing Greenwich und dem Café-Personal gestaltet und gepflegt wurde.

Der Official Poet of the Games, Lemn Sissay, arbeitete mit dem Designer zusammen, um sein Gedicht „Shipping Good" optisch und in lebhaften Farben illustriert auf 34 Sperrholztafeln zu übertragen, die am Gerüst des Caféturms angebracht waren. Mit solchen handgemalten geometrischen Formen wurden auch andere Bereiche des Cafés dekoriert.

03

Mêlant avec humour art, design et fonctionnel, ce local éphémère s'est inscrit dans un projet de rénovation pensé pour coïncider avec les Jeux olympiques de 2012 et en 16 jours seulement, il a vu le jour. L'idée était de créer un espace social permettant d'accueillir une série de spectacles dans un environnement détendu.

La structure en bois a demandé des fondations peu profondes. Elle a hébergé un café, une terrasse et un petit amphithéâtre. Sur le côté, un jardin de plantes comestibles a été installé et entretenu par des bénévoles de Growing Greenwich et par le personnel du café.

Déclaré Poète officiel des JO de Londres, Lemn Sissay a collaboré avec le designer pour modifier son poème intitulé « Shipping Good ». Des couleurs vives illustraient le poème à l'aide de 34 éléments en contreplaqué fixés à la tour en échafaudage. Les mêmes formes géométriques peintes à la main ont servi à décorer d'autres parties du café.

02

Tramshed

Website   chickenandsteak.co.uk
Date Opened   May 2012
Designer   Waugh Thistleton Architects
Cost of Build $$$$+
Size of Build   480 m² / 5,150 ft²
Award   Winner Europe 2013
Address   32 Rivington Street
London EC2A 3LX
UK

"The brief was to bring this hidden gem back to full public enjoyment."

Waugh Thistleton Architects

Built in 1905 as an auxiliary substation, the huge space has become an impressive open-plan restaurant whose design equates simplicity with quality – like the menu, the interior has been kept minimal, letting original elements speak for themselves.

The walls are tiled with Edwardian glazed brick, black metal trusses support pendant lights and a skylight runs the whole length of the space. The extreme verticality was treated with a special commission by Damien Hirst, a formaldehyde work called *Cock and Bull* (2012) that breaks up the large dormitory-style room, while more art can be seen downstairs in the on-site public gallery, Cock n Bull.

Furnishings were regarded as a series of 'interventions', for example, the *111 Navy Chairs* by Emeco use recycled PET plastic from Coca-Cola bottles in keeping with the pared-down industrial theming.

Der große, 1905 als Umspannstation errichtete Raum ist zu einem eindrucksvollen Restaurant mit offenem Grundriss geworden, dessen Gestaltung Schlichtheit mit Qualität verbindet. Ebenso wie die Speisekarte ist auch der Innenraum nur minimal ausgestattet, man lässt die ursprünglichen Elemente für sich sprechen.

Die Wände sind mit glasierten Ziegeln aus edwardianischer Zeit verkleidet. Schwarze Metallbinder tragen Hängeleuchten, und ein Oberlicht führt über die gesamte Länge des Raumes. Der extremen Vertikalität wurde begegnet durch einen speziellen Auftrag an Damien Hirst: ein Bildwerk aus Formaldehyd mit dem Titel *Cock and Bull* (2012), das die große Schlafsaalform des Raumes aufbricht. Weitere Kunstwerke sind im Untergeschoss in der dort öffentlich zugänglichen Galerie Cock n Bull zu sehen.

Die Möblierung wurde als Folge von „Eingriffen" betrachtet. Zum Beispiel wurde für die *111 Navy Chairs* von Emeco PET-Kunststoff aus recycelten Coca-Cola-Flaschen verwendet, um der Themenstellung reduzierter Industrie gerecht zu werden.

Dans cet immense espace, une sous-station auxiliaire construite en 1905 a laissé place à un impressionnant restaurant au design faisant rimer simplicité et qualité. À l'instar du menu, l'intérieur est minimaliste et permet aux éléments d'origine de parler d'eux-mêmes.

Les murs sont carrelés de briques vernissées de l'époque edwardienne, les lampes pendent de poutres en métal noir et une verrière s'étend sur toute la longueur de l'espace. La verticalité extrême a été contrôlée par une œuvre de Damien Hirst : baptisée *Cock and Bull* (2012), cette installation en formaldéhyde vient diviser la grande salle de style dortoir. D'autres œuvres d'art sont exposées à l'étage inférieur dans la galerie Cock n Bull.

Le mobilier a été pensé comme une série d'interventions. Par exemple, les *111 Navy Chairs* d'Emeco ont été fabriquées en plastique PET recyclé à partir de bouteilles de Coca-Cola, en harmonie avec la thématique industrielle épurée.

01

02

01 The ceiling has been painted a sumptuous pea-green and lined with soundproofing panels to reduce the noise level

02 Chesterfield-style leather banquette booths line one of the walls

03 The bright, large-scale painting on the mezzanine, *Beef and Chicken* (2012), by Damien Hirst, was a special commission for the space and depicts the characters Cow and Chicken from the animation broadcast on the Cartoon Network in the 1990s

V'ammos

Website	vammos.gr
Date Opened	November 2012
Designer	Imarchitects
Cost of Build	$$$$
Size of Build	300 m² / 3,250 ft²
Award	Longlist 2013
Address	Karaoli Dimitriou & Sofianopoulou
	18547 Neo Faliro
	Greece

This comfortable and spacious dining area brings elegance to the home of Olympiakos football club, south-west of Athens. The layout of the single-floored restaurant offers exceptional panoramic views of the 32,000-seat Karaiskakis Stadium while a match is in progress.

Amidst crisp white furniture, translucent curtains, steel features and stained dark-wood flooring, diners are further immersed beneath an ebbing and flowing sea of undulating three-dimensional squares. This special parametric design responds to the stadium's close proximity to the sea, illustrating the movement of the waves.

The elongated bar has been built from 300 metal cooking-pots stacked in rows and covered by a wooden bench top, transforming a functional product into an intriguing abstract design which sits in quiet harmony with the ceiling waves overhead.

Dieser komfortable und geräumige Speisesaal verleiht dem Sitz des Fußballvereins Olympiakos im Südwesten von Athen eine gewisse Eleganz. Das eingeschossige Restaurant bietet während der Spiele großartige Panoramablicke zum Stadion Karaiskakis mit 32.000 Sitzplätzen.

Umgeben von reinem, weißem Mobiliar, durchsichtigen Vorhängen, Stahlelementen und dunkel gebeiztem Holzboden tauchen die Gäste in ein auf- und absteigendes Meer aus dreidimensionalen Quadraten. Diese besondere, auf das Wesentliche beschränkte Gestaltung entspricht der Nähe des Stadiums zum Meer und illustriert die Bewegung der Wellen.

Die langgestreckte Bar besteht aus 300 aufgereihten Kochtöpfen und ist mit einer hölzernen Abdeckung versehen. Ein funktionales Produkt wurde hier zu einem interessanten abstrakten Design verbunden, das sich harmonisch der wellenförmigen Decke anpasst.

"Our priorities are integration of landscape and incorporation of the client's vision."

lmarchitects

01 The undulating ceiling feature was actually designed to disguise the building's electronic and structural elements, while still allowing access to them

02 The white tables with either square or round tops were specially designed by lmarchitects

02

Cette salle de restaurant confortable et généreuse confère une touche d'élégance au club de football Olympiakos, au sud-ouest d'Athènes. L'aménagement sur un niveau offre d'exceptionnelles vues panoramiques du stade Karaiskakis de 32 000 places pendant un match.

Au beau milieu de meubles d'un blanc éclatant, de rideaux translucides, d'éléments en acier et d'un parquet foncé, les convives mangent sous le flux et le reflux d'une mer ondulante de carrés en trois dimensions. Ce design paramétrique fait écho à la proximité de la mer du stade et symbolise le mouvement des vagues.

Le bar allongé a été construit en assemblant 300 casseroles en métal et en finissant par un comptoir en bois. Un objet fonctionnel qui donne un design abstrait surprenant, en harmonie avec le plafond vallonné.

Viet Hoa Mess

Website	viethoarestaurant.co.uk
Date Opened	June 1996
Designer	VONSUNG
Size of Build	117 m² / 1,250 ft²
Award	Category winner 2012
Address	70-72 Kingsland Road
	London E2 8DP
	UK

The new addition to Vietnamese-cuisine specialist, Viet Hoa, this basement-level grill has been given a dramatic and minimal stone setting, a stark alternative to the vibrant canteen-style café that can be found on the ground floor.

The two interconnecting restaurants, whilst completely different in style and atmosphere, are linked by way of a vertical five-metre sedimentary stone wall, visible in both spaces.

Once underground, subdued lighting emphasises the space's cave-like character, in which stone and concrete continue throughout – from the square tables placed on concrete block bases to the waxed stone flooring. Theatrical lighting protrudes from the ceiling overhead in the form of deep lava-shaped columns, casting a spotlight on to the diners below and adding to the temple-like atmosphere.

Diese neue Einrichtung des Spezialisten der vietnamesischen Küche, Viet Hoa, das Grillrestaurant im Untergeschoss, hat ein eindrucksvolles und minimalistisches, steinernes Ambiente, eine klare Alternative zum lebendigen Kantinenstil des Cafés im Erdgeschoss.

Die beiden zusammenhängenden, in Stil und Atmosphäre völlig unterschiedlichen Restaurants sind durch eine vertikale, fünf Meter hohe Wand aus Sedimentgestein verbunden, die in beiden Lokalen sichtbar ist.

Im Untergeschoss betont die gedämpfte Beleuchtung den höhlenartigen Charakter des Raumes, der durchgehend aus Naturstein und Beton besteht – von den quadratischen Tischen, die auf einer Betonbasis stehen, bis zum gewachsten Natursteinboden. Hohe Lavalampen stoßen aus der Decke und schicken Lichtstrahlen hinunter auf die Speisenden. Diese theatralische Inszenierung trägt zur tempelähnlichen Atmosphäre des Raumes bei.

01

Aménagé en sous-sol, Viet Hoa est un nouveau restaurant vietnamien à l'intérieur minimaliste et spectaculaire en pierre. Le contraste est saisissant avec la cafétéria haute en couleurs qui occupe le rez-de-chaussée.

Bien que totalement différents en style et en atmosphère, les deux restaurants sont interconnectés par un mur vertical en roche sédimentaire de cinq mètres de haut et visible aux deux niveaux.

L'éclairage tamisé au sous-sol amplifie le sentiment de cave de l'espace entièrement fait de pierre et de béton, qu'il s'agisse des tables carrées reposant sur des blocs de béton ou du sol en pierre lustrée. L'illumination théâtrale sort du plafond sous la forme de colonnes telles des coulées de lave, projetant la lumière sur les tables et augmentant encore l'atmosphère de temple.

02

01 Pietra Medea stone tables contrast with the concrete, each one being equipped with an individual infra-red grill

02 Aluminium furniture gives a utilitarian feel, as well as delicately reflecting the light from the spotlights above

03 A super-minimal waiting area consists of plain concrete blocks with metal chairs

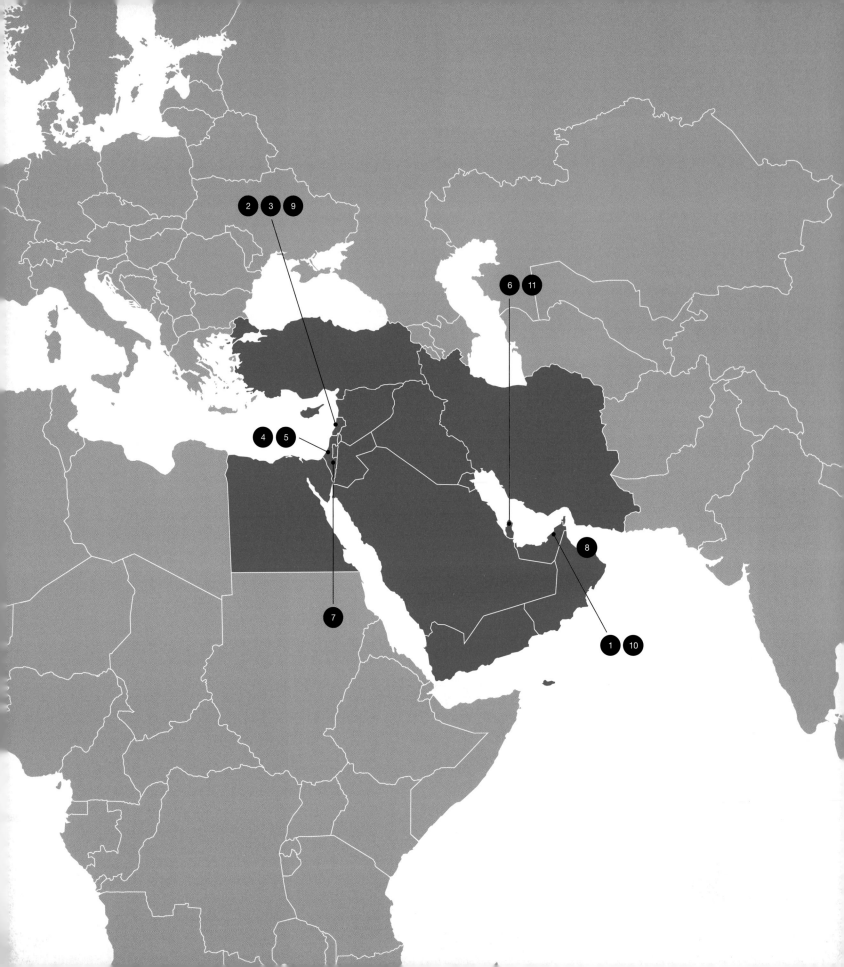

Middle East

Middle East

Karim Rashid
Designer

Karim Rashid is one of the most prolific designers of his generation, with over 3,000 designs in production, over 300 awards and working in over 40 countries. His designs include luxury goods, furniture, lighting, high-tech products, surface design, brand identity, packaging and interiors, and his work features in 20 permanent collections. As a frequent guest lecturer at universities and conferences, he also holds Honorary Doctorates from OCAD, Toronto and from Corcoran College of Art + Design, Washington and his work has been widely featured in numerous magazines and books.

Karim Rashid ist einer der produktivsten Designer seiner Generation. Über 3.000 seiner Entwürfe werden produziert, über 300 Auszeichnungen ergingen an ihn und er ist in 40 Ländern tätig. Von ihm stammen Designs von Luxusgütern, Möbeln, Leuchten, Hightech-Produkten, Oberflächen, Markenidentitäten, Verpackungen und Inneneinrichtungen; seine Arbeiten werden in 20 ständigen Sammlungen gezeigt. Als gefragter Gastdozent an Universitäten und auf Kongressen erhielt er auch die Ehrendoktorwürde der Universität OCAD in Toronto und des Corcoran College of Art + Design in Washington, D.C. Seine Arbeiten wurden in zahlreichen Zeitschriften und Büchern veröffentlicht.

Karim Rashid est l'un des designers les plus prolifiques de sa génération, avec plus de 3 000 designs à son actif, plus de 300 prix décernés et des créations dans plus de 40 pays. Ses designs comptent produits de luxe, mobilier, éclairages, objets high-tech, surfaces, identités de marques, emballages et intérieurs, et sa signature est présente dans 20 collections permanentes. Orateur habituel d'universités et de conférences, il est également Docteur Honoris Causa de l'OCAD (Toronto) et du Corcoran College of Art + Design (Washington). Son travail a été amplement présenté dans de nombreux magazines et ouvrages.

I love the larger experiential impact an interior, space or building can have on people's lives. With hospitality design or public spaces, masses of people have experiences that are about the world we live in now. Guests are physically immersing themselves inside my concepts. I would love to design hotels in every city. We as designers have the power to affect humanity on a social level, whether it is to provide relaxing solitude, community or a pleasurable vacation.

But I believe there is an inclination towards tired archetypes, and/or very cold, sterile minimalism, especially in the case of hospitality. Good design challenges the boundaries of design, to bring a fulgent vibrancy to space. Interiors must have a pulse, must sing and come alive around you, so that guests feel inspired and revitalised.

So many new interiors built in the Middle East are created with the idea of the New and the Future. I am fascinated by Dubai because architecture and design are embraced there without boundaries. It is a blank canvas for the future and for inspiring spaces that touch us in a phenomenal way – underwater hotels, man-made islands, indoor skiing, the world's tallest hotel and tallest building can only exist in the Now!

The Restaurant and Bar Design Awards are an opportunity to promote innovative, responsible, intelligent architecture. The rapid growth of the Middle East has produced a lot of banal architecture but shining examples of good design are all the more powerful. The Middle East has great potential to impact on culture. This is a place of constant growth and astounding optimism and resilience.

Every day I live I believe that we could be living in a world that is full of real contemporary inspiring objects, spaces, places and experiences. Design has been the cultural shaper of our world from the start. We have designed systems, cities, industrialisation – everything, and as the world becomes more competitive, design is exponentially improving the world.

I have great respect for the R&BDA because they are very democratic, nominating not just super-interiors and multi-million-dollar restaurants, but innovative interiors. Good design is not about gaudy luxury. Today, luxury is seamless technology in the hotel, not expensive, heavy, excessive materials. Luxury is perfect lighting in a restaurant. Luxury is new inspiring aesthetics. Luxury is a perfect fluid experience. But whether you design a 50-room hotel or a 600-room hotel the process and work is about the same, and the desire and goal is to make the most progressive, pleasurable, engaging experience.

I think that as designers we tend to clean up the world – we make order from chaos. I want to challenge the boundaries of design, to bring that shining energy to an environment. Our lives are elevated when we experience beauty, comfort, luxury, performance and utility in unison. Design must evolve us – and create beautification and betterment for society. In this way, creating well-designed, provocative, stimulating yet calming environments should be the impetus for everything we embark on.

Ich liebe diese hohe Schlagkraft, die das Erlebnis von Design, eines Raumes oder Gebäudes auf einen Menschen haben kann. Die Gestaltung von Lokalen und öffentlichen Plätzen macht einer breiten Masse die Welt erfahrbar, in der wir heute leben. Die Gäste tauchen physisch in meine Konzepte ein. Gerne würde ich in jeder Stadt Hotels einrichten! Wir Designer haben die Kraft, für Menschen auf sozialer Ebene zu wirken, für erholsame Abgeschiedenheit, gemeinschaftliche Erlebnisse oder angenehme Ferien zu sorgen.

Aber besonders in der Gastronomie wird ein Trend zu überholten Archetypen bzw. sterilem Minimalismus erkennbar. Gute Gestaltung geht an ihre Grenzen, um einen Raum strahlen zu lassen. Innenarchitektur muss pulsieren, beleben, die Gäste anregen.

So viel Interior Design des Nahen Ostens ist beseelt vom Neuen und Zukünftigen. Ich bin fasziniert von Dubai, wo man Architektur und Design grenzenlose Möglichkeiten bietet. Es ist ein noch unbeschriebenes Blatt mit progressiven Bereichen, die uns eindringlich berühren: Unterwasserhotels, künstliche Inseln, Indoor-Skipisten. Das höchste Hotel und das höchste Gebäude der Welt kann es nur jetzt und hier geben!

Die Restaurant and Bar Design Awards fördern innovative, verantwortungsvolle und intelligente Architektur. Das rasche Wachstum im Nahen Osten hat viele banale Bauten hervorgebracht, aber umso eindrucksvoller sind die herausragenden Beispiele guter Architektur. Diese Region bietet mit ihrem konstanten Wachstum, ihrem bewundernswerten Optimismus und ihrer Ausdauer ein hohes kuturelles Bereicherungspotenzial.

Ich bin stets davon überzeugt gewesen, dass wir in einer Welt voll wahrhaft zeitgemäßer, anregender Objekte, Räume, Orte und Erlebnisse leben könnten. Design war seit jeher unser kultureller Impulsgeber. Wir haben alles gestaltet – Systeme, Städte, Industrialisierung –, und je größer der Wettbewerb in der Welt, desto mehr wird sie durch Design exponentiell verbessert.

Ich habe große Hochachtung vor den R&BDA, weil sie sehr demokratisch nicht nur großartige und teure, sondern innovative Restaurants auszeichnen. Gute Gestaltung hat nichts mit protzigem Luxus zu tun. Luxus im Hotel betrifft heute funktionierende Technologie, nicht großartige Materialien. Luxus im Restaurant ist perfekte Beleuchtung, neuartige, anregende Ästhetik, ein erstklassiges Erlebnis. Aber der Ablauf und die Arbeit sind ziemlich die gleichen, ob man ein Hotel für 50 oder 600 Gäste plant, ebenso das Ziel, ein neuartiges, vergnügliches und anregendes Erlebnis zu bieten.

Wir als Designer neigen dazu, die Welt aufzuräumen – Ordnung aus Choas zu machen. Ich möchte die Grenzen von Gestaltung ausloten, die Energie auf ein Umfeld übertragen. Unser Leben wird heiterer, wenn Schönheit, Komfort, Luxus, Inszenierung und Funktionalität übereinstimmen. Design soll uns weiterbilden – und die Gesellschaft verschönern und verbessern. Daher sollte die Schaffung einer gut gestalteten, provokativen, stimulierenden und auch beruhigenden Umgebung Anstoß für alles sein, was wir in Angriff nehmen.

J'aime voir à quel point un intérieur, un espace ou un bâtiment peuvent influencer la vie des gens. Grâce au design d'hôtels ou aux espaces publics, les personnes vivent des expériences liées au monde actuel. Les clients se plongent physiquement dans mes concepts, et j'adorerais être chargé du design d'hôtels dans toutes les villes. Nous autres designers avons le pouvoir d'influencer les hommes au niveau social.

Je crois aussi qu'il existe une propension à des archétypes fatigués et/ou à un minimalisme froid et stérile, notamment dans le cas des hôtels. Un projet réussi remet en cause les limites du design afin de donner un coup d'éclat à un espace. Les intérieurs doivent être vivants pour que les clients y trouvent inspiration et vitalité.

Au Moyen-Orient, les intérieurs sont souvent élaborés selon l'idée de nouveauté et de futur. Dubaï me fascine pour la fusion entre architecture et design, la toile de fond parfaite pour des espaces qui nous influencent grandement : hôtels sous-marins, îles artificielles, pistes de ski couvertes, hôtel le plus haut et bâtiment le plus élevé sont déjà une réalité !

Grâce aux Restaurant and Bar Design Awards, une architecture innovante, responsable et intelligente peut être diffusée. La croissance rapide du Moyen-Orient a donné un lot important d'architecture banale, mais les exemples de design accompli sont aussi des plus brillants. Cette région possède un énorme potentiel pour influencer la culture. Elle ne cesse de se développer avec une dose incroyable d'optimisme et d'adaptation.

Je pense que le monde pourrait être rempli d'objets, d'espaces et d'expériences encourageant l'inspiration. Le design a toujours été un moteur culturel de notre monde. Nous avons conçu des systèmes, des villes, l'industrialisation, tout ; dans un environnement chaque fois plus compétitif, le design est un facteur d'amélioration exponentielle.

Je respecte les R&BDA pour être si démocratiques : les nominations ne se cantonnent pas aux super intérieurs et aux restaurants de plusieurs millions de dollars, elles retiennent les conceptions innovantes. Un bon design ne rime pas avec luxe tape-à-l'œil. Le luxe, c'est une technologie intégrée dans un hôtel, et non des matériaux coûteux et clinquants. Le luxe, c'est un éclairage parfait dans un restaurant. Le luxe, c'est une nouvelle esthétique inspirante. Le luxe, c'est une expérience totalement fluide. Que vous conceviez un hôtel de 50 ou de 600 chambres, le processus et le travail sont identiques, le but recherché étant d'offrir l'expérience la plus naturelle, agréable et motivante.

Les designers ont tendance à « faire le ménage », à ordonner le chaos. Je veux remettre en cause les frontières du design pour dynamiser un environnement. Nous vivons mieux entourés de beauté, de confort, de luxe, d'efficacité et d'utilité. Le design doit nous faire évoluer et viser l'embellissement et l'amélioration de la société. Tous nos projets doivent être stimulés par des environnements bien conçus, provocateurs et motivants, mais aussi empreints de sérénité.

Alegra

Date Opened	February 2012
Designer	Mr. Important Design
Cost of Build	$$$$
Size of Build	300 m² / 3,250 ft²
Award	Shortlist 2013
Address	Al Murooj Rotana
	Sheikh Zayed Road
	Dubai
	United Arab Emirates

Like walking into a three-dimensional broken mirror full of cracks and fissures, this glossy, gold and black restaurant and late-night club is a spectacular assault on the senses.

Intended to cater for the smart set in Dubai, the space was purposely designed as a luxury destination and one that would feature a main bar, shots bar, dining area, DJ station and dance space. Because of the low ceilings and relatively modest area available the bar also had to be flexible, so that it could be easily transformed into a club environment later on in the evenings.

The use of reflecting surfaces and opulent chandeliers and other light fittings results in an explosion of molten light and trapezoidal shapes, amongst the high-resolution installation screens and sleek furnishings.

Als betrete man einen dreidimensionalen, zerbrochenen Spiegel voller Sprünge und Risse, so ergreift dieser in Gold und Schwarz glänzende Ort auf spektakuläre Weise alle unsere Sinne.

Zur Bewirtung der Reichen und Schönen in Dubai war es als Luxusrestaurant geplant, mit einer großen Bar, Shots Bar, Speisesaal, DJ-Pult und Tanzfläche. Wegen der geringen Deckenhöhe und der relativ beschränkten Nutzfläche musste die Bar flexibel gestaltet werden, um sie am späteren Abend problemlos in einen Club umwandeln zu können.

Reflektierende Oberflächen sowie aufwendige Kronleuchter und weitere Leuchtkörper bewirken explosionsartige Lichtströme und trapezförmige Gebilde zwischen High-resolution-Bildschirmen und elegantem Mobiliar.

01

Donnant l'impression d'entrer dans un miroir en trois dimensions craquelé et fissuré, ce restaurant-discothèque aux couleurs or et noir brille de mille feux et stimule tous les sens.

L'espace se veut le lieu de rencontre du Dubaï branché : il a pour cette raison été conçu comme un endroit luxueux, avec un bar principal, un bar à *shots*, une salle de restaurant, une cabine de DJ et une piste de danse. Le plafond est bas et l'espace disponible plutôt modeste ; le bar devait donc être adaptable et facilement transformable en club à partir d'une certaine heure de la nuit.

L'emploi de surfaces réfléchissantes, de lustres opulents et de systèmes d'éclairage originaux crée une explosion de formes trapézoïdales fondues. L'ensemble est assorti d'écrans haute résolution et d'un mobilier élégant.

02

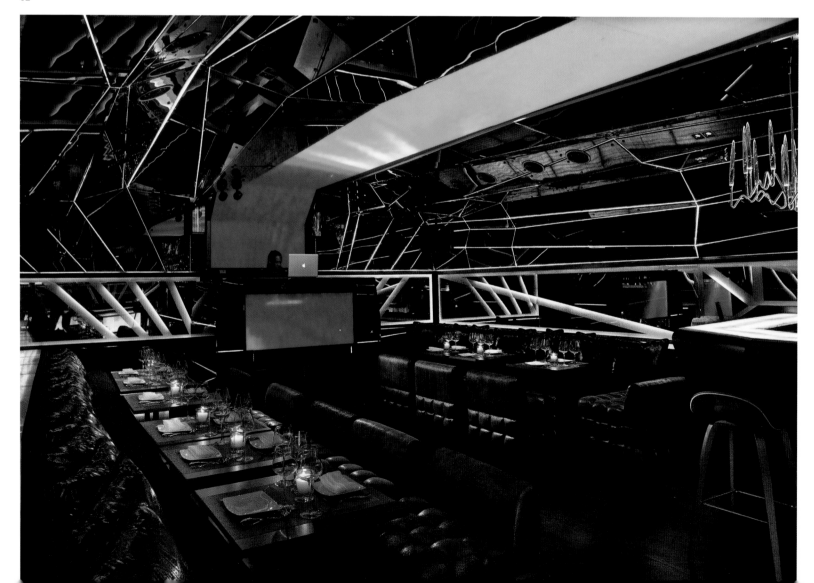

01 Angular filament chandeliers suspended over the bar are an electrifying addition

02 A central break in the ceiling reveals an LED screen for images to match the sounds from the DJ booth

03 Backlit black glass has been used on the walls and ceiling, each facet outlined with gold light to create a stunning effect throughout the space

03

Balthus

Date Opened	September 2012
Designer	Gatserelia Design
Cost of Build	$$$$
Size of Build	250 m² / 2,700 ft²
Award	Longlist 2013
Address	Ghandour Building
	Avenue des Français
	Minet El Hosn
	Beirut
	Lebanon

Steeped in nostalgia, the elegant design of this classic Parisian-style bistro has a timeworn and antiquated feel, transporting guests to an intimate world where they may comfortably lose themselves over lunch or dinner.

The entrance area is enlivened by an installation formed of café chairs climbing the wall and across the ceiling, while the organic curlicues of an art nouveau brass hand-rail lead up to the dining floor.

A snaking light fitting, made from marble alabaster and painted gold, dominates the main space from above the tables and is a counterpoint to the optical illusion with the box design on the floor. A series of distressed mirrored surfaces reflect back on the upholstered leather banquettes, crisp linen tablecloths and brass fittings.

Das von Nostalgie bestimmte, elegante Design dieses klassischen Bistros im Pariser Stil versetzt seine Gäste in die Vergangenheit, in eine intime Welt, in der sie sich bei Lunch oder Dinner wirklich entspannen können.

Den Eingangsbereich belebt eine aus Caféstühlen gebildete Installation, die sich die Wand hinauf und über die Decke zieht, und ein organisch geschwungenes Jugendstilgeländer aus Messing führt hinauf ins Speisegeschoss.

Eine verschlungene, goldfarbene Lichtinstallation aus Marmor-Alabaster über den Tischen beherrscht den großen Raum und bildet einen Kontrast zu der optischen Illusion des Musters auf dem Boden. Mehrere antiquierte Spiegelflächen reflektieren das Licht auf ledergepolsterte Sitzbänke, reine Leinentischtücher und Messingelemente.

01 The light installation has six different settings, offering a range of mood-lighting to suit the time of day

02 The patterned floor is an echo of the interconnected lines and repeating forms in the light installation above

03 Pillars clad in mirrors create an illusionary effect and maximise the impression of space

Empreint de nostalgie, l'élégant design de ce bistro de style parisien a un aspect vétuste. Les convives sont plongés dans un monde intime qui leur fait oublier la réalité le temps d'un repas.

L'entrée est habillée par une installation formée de chaises de café grimpant au mur et envahissant le plafond. Les rinceaux organiques d'une rampe en cuivre Art nouveau mènent à la salle de restaurant.

Une installation lumineuse, faite d'albâtre calcaire et peinte couleur or, serpente au-dessus des tables dans l'espace principal. Elle offre un contrepoint à l'illusion optique créée par le design compartimenté au sol. Une série de surfaces miroitantes projettent des reflets sur les banquettes en cuir, sur les nappes en lin éclatant et sur les finitions en cuivre.

03

Cocteau

Date Opened	August 2011
Designer	Gatserelia Design
Cost of Build	$$$$+
Size of Build	295 m² / 3,200 ft²
Award	Category winner 2012
Address	Palladium Building
	Downtown
	Beirut
	Lebanon

Almost a topsy-turvy city in miniature, with towering columns and curious suspended structures, this spacious restaurant is an enticing venue with abundant detail to attract the eye.

Winner of the Restaurant & Bar Design Awards, Middle East & Africa category, in 2012, the dining hall boasts a high ceiling, a long bar and a large glass façade.

The original open-plan space has been fitted out with a view to creating a fine dining experience. In addition to the larger structural elements the interior is fashioned on the model of a modern brasserie, as typified by flowing lines and the rectangular light cubes, with bronze, leather and glass evoking the dynamic movement of the modern city.

Dieses geräumige Restaurant ähnelt fast einer auf den Kopf gestellten Miniaturstadt mit aufragenden Säulen und sonderbar aufgehängten Gebäuden – ein ansprechender Ort mit vielerlei reizvollen Details.

Besondere Merkmale des 2012 mit dem Restaurant & Bar Design Award, Kategorie Middle East & Africa, ausgezeichneten Lokals sind eine hohe Decke, eine lange Bar und eine große Glasfassade.

Der ursprünglich offene Raum hat durch die neue Struktur an Qualität gewonnen. Zusätzlich zu den größeren baulichen Elementen erhielt er die Ausstattung einer modernen Brasserie mit schwungvollen Linien und Lichtkuben, mit Bronze, Leder und Glas, um die dynamische Bewegung einer modernen Stadt anzudeuten.

Ce restaurant spacieux est comparable à une ville miniature sens dessus dessous, avec ses énormes colonnes et d'étranges structures suspendues. Il forme un local attirant et truffé de détails à admirer.

Lauréate du prix Restaurant & Bar Design Awards dans la catégorie Middle East & Africa en 2012, la salle de restaurant possède un haut plafond, un long bar et une grande façade vitrée.

Le plan ouvert d'origine a été aménagé de façon à offrir une expérience gastronomique agréable. Outre les éléments structurels de grande taille, l'intérieur est conçu comme une brasserie moderne, comme l'illustrent les lignes fluides et les rectangles lumineux. Le bronze, le cuir et le verre viennent traduire la dynamique de la ville moderne.

01 The vertical slats of the
wooden columns are interrupted
by brass belts

02 A high glass wine rack provides
a strong focal point above the bar

03 Suspended rectangular
chandeliers imitate deconstructed
high-rise apartment blocks

03

Jaffa\Tel-Aviv

Date Opened	November 2011
Designer	Baranowitz Kronenberg Architecture
Cost of Build	$$$$+
Size of Build	360 m² / 3,900 ft²
Award	Shortlist 2012
Address	98 Yigal Alon
	6789141 Tel Aviv
	Israel

01

Informed by its multinational environment, this raw and bright space has been sensitively designed with a similar selection of materials. A simple industrial template has been overlaid with a series of distinct, historic features that have elevated the minimal design into a warm and relaxed environment.

The combination of elements is also important, so that the poured terrazzo bar, for example, is coupled with intriguing fittings, such as the large industrial "bell" lights from the Czech Republic running the length of the main floor or the Turkish carpets hung on the walls.

Elevated poplar shutters have been designed to filter the direct sunlight, and are reminiscent of the traditional architecture as found in the old city of Jaffa.

Dieser schlichte und helle, von seinem multinationalen Umfeld geprägte Raum wurde mit entsprechend ausgewählten Materialien einfühlsam gestaltet. Ein einfaches industrielles Gebäude wurde mit unterschiedlichen historischen Elementen ausgestattet, die das minimalistische Design in eine einladende und entspannte Umgebung verwandelt haben.

Auch die Kombination der Elemente war maßgebend. Zum Beispiel wurde die gegossene Terrazzobar über die ganze Geschosslänge mit großen Industrieleuchten aus der Tschechischen Republik ausgestattet, und an der Wand hängen türkische Teppiche.

Im oberen Bereich angebrachte Fensterläden aus Pappelholz filtern das Sonnenlicht und erinnern an die traditionelle Architektur der alten Stadt Jaffa.

02

Influencé par son environnement multinational, cet espace brut et lumineux a été conçu avec sensibilité et les matériaux choisis avec soin. La base industrielle épurée a été enrichie d'une série d'éléments historiques, et le design minimal s'est ainsi converti en un espace accueillant et détendu.

Le mélange d'éléments joue aussi un rôle important. Le bar en terrazzo par exemple est combiné à des éléments originaux, comme les grandes lampes industrielles en forme de cloche de la République tchèque qui s'enfilent sur toute la longueur de l'étage principal, ou encore les tapis turcs accrochés au mur.

Des persiennes en peuplier ont été conçues pour filtrer la lumière directe. Elles rappellent l'architecture traditionnelle dans la vieille ville de Jaffa.

"Guests are invited to sit around the burning fire and watch the 'show'."

Baranowitz Kronenberg Architecture

01 Reclaimed furniture has been paired with Piet Hein Eek scrap-wood chairs and tables

02 Keeping everything on show, the stainless steel kitchen extends to the bar where people can eat

03 Unadorned metal sheeting adds an extra texture, and behind it is the wine walll

03

Little Italy

Date Opened	October 2012
Designer	OPA studio
Cost of Build	$$$
Size of Build	130 m² / 1,400 ft²
Award	Category winner 2013
Address	38 Keren Hayesod Street
	Jerusalem
	Israel

Warm and familiar, yet with a restrained and modern edge, this simple and contemporary Italian restaurant demonstrates a gentle quality in its design.

With inspiration drawn from the updated traditional Italian cuisine on the menu, seating was kept smart but plain while the minimal colour palette and bold graphic work lend a few light touches to bring the restaurant to life and create a refreshing dining experience.

Since quality wine was a prominent feature on the menu as well, this provided the impetus for another detail, with pale wood and iron beams running across the ceiling and down to form a wine rack lining one wall of the restaurant.

Die warme und familiäre, aber auch klare und moderne Atmosphäre dieses schlichten und zeitgemäßen italienischen Restaurants ist das Ergebnis qualitätvollen Designs.

Das italienische Speisenangebot ist traditionell und doch à jour. Entsprechend ist die Möblierung schick, aber auch schlicht gehalten. Die zurückhaltende Farbpalette und auffällige grafische Dekorationen bringen etwas Leichtigkeit und Leben in das Lokal und erzeugen ein entspannendes Ambiente.

Qualitätsweine nehmen eine wichtige Position auf der Speisekarte ein und haben auch ein weiteres Detail bestimmt: Helle Holz- und Eisenbalken führen über die Decke und herab und bilden Weinständer an einer Wand des Restaurants.

02

Chaleureux et classique, mais avec une certaine touche de modernité, ce restaurant italien contemporain présente un design de qualité.

L'inspiration vient du menu qui offre des plats italiens traditionnels revisités. Les chaises sont fonctionnelles et en bois naturel, alors que la palette minimale de couleurs et un graphisme audacieux égayent le restaurant et permettent aux clients de passer un moment agréable.

La carte se distingue aussi par des grands vins, ce qui a motivé l'élaboration d'un porte-bouteilles avec des poutres en bois clair et en fer qui traversent le plafond et descendent le long d'un mur.

01 Bold typography adds character to the otherwise minimal design and binds the space together

02 A modern glass front allows people to sit and look out on to the street

03 Perforated wooden rafters extend down one wall to serve as a wine rack

Pampano

Website	richardsandoval.com
Date Opened	May 2010
Designer	Studio Gaia
Cost of Build	$$$$+
Size of Build	230 m² / 2,500 ft²
Award	Shortlist 2011
Address	1 La Croisette, The Pearl
	Port Arabia
	Doha
	Qatar

A sophisticated and subtle tonal range of sandstone, cream and chiffon is the backdrop for this opulent Mexican restaurant. The use of various textured surfaces and grooved undulating walls, combined with sheer fabric dividers and curved banquettes, creates an intimate and exclusive space.

A choice of dining areas includes the main restaurant, a sunken bar, a large outdoor area and a private upstairs dining-room which overlooks the main space. The restaurant is named after a type of Mexican fish and the aquatic motif is repeated throughout, whether above the bar or in the window designs by photographer Masayoshi Yamada.

Additional special features include the sensual white sculptures by Paloma Torres, an operatic maître-d' stand and a water feature cascading down a black and ruby glass wall.

Den Hintergrund für dieses prächtige mexikanische Restaurant stellt eine intelligente und raffinierte Material- und Farbpalette aus Sandstein, Creme und Chiffon dar. Unterschiedlich strukturierte Flächen und geriffelte, gewellte Wände, vereint mit dünnen Stoffteilern und gekrümmten Sitzbänken, erzeugen ein intimes und exklusives Ambiente.

Das große Lokal ist in verschiedene Bereiche aufgeteilt: eine tiefer gelegene Bar, eine große Sitzfläche im Freien und einen privaten Raum im Obergeschoss mit Blick in den großen Speisesaal. Das Restaurant wurde nach einem mexikanischen Fisch benannt, und das Wassermotiv ist auch überall präsent, über der Bar oder in der Gestaltung der Fenster durch den Fotografen Masayoshi Yamada.

Zu den besonderen Merkmalen zählen die sinnlichen weißen Skulpturen von Paloma Torres, ein Pult für den Chefkellner und ein Wasserspiel, das eine schwarz und rubinrote Glaswand hinabfließt.

01

Cet opulent restaurant mexicain fonctionne dans un camaïeu subtil de grès et de crème. Le recours à des surfaces texturées et les murs ondulants et rainurés créent un espace intime et exclusif, tout comme les séparations en tissu très fin et les banquettes arrondies.

Le local compte plusieurs zones, dont le restaurant principal, un bar en contrebas, un grand espace extérieur et un salon privé à l'étage, surplombant la grande salle. Le restaurant porte le nom d'une espèce de poisson mexicain ; le motif aquatique est omniprésent, au-dessus du bar comme dans les ornements créés par le photographe Masayoshi Yamada pour les fenêtres.

Le restaurant compte d'autres éléments singuliers, comme les sculptures blanches sensuelles de Paloma Torres et une cascade d'eau tombant le long d'un mur en verre noir et rubis.

02

01 Tapered and textured columns
rise up 4.5m into a recess in
the ceiling

02 A 3m screen decorated with
a school of bronze fish descends
from the ceiling above the bar,
which is set low down so the
bartender can make direct eye
contact with people

03 Upstairs a private dining-room
for 12 offers views out across the
main restaurant area

03

Shumis

Date Opened	April 2012
Designer	OPA studio
Cost of Build	$$$
Size of Build	84 m² / 905 ft²
Award	Shortlist 2013
Address	14 Levi Moshe Street
	75658 Rishon le Zion
	Israel

Proving that you can make a big design statement with a modest budget, this fun-loving pizza bar is a punchy homage to the sensationalist, mass-manufactured, mid-century American mainstream.

Located in an industrial area, and with less than 90 square metres to work with, the new restaurant was put together using simple, ready-made materials to realise the design.

01

To bring the playful side of Pop culture to the fore, both side walls are lined floor-to-ceiling with repeating rows of red and white food cans labelled "Shumis Pizza Feel Good Tomato Sauce!" This creates a strong line of perspective which was matched by installing a long, white communal table, offset by the cut-out private booth area, lime-green walls and orange ceiling fans.

Dieses fröhliche Pizzalokal ist der Beweis dafür, dass großartiges Design auch mit einem bescheidenen Etat realisierbar ist, hier als Hommage an den sensationsgierigen, massenproduzierten amerikanischen Mainstream der Jahrhundertmitte.

Der Entwurf für das neue, in einem Industriegebiet gelegene Restaurant mit weniger als 90 Quadratmetern Nutzfläche basiert auf der Verwendung von einfachen Fertigprodukten.

Um den spielerischen Aspekt der Popkultur hervorzuheben, wurden beide Seitenwände raumhoch mit sich wiederholenden Reihen aus rot-weißen Konservendosen mit der Beschriftung „Shumis Pizza Feel Good Tomato Sauce!" ausgekleidet. Dadurch entstand eine stark perspektivische Ausrichtung, passend dazu gibt es einen einzigen langen, weißen Tisch für die Gäste, der durch eine ausgeschnittene private Essnische, lindgrüne Wände und orangefarbene Ventilatoren an der Decke ergänzt wird.

01 3,000 printed cans were used to create the wall installations

02 Written vertically, the illuminated letters read: "All you need is slice"

03 At the front of the space a tricolour neon lighting sculpture stands out against the textured OSB board from which the semi-secluded booth is formed

03

Preuve qu'un design impactant est possible avec
un budget réduit, cet amusant bar à pizzas rend un
hommage percutant à un classique américain
produit en masse au milieu du siècle dernier.

Situé dans une zone industrielle et disposant
de moins de 90 mètres carrés, le nouveau restaurant
a été aménagé avec des matériaux simples et prêt
à l'emploi.

Pour mettre en avant l'aspect ludique de la culture
pop, les deux murs latéraux sont recouverts d'un
alignement de boîtes de conserves rouges et blanches
avec l'étiquette « Shumis Pizza Feel Good Tomato
Sauce! ». Le résultat crée une perspective renforcée
par la longue table collective blanche, qui contraste
avec les banquettes en renfoncement, les murs vert
citron et les ventilateurs orange au plafond.

Slider Station

Website	sliderstation.com
Date Opened	November 2011
Designer	Kuwait Food Concepts
Cost of Build	$$$$+
Size of Build	268 m² / 2,900 ft²
Award	Longlist 2012
Address	Oasis by the Sea
	Shatti AlQorum
	Muscat
	Oman

In homage to the Americana menu on offer, this restaurant design by Basil Al-Salem is modelled on mid-western US gas stations of the 1940s.

Acknowledged as the first 'conveyer-belt burger' restaurant, the open-plan format is characterised by industrial lighting, wood, wire and metal. The original space was long and narrow and this was divided into different seating areas to create a more intimate dining experience.

To achieve an authentic look within a brand-new building careful selection of vintage-inspired items was made, such as the oil-drum seating and tables, tarnished metal fittings, blackboard diagrams and bold use of graphics.

Dieses Restaurant wurde, als Wertschätzung seines amerikanischen Speiseangebots, von Basil Al-Salem nach dem Vorbild der Tankstellen des mittleren Westens aus den 1940er Jahren gestaltet.

Als erstes „Fließband-Burger"-Restaurant aner-kannt, kennzeichnen industrielle Leuchten, Holz, Draht und Metall seinen offenen Grundriss. Der ursprüngliche lange und schmale Raum wurde in verschiedene Ess-bereiche aufgeteilt, damit er intimer erlebt werden kann.

Um dem Lokal in einem brandneuen Gebäude ein authentisches Erscheinungsbild zu geben, wählte man alte Gegenständen zur Ausstattung, etwa Ölfässer als Stühle und Tische, Leuchten aus ange-laufenem Metall, Diagramme auf Wandtafeln und auffällige Grafiken.

À l'image du menu *americana* proposé, le design de ce restaurant signé par Basil Al-Salem s'inspire des stations-service du Midwest des années 40.

Reconnu comme le premier restaurant de burgers équipé d'une bande transporteuse, le plan ouvert se caractérise par un éclairage industriel, du bois, des câbles et du métal. Allongé et étroit, l'espace a été divisé en différentes zones plus intimes.

Pour transmettre une certaine authenticité au sein d'un bâtiment neuf, des éléments *vintage* ont été choisis avec soin, comme les tables et les tabourets en barils de pétrole, les finitions en métal terni, les inscriptions sur tableau noir et l'emploi audacieux de graphismes.

01 The concrete floor combines with pipes and exposed ventilation ducts to accentuate the industrial styling

02 Spot and pendant lighting create a warm feel throughout, balancing the hard surfaces and materials

03 A metallic conveyor-belt snakes across the restaurant to deliver food to the customers

Society Bistro

Website	societybistro.com
Date Opened	October 2012
Designer	Gatserelia Design
Cost of Build	$$$$+
Size of Build	200 m² / 2,150 ft²
Award	Shortlist 2013
Address	Saifi Suites
	Maroun Naccache Avenue
	Beirut
	Lebanon

01

02

A golden and celestial space adorned with images of the smiling faces of Lebanon's social elite, this French-style brasserie makes quite clear which clientele it seeks to attract.

Located within a boutique hotel, the restaurant features a bronze cymbal lighting installation right across the whole ceiling area which scatters its refracted light upwards in a dazzling starry display.

The all-wooden interior is reached by way of a sumptuous translucent red entrance, while effectively placed large mirrors, bronze columns and dividing partitions very much individualise the basic Parisian bistro style with exciting accents.

Diese Brasserie in französischem Stil ist ein gold-farbener, überirdischer, mit Fotos lächelnder Gesichter der libanesischen High Society geschmückter Raum, der keinen Zweifel daran lässt, welche Klientel hier willkommen ist.

Besonderes Merkmal des in einem Boutique-hotel gelegenen Lokals ist eine Installation becken-förmiger Leuchten aus Bronze über der ganzen Deckenfläche, die ihr gebrochenes Licht aufwärts in ein Sternenmuster streut.

Durch einen prächtigen, rot schimmernden Eingangsbereich gelangt man in den ganz mit Holz verkleideten Innenraum. Geschickt angeordnete große Spiegel, Bronzesäulen und Trennwände geben dem grundlegenden Pariser Bistrostil mehr Individualität und spannende Akzente.

03

En optant pour un intérieur doré et céleste, décoré de photos de visages souriants de l'élite sociale du Liban, cette brasserie à la française affiche clairement la clientèle recherchée.

Situé dans un hôtel boutique, le restaurant est éclairé par une installation de cymbales en bronze. Elle orne tout le plafond et l'inonde des reflets de sa lumière réfractée pour donner une belle projection étoilée.

Une somptueuse entrée aux panneaux rouges transparents mène à un intérieur exclusivement en bois. Les grands miroirs judicieusement installés, les colonnes en bronze et les divisions font de ce genre de bistro parisien un endroit aux détails originaux.

01 Lighting consultant Highlights and metal-work company Acid collaborated on the impressive bronze cymbal lighting installation

02 Cheeky pictures of figures from Lebanese high society adorn the walls

03 A free-standing waiters' station in the style of a studded wooden chest lets staff move freely around the restaurant

Switch

Website	meswitch.com
Date Opened	February 2008
Designer	Karim Rashid Inc.
Cost of Build	$$$$
Size of Build	200 m² / 2,150 ft²
Award	Longlist 2010
Address	Dubai Mall
	Doha Street
	Dubai
	United Arab Emirates

Designed as a dazzling futuristic odyssey, this spectacular interior is just the place to take some time out in one of the world's most prestigious shopping destinations.

The sinuous triple curves of the Arabic letter *siin* provided the key element in shaping the design, which is repeated throughout the restaurant both in the structure and form of the walls and echoed in the decoration.

By rotating the letter so that it sits on its side, the free-standing and reduplicating structures form a continuously undulating surface that snakes along the walls and overhead, making guests feel as though they have stepped into a cocoon.

01 The ceiling is backlit and features Arabic calligraphy which gets reflected in the lustrous surfaces

02 Moulded plastic walls bathe guests in an evolving spectrum of bold colours

Dieses spektakuläre, wie eine futuristische Irrfahrt gestaltete Interieur ist der richtige Ort für eine Auszeit von den angesehensten Shoppingzielen der Welt.

Die sinusförmigen Dreifachkurven des arabischen Buchstabens *siin* lieferten das Schlüsselelement für die Gestaltung der Einrichtung; es wiederholt sich im gesamten Restaurant in der Struktur und Form der Wände wie auch in der Dekoration.

Durch seitliche Drehung des Buchstabens bilden die frei stehenden und sich wiederholenden Strukturen eine sich ständig bewegende Oberfläche, die Wände und Decke überzieht und den Gästen das Gefühl vermittelt, in einem Kokon zu stecken.

Conçu comme une odyssée futuriste, cet intérieur spectaculaire est l'endroit parfait où se détendre dans l'une des destinations de shopping les plus prestigieuses au monde.

Les triples courbes sinueuses de la lettre arabe *siin* forment la base du design. Elles se retrouvent dans tout le restaurant, tant dans la structure et la forme des murs que dans la décoration.

La lettre a été pivotée pour reposer sur l'un de ses côtés : les structures autoporteuses se répètent et forment une surface ondulante qui serpente le long des murs et au plafond, donnant aux clients l'impression d'être à l'intérieur d'un cocon.

Tse Yang

Date Opened	June 2010
Designer	Glamorous co., ltd.
Cost of Build	$$$$+
Size of Build	450 m² / 4,850 ft²
Award	Longlist 2011
Address	Parcel 4, The Pearl
	Port Arabia
	Doha
	Qatar

Set in the Qatari sands, this breathtaking Chinese restaurant has had an exquisite and thoroughly triumphant make-over.

The design has been judged to evoke the grandeur of a long-lost past, so that the entrance, for example, is marked by ancient wooden doors which open to reveal the spectacular foyer. The symbolic and instantly recognisable 'Chinese Red' has been used to stunning effect, reflecting off the mirrored glass and polished floors.

The defining element of the design results from a majestic column that occupied the middle of the space. It could not be removed completely for structural reasons, but rather than seek to minimise its presence it became instead the highlight by adorning it with textured fringe furnishings to create a powerfully striking feature.

Dieses atemberaubende, in den Sand von Katar gesetzte chinesische Restaurant hat eine exquisite und durchgehend gelungene Umgestaltung erfahren.

Das Design soll an eine längst vergangene Pracht erinnern: Den Eingang zum Beispiel prägen alte Holztüren, die sich zum spektakulären Foyer öffnen. Das symbolische und sofort erkennbare „chinesische Rot" führt hier zu fantastischen Reflexionen auf den Spiegelglasflächen und polierten Böden.

Die prägende Komponente des Designs resultiert aus einer imposanten Säule, die im Mittelpunkt des Raumes stand. Sie konnte aus baulichen Gründen nicht ganz entfernt werden. Anstatt ihre Präsenz zu verbergen, machte man sie zum Highlight, indem man sie mit roten Quasten schmückte und in ein starkes, auffälliges Element verwandelte.

01

02

01 A towering column has been lined with mirrored boards and adorned with red tassels to transform its mass

02 Wooden beads are strung along the walls in the purple bar area

03 Ornate floor-to-ceiling panelled mirrors continue the theme of elegance and opulence

Installé sur les sables du Qatar, ce somptueux restaurant chinois a connu une rénovation raffinée des plus réussies.

Le design a été pensé pour évoquer la grandeur d'une ère révolue. L'entrée se fait par d'anciennes portes en bois s'ouvrant pour révéler le spectaculaire lounge. Hautement symbolique et facilement reconnaissable, la couleur « rouge chinois » crée un effet garanti en se reflétant dans les miroirs et sur les sols polis.

L'élément caractéristique du design est l'impressionnante colonne plantée au centre de l'espace. Elle existait à l'origine et ne pouvait pas être démolie pour des questions structurelles. Au lieu de chercher à en minimiser la présence, elle est devenue un élément phare, habillée de pompons à franges pour plus d'effet.

03

Designer Index

Koichi Takada Architects
Suite 5.1, 2 Hill Street
Surry Hills, NSW 2010
Australia
www.koichitakada.com
→ 190, 206

Kris Lin Interior Design
Room 301, 4th Building
1163 Hongqiao Road
200051 Shanghai
China
www.krislin.com.cn
→ 106

k-studio
Kalimnou 10, Kato Halandri
15231 Athens
Greece
www.k-studio.gr
→ 258

Kuwait Food Concepts
Fahad Al Salem Street
Kuwait City, 13131
Kuwait
 www.q8fc.com
→ 414

Lazzarini Pickering Architetti
Via delle Mantellate 15/A
00165 Rome
Italy
www.lazzarinipickering.com
→ 218

lmarchitects
Flisvos Marina
17561 Paleo Faliro
Greece
www.lmarchitects.gr
→ 374

Luchetti Krelle
56 Cooper Street
Surry Hills, NSW 2010
Australia
www.luchettikrelle.com
→ 194, 202

m4
Woljeongno 148-2
157-040 Seoul
South Korea
www.designm4.com
→ 110

March Studio
134 Langford Street
North Melbourne, VIC 3051
Australia
www.marchstudio.com.au
→ 182

Martin Brudnizki Design Studio
Unit 1G Chelsea Reach
78-89 Lots Road
London SW10 0RN
UK
www.mbds.com
→ 346

Martin Creed
www.martincreed.com
→ 350

Matsuya Art Works
2F, Nisshin Building
298-2 Funaoka-cho
670-0034 Himeji-shi
Japan
www.matsuya-art-works.co.jp
→ 142

Menu
www.menu.as
→ 302

Michaelis Boyd Associates
108 Palace Gardens Terrace
London W8 4RT
UK
www.michaelisboyd.com
→ 270

Mitchell Taylor Workshop
Wharf Studio, Widcombe Hill
Bath BA2 6AA
UK
www.mitchelltaylorworkshop.co.uk
→ 238

Morag Myerscough
26 Drysdale Street
London N1 6LS
UK
www.studiomyerscough.com
→ 366

Mr. Important Design
3748 Enos Avenue
Oakland, CA 94619
USA
www.misterimportant.com
→ 386

Norm Architects
Frederiksborggade 1A, 4th Floor
1360 Copenhagen
Denmark
www.normcph.com
→ 302

NOUniform
12-13 Clerkenwell Green
London EC1R 0QJ
UK
www.nouniform.com
→ 232

Nuca Studio
50-58, Nuferilor Street
Corp A, 3rd Floor, Ap. 14
13621 Bucharest
Romania
www.nuca-studio.ro
→ 338

One Plus Partnership
9/F New Wing
101 King's Road
Hong Kong
www.onepluspartnership.com
→ 86

OPA studio
15 Sgula Street
68116 Tel Aviv
Israel
www.opastd.com
→ 402, 410

Orbit Design Studio
Unit 2701A, 27th Floor
M. Thai Tower, All Seasons Place
87 Wireless Road
10330 Bangkok
Thailand
www.orbitdesignstudio.com
→ 150

Outline
10 Stoney Street
London SE1 9AD
UK
www.outline-projects.co.uk
→ 250

Paul Burnham Architect
9 Eucla Court
North Fremantle, WA 6159
Australia
www.paulburnham.com.au
→ 198

.PSLAB
PO Box 175636
Beirut
Lebanon
www.pslab.net
→ 74, 254

Ritchie Built
10 Richardson Street
Carlton North, VIC 3054
Australia
www.ritchiebuilt.com
→ 210

Robert Angell Design Studio
504 Metropolitan Wharf Building
70 Wapping Wall
London E1W 3SS
UK
www.robertangelldesignstudio.com
→ 358

Russell & George
170 Peel Street
Windsor, VIC 3181
Australia
www.russellandgeorge.com
→ 214

Sandra Tarruella Interioristas
Madrazo 83, Entl. 2ª
08006 Barcelona
Spain
www.sandratarruella.com
→ 342

Sebastian Mariscal Studio
1 Sparks Place
Cambridge, MA 02138
USA
www.sebastianmariscal.com
→ 38

Sergio Arau
www.sergioarau.com
→ 24

SHH
1 Vencourt Place
London W6 9NU
UK
www.shh.co.uk
→ 254

Sid Lee Architecture
75 Queen Street, Office 1400
Montreal, QC H3C 2N6
Canada
www.sidleearchitecture.com
→ 46

Skylab Architecture
413 SW 13th Avenue, Suite 200
Portland, OR 97205
USA
www.skylabarchitecture.com
→ 66

SOMA
31 W 27th Street, Floor 9
New York, NY 10001
USA
www.soma-architects.com
→ 74

Stefan Bench
www.stefanbench.com
→ 255

STILE/Ietsugu Ohara
2-26-8 Miyakojimanakadori
534-0022 Osaka
Japan
www.go-go-stile.com
→ 146

Studio Arthur Casas
Rua Itápolis, 818
São Paulo-SP, 01245-000
Brazil
www.arthurcasas.com
→ 34

Studio Gaia
245 W 29th Street, 5th Floor
New York, NY 10001
USA
www.studiogaia.com
→ 406

Studio Mode
132 Kniaz Boris Street
1000 Sofia
Bulgaria
www.studiomode.eu
→ 294

SWeeT co., ltd.
Oriental Higashiyama #204
2-2-2 Higashiyama
153-0043 Tokyo
Japan
www.sweetdesign.jp
→ 62

Takeshi Hosaka Architects
Kannai Capital, Building 5F
2-25 Bennten-st
231-0007 Yokohama
Japan
www.hosakatakeshi.com
→ 114

The Metrics
195 Chrystie Street, Ste 600A
New York, NY 10002
USA
www.metricsdesigngroup.com
→ 70

Tom Dixon
Wharf Building, Portobello Dock
344 Ladbroke Grove
London W10 5BU
UK
www.tomdixon.net
→ 158, 321, 330

Tony Hobba Architects
45 Hurst Road
Bells Beach, VIC 3228
Australia
www.hobba.com
→ 226

T.R.O.P.
Nak Niwat 32, 36/66 Soi Sahakon 6
Lat Phrao 71
10230 Bangkok
Thailand
www.tropstudio.com
→ 177

tsk Design
18, 17th Main Road, HAL 2nd A Stage
Bangalore 560008
India
www.tsk-design.com
→ 170

VONSUNG
8B Huguenot Place
Heneage Street
London E1 5LJ
UK
www.vonsung.com
→ 378

Waugh Thistleton Architects
74 Paul Street
London EC2A 4NA
UK
www.waughthistleton.com
→ 370

Wonderwall
3-4-10 Sendagaya
151-0051 Tokyo
Japan
www.wonder-wall.com
→ 138

Yabu Pushelberg
88 Prince Street, 2nd Floor
New York, NY 10012
USA
www.yabupushelberg.com
→ 42

© 2014 TASCHEN GmbH
Hohenzollernring 53,
D-50672 Köln
www.taschen.com

To stay informed about upcoming TASCHEN titles, please subscribe to our free Magazine at www.taschen.com/magazine, find our Magazine app for iPad on iTunes, follow us on Twitter and Facebook, or e-mail us at contact@taschen.com for any questions about our program. Delve in and enjoy!

Printed in Germany
ISBN 978-3-8365-4668-3

Editor
Marco Rebora
Julius Wiedemann

Editorial Coordination
Daniel Siciliano Bretas
Nora Dohrmann

Editorial Assistant
Dani Admiss, London

Design
Mind Design, London

Layout
Daniel Siciliano Bretas
Nora Dohrmann
Jörg Schwellnus

Production
Daniela Schädlich

English Revision
Chris Allen, London

German Translation
Nora Krehl-von Mühlendahl,
Ludwigsburg

French Translation
Valérie Lavoyer for
Delivering iBooks & Design,
Barcelona